DOCUMENTARY HISTORY
OF THE STRUGGLE FOR
RELIGIOUS LIBERTY
IN VIRGINIA

A Da Capo Press Reprint Series

CIVIL LIBERTIES IN AMERICAN HISTORY

GENERAL EDITOR: LEONARD W. LEVY
Claremont Graduate School

DOCUMENTARY HISTORY OF THE STRUGGLE FOR RELIGIOUS LIBERTY IN VIRGINIA

By Charles F. James

DA CAPO PRESS • NEW YORK • 1971

A Da Capo Press Reprint Edition

This Da Capo Press edition of
*Documentary History of the Struggle
for Religious Liberty in Virginia*
is an unabridged republication of the
first edition published in Lynchburg,
Virginia, in 1900.

Library of Congress Catalog Card Number 70-121101

SBN 306-71977-0

Published by Da Capo Press
A Division of Plenum Publishing Corporation
227 West 17th Street, New York, N. Y. 10011

DOCUMENTARY HISTORY
OF THE STRUGGLE FOR
RELIGIOUS LIBERTY
IN VIRGINIA

DOCUMENTARY HISTORY

OF THE

Struggle for Religious Liberty in Virginia.

BY

CHARLES F. JAMES, D. D.,

President of Roanoke Female College,

DANVILLE, VIRGINIA.

LYNCHBURG, VA.:
J. P. BELL COMPANY
1900

TO ALL TRUE LOVERS OF LIBERTY,

BOTH CIVIL AND RELIGIOUS,

AND TO ALL SEEKERS AFTER THE TRUTH OF HISTORY,

THIS VOLUME

IS RESPECTFULLY DEDICATED.

———

"Seize upon truth, wherever found,
On Christian or on heathen ground,
Among your friends, among your foes ;
The plant's divine, where'er it grows."

CONTENTS.

CONTENTS.

APPENDIX.

PREFACE.

In the year 1886, while pastor of the Culpeper Baptist church, I was drawn into a lengthy controversy with the Hon. William Wirt Henry, which forced me to search for and examine for myself all available original sources of information concerning the struggle for religious liberty in Virginia. There had been manifested at various times and on various occasions a disposition to rewrite the history of that struggle, and to rob our Baptist fathers of the peculiar honor which has ever been claimed for them—that of being the foremost, most zealous, and most consistent and unwavering champions of soul liberty. And not a few of our own young brethren were beginning to question the soundness of that claim, and to count as "Baptist brag" much that was spoken on the platform and published in our newspapers during the "Memorial Campaign" of 1873. Hence, to satisfy my own mind, I determined to go back of Howell's "Early Baptists of Virginia," to the sources from which he and others had drawn their information—to the Journal of the Virginia House of Burgesses, or General Assembly, and to the writings of those who participated in the struggle. Being convenient to the Congressional Library, in Washington, and our State Library, in Richmond, I seized every opportunity, during the remainder of my stay in Culpeper, to gather from all sources the evidence in this case. I copied everything of value which I could find, making note of book and page, and arranged the material for future use. For the past ten years I have been hoping to publish it in pamphlet or book form, but my circumstances have been such as to prevent the accomplishment of my original purpose. In a recent correspondence with the editors of the *Religious Herald*, it was suggested that this evidence be first laid before the readers of that paper, and afterwards be published in more permanent form.

The plan of this work is to take the "Journal of the Virginia Assembly" as the thread of the story, and work into it, in chronological order, the memorials and doings of the various religious bodies in the State, together with such letters and other writings of men like Madison and Jefferson as throw light upon the subject in hand. I shall quote freely from the standard histories of those times, and especially from the historians of the several religious denominations, making only such explanatory notes myself as may be deemed necessary for the enlightenment of the general reader and the proper understanding of the situation during the several stages of the conflict. It is, therefore, not a history in the usual sense of that word, but rather a *compilation*—a grouping together of evidence and authorities, so that the reader may see and judge for himself. Hence the name, "*Documentary* History," etc. It will furnish the careful and painstaking student of history a reliable text-book for the study of one of the most important of the great battles that have been fought for human rights and have marked the progress of the human race.

C. F. J.

Danville, Va., December 8, 1898.

INTRODUCTION.

BEFORE entering upon the examination of the records, it will be well to state the meaning of religious freedom, or soul liberty, and give a brief account of the religious sects, or denominations, that participated in the struggle.

By religious freedom, or soul liberty, is meant the natural and inalienable right of every soul to worship God according to the dictates of his own conscience, and to be unmolested in the exercise of that right, so long, at least, as he does not infringe upon the rights of others; that religion is, and must be, a *voluntary* service; that only such service is acceptable to God; and, hence, that no earthly power, whether civil or ecclesiastical, has any right to compel conformity to any creed or to any species of worship, or to tax a man for its support.

This principle gives to "Cæsar" "the things that are Cæsar's," but it denies to Cæsar "the things that are God's." It does not make it a matter of indifference what a man believes or how he acts, but it places all on the same footing before God, the only lord of the conscience, and makes us responsible to him alone for our faith and practice. This doctrine is now very generally accepted, not only in Virginia, but also throughout the United States. It has been incorporated into our National and State Constitutions, and it is the basis of our civil liberties. And yet at the date of the American Revolution it was not so. No government in the Old World had recognized this doctrine, and, unless Rhode Island be an exception, it did not find full and unequivocal recognition in any of the colonies

of the New World. Virginia was the first to recognize it
in her organic law, and this she did in Article XVI. of her
Bill of Rights, which was adopted on the 12th day of
June, 1776. From that time down to January 19, 1786,
when Jefferson's "Bill for Establishing Religious Freedom" became the law of the State, the battle for soul
liberty was on.

Of the several religious sects in the Commonwealth at
that time, the Episcopalians, Presbyterians, and Baptists
were the only ones that were prominent in the struggle.
The Lutherans and Quakers were not numerous, and
seldom acted independently. The Methodists were more
numerous, perhaps, but they were a part of the Episcopal
communion, and acted with that church until 1784, when
the Methodist Episcopal Church of America was organized
in the city of Baltimore.

EPISCOPALIANS, OR CHURCH OF ENGLAND.

The history of the Episcopal church in Virginia dates
from the founding of the colony, at Jamestown, in 1607.
It was known as the Church of England down to the
Revolution, when the colony declared independence of
Great Britain. It was known, also, as the "Established
Church," because it was made, by legal enactment, the
church of the State and was supported by taxation. Not
only so, but it was designed to be the established church,
to the exclusion of all others. Rigid laws, with severe
penalties affixed, were passed, having for their object the
exclusion of all Dissenters from the colony, and the compelling of conformity to the established, or State religion.
Even after the Revolution of 1688, which placed William
and Mary upon the throne of England and secured the
passage of the "Act of Toleration" the following year,

the "General Court of the Colony" of Virginia construed that act to suit themselves, and withheld its benefits from Dissenters, as we shall hereafter see, until they were compelled to yield to force of circumstances.

PRESBYTERIANS.

The first Presbyterian church in America was organized in Philadelphia in 1701, the first Presbytery in 1705, and the first Synod in 1717. Dr. Justin A. Smith, in his "Modern Church History" (page 210), says: "Quite a number of Scotch Presbyterians settled upon Elizabeth river, in Virginia, during the ten years from 1670 to 1680." But there seems to have been no organization there, and they receive no mention in the "Sketches of Virginia," by their historian, Dr. William Henry Foote. Foote tells of the work of one Francis Makemie, in Accomac county, who began preaching there in 1699; but his work does not seem to have been productive of permanent results. "For about thirty years after the death of Makemie," says Dr. Foote, "the number and influence of Presbyterians in Virginia were small. Not one flourishing congregation could be found, nor one active minister lived in her borders." Sketches of Virginia, page 84.

It was Pennsylvania, the land of William Penn, son of an English Baptist, that offered the greatest attractions in this New World to the Presbyterian emigrants from Ireland. Thousands settled there, in the unoccupied regions east of the Blue Ridge, whence the tide of emigration flowed southward into Maryland, Virginia, and North Carolina. In the year 1738, an agreement was entered into between the Presbyterian Synod of Philadelphia and Governor William Gooch, of Virginia, according to which Presbyterian emigrants were allowed to occupy the frontier portions of the colony and enjoy the benefits of the Act of Toleration. The terms of this agreement will be given in Chapter I. It is sufficient to say here that the result of this movement was the establishment of Presbyterian settlements, of Scotch-Irish origin, not only in the Valley of Virginia and along the eastern base of the Blue Ridge, but also in the counties of Prince Edward, Charlotte, and Campbell. But perhaps the most influential body of Presbyterians in Virginia took their rise in Hanover county, about the year 1743. William Robinson, an English Presbyterian, began the work ; but the real founder of " Tidewater Presbyterianism " was the great Samuel Davies, whom Robinson helped to educate for the ministry. It was from this county that " the first Presbytery south of the Potomac " took its name, and it is this " Hanover Presbytery " that will be heard from hereafter as the official representative of the Presbyterians of Virginia.

BAPTISTS.

"The Baptists of Virginia," according to Semple, "originated from three sources." The *first* were emigrants from England, who settled in the southeast parts of the State about the year 1714. Dr. Foote (page 314) says: "There was a Baptist church gathered in Isle of Wight county, by a minister from England, as early as the year 1714." The *second* party came from Maryland about 1743, and settled in the northwest. This was the beginning of the Ketocton Association, whose "History" was written by William Fristoe and published in 1808, two years before the publication of Robert B. Semple's "History of the Baptists of Virginia." The Ketocton Association was composed of " Regular Baptists," as they were then called, and it extended from King George county, in the Northern Neck, to Redstone Settlement, back of the Alleghany Mountain, and from Orange county, south of the Rapidan, to Fredericktown, in Maryland—in length about 300 miles, and in width about 100. A *third* party, styled "Separate Baptists," came from New England, about the year 1754, under the lead of Shubal Stearns. They were originally Presbyterians, who were converted under the preaching of George Whitfield, and who "separated themselves from the established churches" in New England, and set up for themselves as "Separates," on the plan of the "Independents," which put all power in the hands of the local church. They took their rise about the year 1744. In 1751, Shubal Stearns, their leading preacher, formed the acquaintance of some Baptists, and was convinced of the duty of believers' baptism. He became a Baptist, and in 1754 he and a few of his members took their leave of New England and started southward, in obedience to a divine call. See Semple, pages 1 and 2. "They halted first at Opeckon, in Berkeley county, Virginia, where they found a Baptist church, under the care of Rev. John Garrard." Moving on southward, they came to Sandy Creek, Guilford county, North Carolina, where Stearns took up his permanent residence, and began a work which spread rapidly over Virginia, North and South Carolina, and Georgia. It was these "Separate Baptists," who, as Fristoe says, were "first Separate Presbyterians," that were most active in evangelizing Virginia and most severely persecuted, and who had the largest share of the work of pulling down the "Establishment" and securing religious liberty for all. In 1760, they formed the first "General Association" in Virginia, representing the "Separate Baptists," while the "Ketocton" represented the "Regulars." This "General Association" continued until 1783, when it was divided into four district associations, two on each side of James river. But at the same meeting at which this division took place a "General Committee" was appointed, to be "composed of not more than four delegates from each district association, to meet annually and to consider matters that may be for the good of the whole society." This "General Committee" continued its work until 1799, when, its mission having been fulfilled, it gave place to the "General Meeting of Correspondence," the object of which was "to promote and preserve union and harmony among the churches." Semple, pages 68 and 86.

Of the Baptists, at least, it may be truly said that they entered the conflict in the New World with a clear and consistent record on the subject of soul liberty. "Freedom of conscience" had ever been one of their fundamental tenets. John Locke, in his "Essay on Toleration," says : "The Baptists were the first and only propounders of absolute liberty, just and true liberty, equal and impartial liberty." And the great American historian, Bancroft, says : "Freedom of conscience, unlimited freedom of mind, was from the first a trophy of the Baptists." Vol. II., pages 66, 67.

The history of the other denominations shows that, in the Old World, at least, they were not in sympathy with the Baptist doctrine of soul liberty, but in favor of union of Church and State, and using the civil power to compel conformity to the established church. While the Revolution of 1688 marked an epoch in English history, and led to the passage of the *Toleration Act* in 1689, it did not secure *religious liberty* to His Majesty's subjects. As Dr. Foote (page 5) says : "The Protestant religion was established as the religion of the State—in *England*, under the form of *prelacy;* in *Scotland*, of *presbytery.*" (Italics mine.)

The Reformation which began with Martin Luther corrected many errors of faith and practice among those who came out of the corrupt and apostate church, but not all. It was left to the sect once "everywhere spoken against" to teach their Protestant brethren the lesson of soul liberty, and this they did in the school of adversity in this New World.

DOCUMENTARY HISTORY

OF THE

Struggle for Religious Liberty in Virginia.

BY REV. C. F. JAMES, D. D.

FIRST PERIOD—BEFORE REVOLUTION.

CHAPTER I.

Intolerance and Toleration.

"TOLERATION in the forms of religion was unknown in Virginia in 1688. From the commencement of the colony, the necessity of the religious element was felt. The company knew not how to control the members composing the colony but by religion and law. They exercised a despotism in both." Foote's "Sketches of Virginia," page 25.

In Hening's "Statutes at Large" (Vols. I. and II.) may be found the various laws which were passed by the colonial government against dissenters or non-conformists of every name. It will be sufficient to give a description of these laws. Semple (page 28) says: "By the first act of 1623, it is provided that in every plantation, or settlement, there shall be a house or room set apart for the worship of God. But it soon appears that this worship was only to be according to the canons of the Church of England, to which a strict uniformity was enjoined. A person absenting himself from divine service on a Sunday without a reasonable excuse forfeited a pound of tobacco, and he that absented himself a month forfeited fifty pounds. . . Whoever disparaged a minister, whereby the minds of his parishioners might be alienated, was compelled to pay 500 pounds of tobacco, and ask the minister's pardon publicly in the congregation. No man was permitted to dispose of any of his tobacco till the minister was satisfied, under the penalty of forfeiting double his part of the minister's salary. . . . To preserve the 'purity of doctrine and unity of the church,' it was enacted, in 1643, that all ministers should be conformable to the orders and constitutions of the Church of England, and that no others be permitted to teach or preach, publicly or privately. It was further provided that the Governor and Council should take care that all non-conformists departed the colony with all con-veniency.''

Winsor's '' Narrative and Critical History of America '' (Vol. III., page 148,) has the following notice of that act of 1643. After stating that Sir William Berkeley became Governor in 1642, he says: '' During the year, three Con-gregational ministers came from Boston to Virginia to dis-seminate their doctrines. Their stay, however, was but short; for, by an enactment of the Assembly, all ministers other than those of the Church of England were compelled to leave the colony.''

Hassell, in his '' Church History '' (page 523), says: '' In 1643, Sir William Berkeley, Royal Governor of Vir-ginia, strove, by whippings and brandings, to make the inhabitants of that colony conform to the Established church, and thus drove out the Baptists and Quakers, who found a refuge in the Albemarle country of North Caro-lina, a colony which ' was settled,' says Bancroft, ' by the freest of the free—by men to whom the restraints of other colonies were too severe.' "

Semple (page 29) says that "the Quakers made their first appearance in Virginia in 1659–'60," and that "the utmost degree of persecution was exercised towards them."

Foote's "Sketches of Virginia" (pages 28–40) gives a full account of the laws of that period, all tending to uphold and strengthen the Established church, and to suppress or drive out all who were opposed to the Church of England.

In 1661–'2, the following act was passed:

"Whereas many schismatical persons, out of their averseness to the orthodox established religion, or out of the new-fangled conceits of their own heretical inventions, refuse to have their children baptized; be it, therefore, enacted, by the authority aforesaid, that all persons that, in contempt of the divine sacrament of baptism, shall refuse, when they may carry their child [children] to a lawful minister in that county to have them baptized, shall be amerced two thousand pounds of tobacco, half to the informer, half to the public." Foote, page 34. Hening, Vol. II., pages 165, 166.

This was immediately after the restoration of Charles II., which happened in May, 1660. During the period of the Commonwealth in England, there had been a kind of interregnum as to both Church and State in Virginia; but "in 1661 the supremacy of the Church of England was again fully established." "No minister was permitted to preach unless he had received ordination from some bishop in England." Semple, page 30, and Foote, pages 33, 34. "Any minister admitted into a parish was entitled to all the spiritual and temporal rights thereof, and might maintain an action against any person who attempted to disturb him in his possession." Semple, page 31. "Under the old ecclesiastical establishment, no person could celebrate the rites of matrimony but a minister of the Church of England, and according to the ceremony prescribed in the Book of Common Prayer.'' Semple, page 34.

FIRST CASES OF TOLERATION.

The "Act of Toleration" was passed by the British Parliament in 1689, but its provisions were unknown to the people of Virginia until 1699, when Francis Makemie, a Presbyterian minister of Accomac county, applied for and received license to preach at two designated places on his own property. Dr. Foote speaks of him as the first consistent Presbyterian minister in Virginia, and as ''the first minister, dissenting from the Church of England, that had leave from the constituted authorities to preach in Virginia.'' Sketches of Virginia, pages 40, 41. The license issued to Makemie is given by Foote (page 44), and is taken from the records of the county of Accomac. It is given here as a sample, and bears date of October 15, 1699 :

"Whereas Mr. Francis Makemie made application by petition to this court, that being ready to fulfill what the law enjoins to dissenters, that he might be qualified according to law, and prayed that his own dwelling-house at Pocomoke, also his own house at Ononcock, next to Captain Jonathan Lively's, might be places recorded for the meeting ; and having taken the oaths enjoined by act of Parliament instead of the oaths of allegiance and supremacy, and subscribed the test, as likewise that he did, in compliance with what the said law enjoins, produce certificate from Barbadoes of his qualifications there, did declare in open court of the said county and owned the articles of religion mentioned in the statute made in the 13th year of Queen Elizabeth, except the 34th, 35th, and 36th, and those words of the 20th article—viz., the church hath power to decide rights and ceremonies, and authority in controversies of faith—which the court have ordered to be registered and recorded, and that the clerk of court give certificate thereof to the said Makemie, according as the law enjoynes.''

Foote adds:

"This is the first certificate of qualifiation under the Toleration Act known to be on record.'' Page 45.

By way of explaining this exhibition of a tolerant spirit by those who were generally intolerant, Dr. Foote (page 51) quotes the following from Beverly's '' History and Present State of Virginia '':

"They [dissenters] have no more than five conventicles amongst them—namely, three small meetings of Quakers and two of Presbyterians. 'Tis observed that those counties where the Presbyterian meetings are produce very mean tobacco, and for that reason can't get an orthodox minister to stay amongst them.''

Foote adds :

"So it appears on account of the poorness of the tobacco the established clergy left some counties, although in 1696 their salary had been fixed at sixteen thousand pound weight of that commodity. If this statement be true, we can the more easily understand why Makemie had not been more molested. We suppose he took his residence in Accomac soon after his marriage. There was no Episcopal minister to complain of him, and many of the inhabitants preferred to hear Makemie to passing silent Sabbaths, and many others were true Presbyterians.'' Sketches of Virginia, page 51.

In 1725, a similar license was granted to certain parties (doubtless Presbyterians) in the county of Richmond, as will be seen from the following minute taken from the "journal of the Governor's Council,'' bearing date May 4, 1742:

"This Board having considered the representation of the justices of Richmond county, together with the opinion of His Majesties' Attorney-General, and of John Holloway and John Randolph, Esqs., to whom it was referred to report their opinion how far the act of Parliament, made in the first year of the reign of their Majesties, King William and Queen Mary, entitled an 'Act for exempting their

Majesties' Protestant subjects dissenting from the Church of England from the penalties of certain laws,' were in force in this colony, and having also considered His Majesty's instruction to the Governor for allowing a liberty of conscience to all Christians except papists. It is the opinion of this Board, and accordingly ordered, that the dissenters in Richmond county and their preacher, on their application to the court of the said county, respectively taking such oaths and subscribing such declaration as are prescribed and enjoined by the said act, have the free exercise of their religion at such place of public worship in the said county as they shall desire to be recorded by the county court for that purpose, so as they also observe the directions of the said act of Parliament at their meetings at such place of public worship set apart as aforesaid." See Journal, in State Library.

AGREEMENT BETWEEN THE PRESBYTERIAN SYNOD OF PHILADELPHIA AND GOV. WM. GOOCH, OF VIRGINIA.

From about 1732 down to 1738, Presbyterian families had been moving into the Valley of Virginia from Pennsylvania and Maryland. In 1738, the number had become so large that steps were taken by the Synod of Philadelphia to secure from Governor Gooch assurance that Presbyterian ministers should have the privileges of the Act of Toleration of Virginia. Foote, on pages 103, 104, gives the letter of the Synod to Governor Gooch, and also the Governor's reply.

LETTER OF SYNOD.

"To the Honorable William Gooch, Esquire, Lieutenant-Governor of the Province of Virginia, the humble address of the Presbyterian ministers convened in Synod, May 30, 1738. May it please your Honour, we take leave to address you in behalf of a considerable number of our brethren who are meditating a settlement in the remote parts of your government, and are of the same persuasion as the Church of Scotland. We thought it our duty to acquaint your Honour with this design, and to ask your favour in allowing them the liberty of their consciences, and of worshipping God in a way agreeable to the principles of their education. Your Honour is sensible that those of our profession in Europe have been remarkable for their inviolable attachment to the house of Hanover, and have upon all occasions manifested an unspotted fidelity to our gracious sovereign, King George, and we doubt not but that these, our brethren, will carry the same loyal principles to the most distant settlements, where their lot may be cast, which will ever influence them to the most dutiful submission to the government which is placed over them. This, we trust, will recommend them to your Honour's countenance and protection, and merit the free enjoyment of their civil and religious liberties. We pray for the divine blessing upon your person and government, and beg leave to subscribe ourselves your Honour's most humble and obedient servants."

LETTER OF GOV. GOOCH TO MODERATOR OF SYNOD.

"*Sir*,—By the hands of Mr. Anderson, I received an address signed by you, in the name of your brethren of the Synod of Philadelphia. And as I have been always inclined to favour the people who have lately removed from other provinces to settle on the western side of our great mountains, so you may be assured that no interruption shall be given to any minister of your profession who shall come among them, so as they conform themselves to the rules prescribed by the Act of Toleration in England, by taking the oaths enjoined thereby, and registering the place of their meeting, and behave themselves peaceably towards the government. This you may please to communicate to the Synod as an answer to theirs."

EXPLANATION.

Commenting on this, Dr. Foote (page 99) says :

"Poverty and intolerance drove them [Presbyterians] from their mother country, and the necessity of providing a frontier line of brave people west of the Blue Mountains compelled Virginia to relax her rigor and open her borders ;" and again (on page 105) : "The reasons that actuated Governor Gooch to promise protection in the exercise of their religious forms, in a State whose laws for uniformity were precise and enforced with rigor, were two : 1st. He wished a frontier line at a greater distance from Williamsburg ; if possible, west of the great mountains. 2d. He knew these people to be firm, enterprising, hardy, brave, good citizens and soldiers. To form a complete line of defense against the savage inroads, he welcomed these Presbyterian emigrants, the Quakers, and colonies from the different German States to the beautiful and luxuriant prairies of the great Valley of the Shenandoah, on the head waters of the James, and along the Roanoke. At so great a distance from the older settlements, he anticipated no danger or trouble to the established church of the colony ; perhaps he never seriously considered the subject in the probable influence of the necessary collision of religious opinions.''

The above quotations are important as showing the nature and restrictions of the licenses granted to dissenters, and also the conditions under which the Presbyterians were given permission to settle in the colony and to enjoy the benefits of the Toleration Act. They were not only to settle in the frontier counties as a buffer between the Churchmen and the Indians, but they had to swear allegiance to ''His Majesty's person and government,'' pay the taxes levied for the support of the Established Church, and never by word or deed seek to injure the said church. That this does not over-state the case, is proven by certain trials before the Governor's Council, of which an account is given in Foote's Sketches (pages 160-162), which trials were not merely for preaching without license, but for ''speaking against the canons of the Church of England,'' or ''for reviling the bishops and clergy.''

And yet some modern writers are claiming that the Presbyterians were foremost in the attack upon the Establishment and in the battle for religious liberty in Virginia, forgetting that they were estopped from all such action by their agreement with Governor Gooch, and by their oaths of allegiance, etc. To the honor of those early Presbyterians of Virginia be it said, that they did not break their promise nor violate their oaths. The records will show that, up to the date of the Revolution, they never demanded anything more than their rights under the Act of Toleration, and that not until the Revolution was accomplished, and Virginia had thrown off allegiance to Great Britain, did they (the Presbyterians) strike hands with the Baptists in the effort to pull down the Establishment. Being no longer subjects of King George, but citizens of Virginia, they were absolved from their oaths and were free to act according to their judgment and interests under the new government.

But while the Presbyterians enjoyed to a limited extent the benefits of the Toleration Act, it was not until the outbreak of the French and Indian war that they enjoyed any great degree of freedom. The colonial government was provokingly slow in granting licenses.

"Houses for public worship could not be occupied without permission from the civil authorities, and each application for a house of worship was heard on its own merits." But "what was not granted to petition and argument and English construction of colonial law was yielded to force of circumstances. The French and Indian war, commonly known as Braddock's war, which, after many provocations and preliminary atrocities, broke out in its fury in 1755, by the strange agency of fire and sword, the tomahawk and scalping knife, plead the cause of freedom of conscience with a success hitherto unknown. . . . During the confusion of this savage warfare, the Presbyterians east of the Blue Ridge chose houses for worship and occupied them without license or molestation." Foote's Sketches, pages 307, 308.

It was in that fateful year of 1755 that the clergy of the Establishment began their suicidal contest with the people over their salaries, in what is known as the "Parsons'

Cause," and which culminated in 1763 in a crushing defeat of the parsons by the maiden speech of Patrick Henry. And it was in that same year (1755) that Shubal Stearns, the leader of the Separate Baptists, passing through Virginia, settled ·in North Carolina, and began the great work of evangelization to which he felt called of God when he set out from his home in New England. The Lord was marshalling his hosts for the liberation of this fair land from the domination and curse of a priestly hierarchy, and the souls of men from bondage to human law and custom.

BAPTISTS AND TOLERATION.

As there were different bodies of Baptists in Virginia during the colonial period, so there was some difference of action in the matter of taking out license for preachers and preaching places under the Toleration Act. The records indicate that some, at least, of the " Regular Baptists" conformed to the custom of the Presbyterians, by applying for license and taking the prescribed oaths. With the "Separate Baptists," however, it was different. With few exceptions, if any, these did not recognize the right of any civil power to regulate preaching or places of meeting. While yielding a ready obedience to the civil authorities in all civil affairs, in matters of religion they recognized no lord but Christ. They were truly apostolic in refusing to obey man rather than God. It was this body that spread so rapidly throughout the State from 1755 to the date of the Revolution.

FAVORABLE CONDITIONS.

The conditions were favorable for the rapid growth of their principles. First, the distress of the colonists, consequent upon the French and Indian wars, inclined them towards religion.

"Rev. Mr. Wright, the Presbyterian minister in Cumberland county, which was then a frontier, under date of August 18, 1755, says: 'People generally begin to believe the divine government, and that our judgments are inflicted for our sins. They now hear sermons with solemnity and attention; they acknowledge their wickedness and ignorance, and believe that the new-light clergy and adherents are right.'" Foote's Sketches, page 308.

Secondly, the character of the clergy of the Establishment made it impossible for the distressed people to find solace or comfort there. Says Semple (page 25):

"The great success and rapid increase of the Baptists in Virginia must be ascribed primarily to the power of God working with them. Yet it cannot be denied but that there were subordinate and cooperating causes; one of which, and the main one, was the loose and immoral deportment of the Established clergy, by which the people were left almost destitute of even the shadow of true religion. 'Tis true, they had some outward forms of worship, but the essential principles of Christianity were not only not understood among them, but by many never heard of. Some of the cardinal precepts of morality were disregarded, and actions plainly forbidden by the New Testament were often proclaimed by the clergy as harmless and innocent, or, at worst, foibles of but little account. Having no discipline, every man followed the bent of his own inclination. It was not uncommon for the rectors of parishes to be men of the lowest morals. The Baptist preachers were, in almost every respect, the reverse of the Established clergy.'"

If they did not have scholarship, they had personal piety and knew the Bible. If they did not have position in society, they had "favor with God," and that always gives "favor with men."

That Dr. Semple does not overstate the case, is evidenced by the statements of some of their own authorities.

Dr. Foote (page 38) quotes from the Bishop of London, as follows:

"The Bishop of London said of them, about this time [1743], in his letter to Dr. Doddridge: 'Of those who are sent from hence, a great part are the Scotch or Irish, who can get no employment at home, and enter into the service more out of necessity than choice. Some others are willing to go abroad to retrieve either lost fortune or lost character.'"

Bishop Meade in his "Old Parishes and Families of Virginia" (Vol. I., 118, 385, etc.), says:

"Many of them had been addicted to the race-field, the card-table, the theatre—nay, more, to drunken revel, etc."

Dr. Hawks, in his History of the Protestant Episcopal Church of Virginia (page 65), says:

"They could babble in a pulpit, roar in a travern, exact from their parishioners, and rather by their dissoluteness destroy than feed the flock."

In confirmation of the above, note the following law passed by the Assembly in 1776:

"Be it further enacted by this Grand Assembly, and by the authority thereof, that such ministers as shall become notoriously scandalous by drunkenness, swearing, fornication, or other heinous and crying sins, and shall thereof be lawfully convicted, shall, for every such their heinous crime and wickedness," etc.   Hening's Statutes, Vol. II., page 384.

It will be seen from the above that the Established church in Virginia was in very much the same plight as the sect of the Pharisees in our Lord's day; and as "the common people heard him gladly" and joined themselves unto him, so did the distressed burden-bearers of Virginia turn away from a corrupt and apostate church, with its hireling ministry, to find the consolations of the Christian religion among those who not only knew what Christianity was, but who also exemplified it in their lives.

CHAPTER II.

Legal Persecutions, 1768–1774.

SEMPLE (page 14), says: "It seems by no means certain that any law in force in Virginia authorized the imprisonment of any person for preaching. The law for the preservation of peace, however, was so interpreted as to answer this purpose, and accordingly, whenever the preachers were apprehended, it was done by a peace warrant." On page 15, he says: "The first instance of actual imprisonment, we believe, that ever took place in Virginia was in the county of Spotsylvania. On the 4th of June, 1768, John Waller, Lewis Craig, James Childs, etc., were seized by the sheriff and haled before three magistrates," etc. "They offered to release them, if they would promise to preach no more in the county for a year and a day. This they refused, and, therefore, were sent into close jail."

This work went on until the year 1774. Semple gives only a few sample cases of imprisonment, saying that there were many others besides. In December, 1770, William Webber and Joseph Anthony were imprisoned in Chesterfied jail, and in May, 1774, David Tinsley, Augustin Eastin, John Weatherford, John Tanner, and Jeremiah Walker were imprisoned in the same jail. In Middlesex county, William Webber, John Waller, James Greenwood, and Robert Ware were imprisoned in August, 1771. Semple, pages 17, 18. In Caroline county, Lewis Craig, John Burrus, John Young, Edward Herndon, James Goodrich, and Bartholomew Chewing were imprisoned, but the year

is not given. See Taylor's Virginia Baptist Ministers,
Vol. I., pages 81, 82. In King & Queen county, James
Greenwood and William Lovall were imprisoned in August, 1772, and John Waller, John Shackleford, Robert
Ware, and Ivison Lewis in March, 1774. See Semple,
page 22. Dr. Taylor, in his sketch of Elijah Craig, says
he was imprisoned in Orange county, but does not give
the year. According to Taylor's Virginia Baptist Ministers, there were confined in Culpeper jail, at different times,
James Ireland, John Corbeley, Elijah Craig, Thomas
Ammon, Adam Banks, and Thomas Maxfield.

Semple, writing of the year 1771 (page 19), says:

"The rage of the persecutors had in no wise abated; they seemed
sometimes to strive to treat the Baptists and their worship with as
much rudeness and indecency as was possible. They often insulted
the preacher in time of servce, and would ride into the water and
make sport when they administered baptism. They frequently
fabricated and spread the most groundless reports, which were injurious to the characters of the Baptists. When any Baptist fell
into any improper conduct, it was always exaggerated to the utmost
extent."

William Fristoe, in his "History of the Ketocton Baptist Association," writes as follows (beginning at page
69):

"The enemy, not contented with ridicule and defamation, manifested their abhorrence to the Baptists in another way. By a law
then in force in Virginia, all were under obligation to go to church
several times in the year; the failure subjected them to fine. Little
notice was taken of the omission, if members of the Established
church ; but so soon as the ' New Lights' were absent, they were
presented by the grand jury, and fined according to law." And
again (on page 70): ' Soon they began to take other steps to deter
the Baptist preachers and obstruct the progress of the gospel, by ob-
jecting to their preaching until they obtained license from the General Court, whose place of sitting at that time was old Williamsburg.

Until such times that license was obtained, they were exposed to be apprehended and imprisoned.' Again (on pages 79, 80): 'When persecutors found religion could not be stopped in its progress by ridicule, defamation, and abusive language, the resolution was to take a different step and see what that would do ; and the preachers in different places were apprehended by magisterial authority, some of whom were imprisoned and some escaped. Before this step was taken, the parson of the parish was consulted (in some instances, at least), and his judgment confided in. His counsel was that the 'New Lights' ought to be taken up and imprisoned, as necessary for the peace and harmony of the old church. As formerly the high priests took the lead in persecuting the followers of Christ, in like manner the high priests have conducted in latter days, and seldom there has been a persecution but what an high priest has been at the head of it, or exercised influence."

Now let Dr. Hawks, an Episcopalian, testify. In his "History of the Protestant Episcopal Church of Virginia" (page 121), he says:

" No dissenters in Virginia experienced, for a time, harsher treatment than did the Baptists. They were beaten and imprisoned, and cruelty taxed its ingenuity to devise new modes of punishment and annoyance."

PETITIONS.

Returning now to 1769, the year after the county officials began to imprison Baptist preachers, and layman also, we find petitions beginning to appear before the House of Burgesses. The first is from members of the Established church, and it indicates great concern about the spread of Baptist principles, which the petitioners are pleased to style "pernicious doctrines."

EPISCOPAL PETITION OF MAY 5, 1769.

Journal notice: "A petition was presented from 'the minister and sundry inhabitants of the parish of Hamilton,' praying for a division of the parish into two, the reason being that the parish was 'so large that many of the inhabitants reside so far from their parish churches that they can but seldom attend public worship; from which causes, dissenters have opportunity and encouragement to propagate their pernicious doctrines.' "

A year later, there appears a petition from the oppressed and persecuted Baptists.

FIRST BAPTIST PETITION.

The journal of May 26, 1770, has the following:

"A petition of several persons, being Protestant dissenters of the Baptist persuasion, whose names are thereunto subscribed, was presented to the House and read ; setting forth the inconveniences of compelling their licensed preachers to bear arms under the militia law and to attend musters, by which they are unable to perform the duties of their function ; and further setting forth the hardships they suffer from the prohibition to their ministers to preach in meeting-houses, not particularly mentioned in their licenses ; and, therefore, praying the House to take their grievances into consideration, and to grant them relief."

This petition was referred to "Committee for Religion," which reported, June 1st, as follows:

"*Resolved*, That it is the opinion of this committee that so much of the said petition as prays that the ministers or preachers of the Baptist persuasion may not be compelled to bear arms or attend musters be rejected." "Agreed to by the House."

This action of the House of Burgesses, which was composed almost exclusively, if not entirely, of "Churchmen," shows the spirit of that body towards the Baptists. The time is not distant, however, when another great war cloud will overshadow the land, and a new spirit will then pervade the Assembly. The "Stamp Act" of 1765 had alarmed the colonists, and it was in opposition to the principle involved in that act that Patrick Henry, who had just entered the Assembly, made the boldest speech of his life, and placed himself at the head of the opposition in Virginia. Thomas Jefferson joined him in the same House, in 1769. When the House assembled on the 6th of February, 1772, Patrick Henry was present, and was a member of the "Committee of Propositions and Grievances," and also of the "Committee of Religion." The "Committee on Propositions and Grievances" was appointed with instructions to meet and adjourn from day to day, and "to take into their consideration all propositions and grievances that shall come legally certified to this Assembly, and to report their proceedings, with their opinions thereupon, from time to time, to the House; and such propositions and grievances are to be delivered to the clerk of the House, and by him to the said committee of course, and said committee are to have power to send for persons, papers, and records for their information."

MORE BAPTIST PETITIONS.

Journal entry, February 12, 1772: "A petition of several persons of the county of Lunenburg, whose names are thereunto subscribed, was presented to the House and read ; setting forth that the petitioners, being of the society of Christians called Baptists, find themselves restricted in the exercise of their religion, their teachers imprisoned under various pretences, and the benefits of the Toleration Act denied them, although they are willing to conform to the true spirit of that act, and are loyal and quiet subjects; and, therefore, praying that they may be treated with the same indulgence, in religious matters, as Quakers, Presbyterians, and other Protestant dissenters enjoy."

February 22, appears an exactly similar petition from Mecklenburg county, and on the 24th another from Sussex. On the same day, February 24, a petition from Amelia county appears, differing from the others in this :

"If the Act of Toleration does not extend to this colony, they are exposed to severe persecution ; and if it does extend hither, and the power of granting licenses to teachers be lodged, as is supposed, in the General Court alone, the petitioners must suffer considerable inconveniences, not only because that Court sits not oftener than twice in the year, and then at a place far remote, but because the said Court will admit a single meeting-house, and no more, in one county."

Fristoe, in his History, confirms the above statement as to the rule of the General Court, when he says (page 73):

"I knew the General Court to refuse a license for a Baptist meet-ing-house in the county of Richmond, because there was a Presby-terian meeting-house already in the county, although the Act of Toleration considered them distinct societies."

The Journal of February 25, 1772, gives the first fa-vorable action of the House, as follows:

"Mr. Treasurer reports from the Committee on Religion." . .

"Resolved, That it is the opinion of this committee that the pe-titions of sundry inhabitants of the counties of Lunenburg, Mecklen-burg, Sussex, and Amelia, of the society of Christians called Bap-tists, praying that they may be treated with the same kind indul-gence, in religious matters, as Quakers, Presbyterians, and other Protestant dissenters enjoy, so far as they relate to allowing the peti-tioners the same toleration, in matters of religion, as is enjoyed by His Majesty's dissenting Protestant subjects of Great Britain, under different acts of Parliament, is reasonable."

This "resolution" was agreed to by the House, and the "Committee for Religion" was ordered to bring in a bill in accordance therewith. And on the 27th of Febru-ary appears the following entry:

TOLERATION BILL PROPOSED.

"A bill for extending the benefit of the several Acts of Tolera-tion to His Majesty's Protestant subjects in this colony, dissenting from the Church of England, was read a second time," and "com-mitted to the Committee for Religion."

March 14, another petition is presented from Caroline county, the Journal notice of which is exactly like the notice of the one from Lunenburg. The petition was "laid on the table."

March 17, "Mr. Treasurer reported from Committee for Religion, to whom the bill for extending the benefit of the several Acts of Toleration to His Majesty's Protestant subjects in this colony, dissenting from the Church of England, was committed." The bill was engrossed and ordered to be read the third time, July 1, 1772. This bill, as we shall see hereafter, was very objectionable to both Baptists and Presbyterians, and it never became a law. The House was prorogued April 11, to the "25th day of June next." But there is no entry in the Journal until March 4, 1773. March 15, the House was prorogued again by Lord Dunmore, who had succeeded Botetourt as Governor. They met again June 17, and were prorogued continually until May 5, 1774. The explanation of this action of the Governor is found in the antagonism between him and the House. "Early in the session of 1773, Henry, Jefferson, the two Lees, and Dabney Carr met in Raleigh Tavern and originated that great machine, the 'Committee of Correspondence, for the dissemination of intelligence between the colonies.' The Burgesses promptly acted upon the suggestion, and were as promptly dissolved by Lord Dunmore. They were all re-elected by the people, and resumed their seats in the spring of 1774." See American Cyclopedia, VIII., 663.

JAMES MADISON'S TESTIMONY.

Before examining the Journal of that session, the reader should hear from James Madison, who had graduated from Nassau Hall, Princeton, in 1771, and, after taking a post-graduate course of one year, had returned to his home in Orange county, Va., at the age of twenty-one. In a letter to his old college friend, Bradford, of Philadelphia, dated January 24, 1774, he says:

"I verily believe the frequent assaults that have been made on America (Boston especially) will in the end prove of real advantage. If the Church of England had been the established and general religion in all the Northern colonies, as it has been among us here, and uninterrupted harmony had prevailed throughout the continent, it is clear to me that slavery and subjection might and would have been gradually insinuated among us. Union of religious sentiments begets a surprising confidence, and ecclesiastical establishments tend to great ignorance and corruption, all of which facilitates the execution of mischievous projects. . . . I want again to breathe your free air. I expect it will mend my constitution and confirm my principles. I have, indeed, as good an atmosphere at home as the climate will allow, but have nothing to brag of as to the state and liberty of my country. Poverty and luxury prevail among all sorts ; pride, ignorance, and knavery among the priesthood, and vice and wickedness among the laity. This is bad enough ; but it is not the worst I have to tell you. That diabolical, hell-conceived principle of persecution rages among some, and, to their eternal infamy, the clergy can furnish their quota of imps for such purposes. There are at this time in the adjacent country not less than five or six well-meaning men in close jail for publishing their religious sentiments, which, in the main, are very orthodox. I have neither patience to hear, talk, or think of anything relative to this matter ; for I have squabbled and scolded, abused and ridiculed so long about it, to little purpose, that I am without common patience. So I must beg you to pity me, and pray for liberty of conscience to all." Rives' Life and Times of Madison, Vol. I., page 43.

Again, April 1, 1774, Madison wrote to Bradford as follows:

"Our Assembly is to meet the 1st of May, when it is expected something will be done in behalf of the dissenters. Petitions, I hear, are already forming among the persecuted Baptists, and I fancy it is in the thought of the Presbyterians also to intercede for greater liberty in matters of religion. For my own part, I cannot help being very doubtful of their succeeding in the attempt. The affair was on the carpet during the last session ; but such incredible and extravagant stories were told in the House of the monstrous effects of the enthusiasm prevalent among the sectaries, and so greedily swallowed by their enemies, that I believe they lost footing by it. And the bad name they still have with those who pretend too much contempt to examine into their principles and conduct, and are too much devoted to ecclesiastical establishment to hear of the toleration of the dissentients, I am apprehensive, will be again made a pretext for rejecting their requests. . . . The sentiments of our people of fortune and fashion on this subject are vastly different from what you have been used to. That liberal, catholic, and equitable way of thinking, as to the rights of conscience, which is one of the characteristics of a free people, and so strongly marks the people of your province, is little known among the zealous adherents to our hierarchy. We have, it is true, some persons in the Legislature of generous principles, both in religion and politics ; but number, not merit, you know, is necessary to carry points there. Besides, the clergy are a numerous and powerful body, have great influence at home by reason of their connection with and dependence on the bishops and crown, and will naturally employ all their arts and interest to depress their rising adversaries ; for such they must consider dissentients, who rob them of the good will of the people, and may in time endanger their livings and security.'' Rives, page 53.

These two letters are quoted thus fully because they throw so much light upon the condition of the country at that time, and the apparent hopelessness of any attempt to secure relief for the persecuted Baptists. According to the testimony of Madison, himself not a Baptist, the Baptist preachers were in the main orthodox, and the persecution waged against them was often led by clergymen of the Establishment—clergymen who were prompted, not by any due regard for religion and morals, but by considerations of self-interest.

Semple (page 20) describes the dilemma in which the leaders found themselves at this juncture:

"The zealots for the old order were greatly embarrassed. 'If,' say they, 'we permit them to go on, our church must come to nothing; and yet, if we punish them as far as we can stretch the law, it seems not to deter them; for they preach through prison windows, in spite of our endeavors to prevent it.'"

Such was the status of things when the House of Burgesses met, in May, 1774. They met on the 5th, and on the 12th the following entry appears in the Journal:

BAPTIST PETITION OF 1774.

"A petition of sundry persons of the community of Christians called Baptists, and other Protestant dissenters, whose names are thereunto subscribed, was presented to the House and read, setting forth that the toleration proposed by the bill ordered at the last session of the General Assembly to be printed and published not admitting public worship, except in the daytime, is inconsistent with the laws of England, as well as the practice and usage of the primitive churches, and even of the English church itself; that the night season may sometimes be better spared by the petitioners from the necessary duties of their callings; and that they wish for no indulgences which may disturb the peace of government; and therefore praying the House to take their case into consideration, and to grant them suitable redress." This petition was "referred to Committee for Religion."

PETITION OF KETOCTON ASSOCIATION.

May 16, 1774, the House "ordered that the Committee of Propositions and Grievances be discharged from proceeding upon the petition of sundry Baptist ministers, from different parts of this country, convened together in Loudoun county, at their annual Association, which came certified to this Assembly, praying that an Act of Toleration may be made, giving the petitioners, and other Protestant dissenting ministers, liberty to preach in all proper places and at all seasons, without restraint.'' It was ordered that said petition be '' referred to the consideration of the Committee for Religion.''

This is the first reference on the pages of the Journal to this petition of the ministers of the Ketocton Association; but the reference indicates that it has been in the hands of the '' Committee of Propositions and Grievances '' for some time. It seems impossible to arrive at the date of the meeting of the Association at which it originated. It could not have been later than August, 1773. The fact that it does not refer to the '' Toleration Bill '' proposed in February, 1772, but prays '' that an Act of Toleration may be made,'' etc., would indicate that it dates as far back as the August meeting of 1771, and was one of those numerous petitions which began to pour in upon the Assembly in 1772, and led to the Toleration Bill of that session.

FIRST PRESBYTERIAN PETITION, 1774.

The next petition comes from the Presbyterians. According to the Journal of May 17, 1774, a petition was received from some Presbyterians in Bedford county, stating that some of their liberally disposed brethren wanted to make grants for the support of their ministry, but, *as they were not incorporated,* they could not receive and hold such, *complaining of the unsatisfactory plan of supporting them by subscriptions,* and asking for such act as would enable them '' *to take and hold lands and slaves to such use.''*

Attention is called, by the use of italics, to certain portions of the above memorial, as indicating that those Presbyterians, at least, did not like the voluntary plan of supporting the ministry, but were seeking legislation that would enable them to receive and to hold both lands and slaves for ministerial support. No petition has yet appeared from the Hanover Presbytery.

By reference to Foote's Sketches, page 320, it is found that, in their meeting of October 15, 1773—

"Presbytery took the Bill of Toleration into consideration, and judge it expedient that some two persons do attend the Assembly as commissioners of the Presbytery to transact that affair in their name and behalf. The Presbytery do, therefore, appoint the Rev. John Todd and Captain John Morton, a ruling elder, to attend the Assembly on that business, and wish they may not fail in business of that importance. The Presbytery do trust the matter entirely to them, to act as their prudence may direct and the nature of the case may require."

This shows caution.

Foote adds:

"Nothing was done in the Assembly that year to remedy the disabilities of dissenters. No laws of any kind were passed in 1774, owing to the disagreement between the Governor and the Assembly." Page 320.

In the meeting of Presbytery, October 14, 1774, it was agreed "to meet on the second Wednesday of November next, at the house of Colonel William Cabell, of Amherst, to remonstrate against a bill entitled 'A Bill for Extending the Benefit of the Act of Toleration to His Majesty's Subjects Dissenting from the Church of England in the Colony of Virginia.'" Pages 320, 321.

Their petition was presented to the House of Burgesses the following spring, and is thus described in the Journal of June 5, 1775:

PETITION OF HANOVER PRESBYTERY, 1775.

"A petition of the Presbytery of Hanover in behalf of themselves, and all the Presbyterians in Virginia, and of all Protestant dissenters elsewhere, was presented to the House and read ; setting forth that, in or about the year 1738, many thousand Presbyterian families, relying upon the assurances of Government that they should enjoy the free exercise of their religion, removed from the northern colonies and settled in the frontiers of this, forming a barrier for the lower parts thereof ; and taking notice of a bill for granting a toleration for His Majesty's dissenting Protestant subjects, which in the year 1772 was presented to the House, and afterwards ordered to be printed, and pointing out several objections thereunto ; and praying that no bill may pass into a law but such as will secure to the petitioners equal liberties and advantages with their fellow-subjects." It was "ordered that the said petition do lie upon the table."

BAPTIST PETITION, 1775.

June 13, 1775 : "A petition of sundry persons of the community of Christians called Baptists, and other Protestant dissenters, whose names are thereunto subscribed, was presented to the House and read ; setting forth that the toleration proposed by the bill, ordered at a former session of the General Assembly to be printed and published, not admitting public worship, except in the daytime, is inconsistent with the laws of England, as well as with the practice and usage of the primitive churches, and even of the English church itself ; that the night season may sometimes be better spared by the petitioners from the necessary duties of their callings ; and that they wish for no indulgences which may disturb the peace of Government ; and, therefore, praying the House to take their case into consideration and to grant them suitable redress." This petition, too, was ordered "to lie upon the table."

This Baptist petition was essentially the same as one which had been presented to the House in May, 1774, while the petition of the Hanover Presbytery is presented now (June 5, 1775,) for the first time. Although the Baptists had been suffering persecution from 1768 down to and including the year 1774, the Hanover Presbytery has not been heard from. And the explanation of this silence is not difficult. *They* were enjoying the benefits of the Act of Toleration, according to the agreement entered into in 1738 between the Presbyterian Synod and Governor Gooch. And it was not until the Assembly had, in the year 1772, in response to Baptist petitions, prepared a new Toleration Bill, which contained very annoying and oppressive restrictions, that the Hanover Presbytery broke their silence and came out in earnest protest against the changes proposed.

PETITION OF THE PRESBYTERY OF HANOVER.

This petition of the Hanover Presbytery was published in full in the *Central Presbyterian* of May 16, 1888, and heralded as the "advance guard of that army of remonstrances which so vigorously attacked the Establishment, and finally overpowered it and established perfect religious liberty on its ruins." The editor referred to it as proof "that the Presbyterians anticipated the Baptists in their memorials asking for religious liberty." That the reader may judge for himself, that memorial is given here in full:

"*To the Honorable the Speaker, and the Gentlemen of the House of Burgesses:*

The petition of the Presbytery of Hanover, in behalf of themselves and all the Presbyterians in Virginia in particular, and all Protestant dissenters in general, humbly showeth, That upon application made by the Rev. Mr. James Anderson in behalf of the Synod of Philadelphia, the honorable Governor Gooch, with the advice of the Council, did, in the year 1738, or about that time, for the encouragement of all Presbyterians who might incline to settle in the colony, grant an instrument of writing under the seal of the colony, containing the most ample assurances that they should enjoy the full and free exercise of their religion, and all the other privileges of good subjects. Relying upon this express stipulation, as well as upon the justice and catholic spirit of the whole legislative body, several thousand families of Presbyterians have removed from the Northern provinces into the frontiers of this colony, exposed themselves to a cruel and savage enemy, and all the other toils and dangers of settling a new country, and soon became a barrier to the former inhabitants who were settled in the more commodious parts of the colony. Ever since that time we have been considered and treated upon an equal footing with our fellow-subjects ; nor have our ministers or people been restricted in their religious privileges by any law of the colony. Your humble petitioners further show, that with gratitude they acknowledge the catholic design of our late honorable Assembly to secure by law the religious liberties of all Protestant dissenters in the colony ; accordingly they did, in the year 1772, prepare and print a Toleration Bill ; but, as the subject was deeply interesting, it was generously left open for amendment. But, notwithstanding we are fully persuaded of the catholic and generous design of our late representatives ; yet we are deeply sensible that some things in the above named bill will be very grievous and burdensome to us, if passed into a law. Therefore, we humbly and earnestly pray that the said bill may not be established without such alterations and amendments as will render it more agreeable to the principles of impartial liberty and sound policy, which, we presume, were the valuable ends for which it was first intended. Therefore, we humbly beg leave, while we are making the prayer of our petition in a more particular way, to lay before this honorable House in the most respectful manner a few remarks upon the bill.

The preamble is agreeable to what we desire, only we pray that the preamble and every other part of the bill may be so expressed as will be most likely to obtain the royal assent.

We are also willing that all our clergymen should be required to take the oaths of allegiance, etc., usually taken by civil officers, and to declare their belief of the Holy Scriptures.

Likewise, as is required in the said bill, we shall willingly have all our churches and stated places for public worship registered, if this honorable House shall think proper to grant it. But every minister of the gospel is under indispensable obligations to follow the example of our blessed Saviour, "who went about doing good," and the example of his apostles, who not only "taught in the temple, but in every house where they came they ceased not to teach and preach Jesus Christ." From which, and their constant practice of travelling into every quarter of the world, we humbly trust that it will appear to this Assembly that we cannot, consistent with the duties of our office, wholly confine our ministrations to any place or number of places; and to be limited by law would be the more grievous, because in many parts of this colony, even where the majority of the inhabitants are Presbyterians, it is not, and perhaps it may not in any short time be easy to determine where it would be the most expedient to fix upon a stated place for public worship; and, indeed, where we have houses for worship already built, generally the bounds of our congregations are so very extensive that many of our people, especially women, children and servants, are not able to attend by reason of the distance, which makes it our duty, as faithful ministers of Christ, to double our diligence, and frequently to lecture and catechise in the remote corners of our congregations. This restriction would also be very grievous to us in many other respects. We only beg leave to add : That the number of Presbyterians in this province is now very great and the number of clergymen but small ; therefore, we are obliged frequently to itinerate and preach through various parts of the colony, that our people may have an opportunity to worship God and receive the sacraments in the way agreeable to their own consciences. As to our having meetings for public worship in the night, it is not in frequent practice among our churches ; yet sometimes we find it expedient to attend night meetings, that a neighborhood may hear a sermon or a lecture, or be catechised, without being much interrupted in their daily labor. And so long as our fellow-subjects are permitted to meet together by day or by night for the purposes of business or diversion, we hope we shall not be restrained from meeting together as opportunity serves us, upon business of all others the most important ; especially if it be considered that the apostles held frequent societies by night, and once St. Paul continued his speech till midnight ; accordingly it is well known that in city and collegiate churches evening prayers and lectures have long been esteemed lawful and profitable exercises. As to any bad influence this practice may have upon servants or any others, it is sufficient to say that there is nothing in our principles or way of worship that tends to promote a spirit of disobedience or disorder, but much to the contrary ; and if any person shall be detected in doing or teaching anything criminal in this respect, we presume he is liable to punishment by a law already in being ; therefore, we pray that no dissenting minister, according to law, may be subjected to any penalty for preaching or teaching at any time or in any place in this colony.

We confess it is easy for us to keep open doors in time of divine service, except in case of a storm or other inclemencies of the weather; yet we would humbly represent that such a requirement implies a suspicion of our loyalty, and will fix a stigma upon us to after ages, such as, we presume, our honorable representatives will not judge that we have anyhow incurred ; therefore we pray that this clause may also be removed from the bill.

And as to baptizing or receiving servants into our communion, we have always anxiously desired to do it with the permission of their masters ; but when a servant appears to be a true penitent and makes profession of his faith in Christ, upon his desire it is our indispensable duty to admit him into our church, and if he has never been baptized, we are to baptize him according to the command of Christ : "Go ye, therefore, and teach all nations, baptizing them in the name of the Father, and of the Son, and of the Holy Ghost, teaching them to observe all things whatsoever I have commanded you ; and, lo, I am with you alway, even unto the end of the world. Amen." And we are so confidently persuaded of the liberal sentiments of this House, that in obeying the laws of Christ, we shall never be reduced to the necessity of disobeying the laws of our country.

And we also, having abundant reasons to hope that we shall be indulged in every other thing that may appear reasonable, your petitioners further pray :

For liberty and protection in the discharge of all the functions and duties of our office as ministers of the gospel, and that the penalties to be inflicted on those who may disturb any of our congregations in the time of divine service, or misuse the preacher, be the same as on those who disturb the congregation or misuse the preachers of the Church of England, and that the dissenting clergy, as well as the clergy of the Established church, be excused from all burdensome offices. All which we conceive is granted in the English Toleration Act.

And we pray for that freedom in speaking and writing upon religious subjects which is allowed by law to every member of the British Empire in civil affairs, and which has long been so friendly to the cause of liberty.

And also we pray for a right by law to hold estates, and enjoy donations and legacies for the support of our churches and schools for the instruction of our youth. Though this is not expressed in the English Act of Toleration, yet the greatest lawyers in England have pled, and the best judges have determined, that it is manifestly implied.

Finally, we pray that nothing in the Act of Toleration may be so expressed as to render us suspicious or odious to our countrymen, with whom we desire to live in peace and friendship; but that all misdemeanors committed by dissenters may be punished by laws equally binding upon all our fellow-subjects, without any regard to their religious tenets. Or if any non-compliance with the conditions of the Act of Toleration shall be judged to deserve punishment, we pray that the crime may be accurately defined and the penalty ascertained by the Legislature, and that neither be left to the discretion of any magistrate or court whatsoever.

May it please this honorable Assembly, There are some other things which we omit, because they are less essential to the rights of conscience, and the interest of our church. We trust that we petition for nothing but what justice says ought to be ours; for as ample privileges as any of our fellow-subjects enjoy. "To have and enjoy the full and free exercise of our religion, without molestation or danger of incurring any penalty whatsoever." We are petitioning in favor of a church that is neither contemptible nor obscure. It prevails in every province to the northward of Maryland, and its advocates in all the more Southern provinces are numerous and respectable; the greatest monarch in the north of Europe adorns it; it is the established religion of the populous and wealthy states of Holland; it prevails in the wise and happy cantons of Switzerland; and it is the possession of Geneva, a state among the foremost of those who, at the Reformation, emancipated themselves from the slavery of Rome; and some of the first geniuses and writers in every branch of literature were sons of our church.

The subject is of such solemn importance to us that, comparatively speaking, our lives and our liberties are but of little value; and the population of the country, and the honor of the Legislature, as well as the interest of American liberty, are certainly most deeply concerned in the matter: Therefore, we would willingly lay before this honorable House a more extensive view of our reasons in favor of an unlimited, impartial toleration; but fearing we should transgress upon the patience of the House, we conclude with praying that the alwise, just and merciful God would direct you in this, and all your other important determinations.

Signed by order of Presbytery.

DAVID RICE, Moderator.
CALEB WALLACE, Clerk.

At a session of the Presbytery in Amherst county, November 11th, 1774."

The reader will look in vain for any "attack upon the Establishment," or any sign of hostility to it. It professes the greatest loyalty to King George and to the Colonial Government. It contemplates nothing more than securing for Presbyterians and others in Virginia the same privileges and liberties which they enjoyed in England under the Act of Toleration. As has already been said, in the comment upon the agreement between the Presbyterian Synod and Governor Gooch, the Presbyterians were bound by that agreement to be loyal to the government and to support the Establishment, and they do not violate their word in the above petition. Nor do they ever take any step against the Establishment until the Colonial Government has been overturned and the colony has become a sovereign and independent State.

This closes the period of "Intolerance, Toleration, and Persecution." The colony is involved in trouble with the mother country. Virginia has denounced the "Boston Port Bill," and made common cause with Massachusetts. The First Continental Congress has already met in Philadelphia. Patrick Henry has electrified the country by his memorable speech in the popular Convention which met March, 1775, in the old St. John's church, in Richmond. The battles of Lexington and Concord have been fought (April 19), and Virginia has taken steps to enroll companies of volunteers in every county. The war of the

Revolution is on, and the times call for union and harmony among all classes. Hence there is no more persecution of Baptists. There are no imprisonments in 1775, and that obnoxious Toleration Bill is indefinitely postponed. The same ruling class that admitted the Presbyterians to Virginia and to the benefits of the Act of Toleration, on condition that they occupied the frontier counties, and thus protected them against Indian raids, are now inclined to tolerate, not only the Presbyterians, but the Baptists also, with all their "pernicious doctrines," if only they will help in the struggle with Great Britain. The Baptists will help, and not a Tory will be found among them. But they will strike for something more and something dearer to them than civil liberty—for freedom of conscience, for "just and true liberty, equal and impartial liberty."

CHAPTER III.

The Colonial Convention of 1775.

THE "Popular Convention," which met in St. John's church, Richmond, March 20, 1775, had responded to Patrick Henry's "Give me liberty or give me death" oration, by adopting the resolutions which he had proposed, and taking active steps towards putting the colony in a state of defense. The second Continental Congress had met in Philadelphia, May 10, and on the 17th of June, the day of the battle of Bunker Hill, they elected George Washington "commander-in-chief" of the "Continental army." Governor Dunmore had called the House of Burgesses together on the 1st day of June; but becoming alarmed at the rebellious proceedings of that body, he fled, with his family, from Williamsburg, and took refuge on a man-of-war. The House declared that the Governor had by this act abdicated his post, and they made the president of the Council the head of the government. They then adjourned to meet in Richmond, July 17, "as a convention"; so that the "Colonial Convention of 1775" was simply the House of Burgesses under a new name and in a different character.

But while these things were going on in the political world, certain important steps were being taken by the persecuted Baptists, the only body of dissenters that appeared before this Convention and sought to influence its action. Their remarkable growth and rapid spread dur-

ing the years of persecution had emboldened them to "undertake great things for God" and to "expect great
things from God." On page 25 of his History, Semple
says:

"So favorable did their prospects appear, that towards the close
of the year 1774 they began to entertain serious hopes, not only of
obtaining liberty of conscience, but of actually overturning the
church establishment, from whence all their oppressions had arisen.
Petitions for this purpose were accordingly drawn and circulated
with great industry. Vast numbers readily, and indeed eagerly,
subscribed to them."

This statement accords with what Madison had said in
his letter to Bradford, and it is given here to show how
early the Baptists began to take steps looking towards the
fullest and freest liberty.

The General Association of Separate Baptists had divided into two divisions, one for the north side and the
other for the south side of the James river ; but in the fall
of 1774 "both of the associations appointed their next
session to be holden at Manokin Town, or Dover meeting-
house, the fourth Saturday in May, 1775." At that
meeting, it was determined that the two districts should
meet jointly at their next session, and they appointed Dupuy's meeting-house, Powhatan (then Cumberland)
county, as the place, and the second Saturday in August,
1775, as the time.

IMPORTANT BAPTIST MEETING.

As to this meeting, Semple (page 62) has the following:

"It seems that one great object of uniting the two districts at
this time was to strive together for the abolition of the hierarchy,
or church establishment, in Virginia. The discontents in America,
arising from British oppression, were now drawing to a crisis ; most

of the colonies had determined to resist, and some were for independence. This was a very favorable season for the Baptists. Having been much ground under the British laws—or, at least, by the interpretation of them in Virginia—they were to a man favorable to any revolution by which they could obtain freedom of religion. They had known from experience that mere toleration was not a sufficient check, having been imprisoned at a time when that law was considered by many as being in force. It was, therefore, resolved at this session to circulate petitions to the Virginia Convention, or General Assembly, throughout the State, in order to obtain signatures. The prayer of these was that the church establishment should be abolished, and religion left to stand upon its own merits ; and that all religious societies should be protected in the peaceable enjoyment of their own religious principles and modes of worship. They appointed Jeremiah Walker, John Williams, and George Roberts to wait on the Legislature with these petitions. They also determined to petition the Assembly for leave to preach to the army, which was granted."

Dr. Howell, in his account of the meetings at Manokin Town and Dupuy's, is somewhat fuller and more definite. He says that at the first meeting a committee was appointed to prepare an address to the Convention soon to meet in Richmond, which "would embody their opinions and desires in the existing political crisis of the country." This committee was to report at the next meeting, at Dupuy's. And on page 142 Howell says:

"The General Association assembled at the time and place appointed. The committee reported the address, which was carefully canvassed, and, after a deliberation of two days, unanimously adopted. Rev. Messrs. Jeremiah Walker, John Williams, and George Roberts were appointed commissioners on the part of the Baptists of Virginia to present their address to the Convention ; and these gentlemen were especially instructed to remain at the Capitol during the session, to mingle and converse freely with the members of the Convention, and to employ every honorable means to attain the ends proposed."

And on page 143 he adds: "The address, which was adopted, and which was filed among the State papers of Virginia, contemplated two objects—the freedom of the colony from British rule, and the freedom of religion from all government trammels and direction. The former of these objects is thus noticed in the journals of the Convention:" [Here Howell gives the Journal entry, which will be found below.]

The Convention assembled in Richmond on the 17th day of July, and on the 12th of August (second Saturday) the Baptist Association met at Dupuy's. Four days thereafter, August 16, the Baptist address was laid before the Convention, as the following extract from the Journal of that day shows:

BAPTIST ADDRESS.

[Journal of Convention, August 16, 1775.]

"An address from the Baptists in this colony was presented and read, setting forth that, however distinguished from the body of their countrymen by appellations and sentiments of a religious nature, they, nevertheless, considered themselves as members of the same community in respect to matters of a civil nature, and embarked in the same common cause ; that, alarmed at the oppression which hangs over America, they had considered what part it would be proper to take in the unhappy contest, and had determined that in some cases it was lawful to go to war ; and that they ought to make a military resistance against Great Britain in her unjust invasion, tyrannical oppression, and repeated hostilities; that their brethren were left at discretion to enlist without incurring the censure of their religious community ; and, under these circumstances, many had enlisted as soldiers, and many more were ready to do so, who had an earnest desire that their ministers should preach to them during the campaigns ; that they had, therefore, appointed four of their brethren to make application to this Convention for the liberty of preaching to the troops at convenient times, without molestation or abuse, and praying the same may be granted them."

Fortunately, this one of the many memorials of the Baptists can be produced in full. It was found in the old State papers in the Capitol building by Hon. William Wirt Henry, and, through his courtesy, published in the *Religious Herald* of July 19, 1888. [See Appendix.]

RESOLUTION OF CONVENTION.

The Convention was in a conciliatory frame of mind just then, and the following resolution was passed:

"*Resolved*, That it be an instruction to the commanding officers of the regiment or troops to be raised, that they permit dissenting clergymen to celebrate divine worship, and to preach to the soldiers, or exhort from time to time, as the various operations of the military service may permit, for the ease of such scrupulous consciences as may not choose to attend divine service as celebrated by the chaplain."

Those words, "for the ease of such scrupulous consciences," etc., have in them a little sting, and suggest the thought that the framers of that resolution were swallowing a bitter pill. Only the year before, Jeremiah Walker and others had been imprisoned in Chesterfield jail for preaching the gospel, and now he comes, with Williams and Roberts, to ask in behalf of their persecuted brethren that they might have the privilege of preaching to the soldiers whom they sent to the patriot army. But, bitter as the pill was, it was sufficiently sugar-coated with the promise of their much needed help in the struggle with Great Britain to enable them to swallow it. It was the same class (the ruling class) that had, a few years before, made concessions to the brave and hardy Scotch-Irish Presbyterians, on condition that they settled in the western counties, and thus formed a frontier line of defense against the Indians, and now, when the services of all the people are needed against a stronger and mightier foe, even Baptist preachers, whose petition for exemption from musters and other military duties had been contemptuously spurned hitherto, are now welcomed as co-laborers in the common cause and placed upon an equality with the clergy of the Established church, *so far as the army is concerned.*

Dr. Hawks says:

"This, it is believed, was the first step made towards placing the clergy of all denominations upon an equal footing in Virginia." History, etc., page 138.

Dr. Foote (322) makes this comment:

"The action of the Legislature shows how far the principle of religious toleration had advanced. When all men were called to defend their common country against an alarming danger, as in the French and Indian war, then the law-makers discovered that those who fought their battles ought to be indulged with freedom of conscience. Granted in one position and one set of circumstances, there was no stopping till it was granted to all men and in all cases."

"The Baptists," says Dr. Hawks (137), "were not slow in discovering the advantageous position in which the political troubles of the country had placed them. Their numerical strength was such as to make it important to both sides to secure their influence. They knew this, and therefore determined to turn the circumstance to their profit as a sect. Persecution had taught them not to love the Establishment, and they now saw before them a reasonable prospect of overturning it entirely. In their Association, they had calmly discussed the matter, and resolved upon their course ; in this course they were consistent to the end, and the war which they waged against the church was a war of extermination."

This bold and advanced attitude of the Baptists will be better appreciated when it is considered that the political leaders in Virginia did not, at this time, contemplate independence of Great Britain, but only a struggle for their rights "in the union." By reference to chapter 4 of ordinances of this convention, it will be seen that they ordered a new convention to be elected by the people every April. But, what is more to the point, they drew and passed "A Declaration of Delegates," August 26, containing the following:

"But, lest our views and designs should be misrepresented and misunderstood, we again and for all publicly and solemnly declare, before God and the world, that we do bear faith and true allegiance to His Majesty, George the Third, our only lawful and rightful King," etc.

This needs no comment. It is evident that this body was opposed to separation from the mother country. And such was the attitute of the colonies generally. Rayner, in his "Life of Jefferson" (page 127), says: "All historians concur in testifying that total emancipation was not contemplated until the spring of '76."

The Convention met again in Richmond, December 1, 1775, and adjourned the same day to meet in Williamsburg, the capital, December 4. They adjourned January 20, 1776, to meet again April 2. The election that month resulted in some changes and additions. Twenty-nine new members were elected, and seventy of the old ones returned. They will meet in Williamsburg, May 6, and decide the future destiny of Virginia, and also exert a material influence upon the Continental Congress in Philadelphia. In the meantime, those petitions ordered by the General Association in their meeting at Dupuy's are being circulated all over the State, and signatures are being obtained from all classes, including many noble members of the Established church, and in due time they will be presented to the Virginia General Assembly for legislative action.

CORRECTION.

It was the opinion of the writer, at one time, that the address which was presented to the Convention of '75 embraced all of the subjects that were considered and acted upon by the General Association of that year. That opinion was based upon the accounts given by Semple and Howell, which, while clear enough as to what the Baptists resolved upon and what they actually did, are not always clear as to times and places. They do not seem to distinguish between the Convention of '75, the Convention of '76, and the General Assembly of '76—an omission which is attributed partly to the fact that they were writing, not a history of political affairs, but a brief account of the Baptists, and partly, also, to the fact that these three bodies were, as to their personnel, essentially the same ; for the lower house (House of Delegates) of the first Assembly under the Constitution and Bill of Rights was the same as the Convention of '76, which framed the Constitution, and of that Convention there were, as has already been stated, only twenty-nine members that were not in the Convention of '75. Hence Semple (and Howell, too,) might very well use Convention and Assembly interchangeably; but, in doing so, he leaves the reader in the dark as to what was presented to the one and what to the other. But the discovery and publication of the address itself removes all doubt and uncertainty, and shows that, while the Baptists had determined on the overthrow of the Establishment, and to circulate petitions to that end, yet, in their address to that Convention, met for the consideration of measures for the defence of the colony, they expressed themselves on that subject only, declaring in favor of military resistance to British oppression, offering the services of their young men as soldiers, and asking only that, so far as the army was concerned, their ministers might enjoy like privileges with the clergy of the Established church.

There was consummate wisdom in this ; for, as subsequent developments will show, it would have been very impolitic, even if their petitions had been ready, to have sprung the question of disestablishment upon that body before they had committed themselves to the cause of independence.   And as it is matter of history that the Baptists had already won the sympathies and friendship of such men as Patrick Henry, Thomas Jefferson, and James Madison, it is not unreasonable to suppose that, in the management of their long and desperate struggle for religious freedom, they were guided to some extent, at least, by the advice of these great men.   But, however that may be, they showed "the wisdom of the serpent" and "the harmlessness of the dove" in their address to the Convention of '75, and the journal of that body records the first complimentary notice of Baptist petitions, and the "first step made towards placing the clergy of all denominations upon an equal footing in Virginia."

CHAPTER IV.

The Convention of 1776.

This body was elected in April and assembled in Williamsburg on the 6th of May. A comparison of the lists of delegates in attendance shows that there were twenty-nine new members in this Convention that were not in the last Convention of '75. It is impossible to explain all of these changes, but it is quite certain that some of them were due to the rising tide of Baptist principles and the solidarity of Baptist votes. The following significant statement of William Fristoe, at page 90 of his History, will explain:

"The business then [1776] was to unite as an oppressed people in using our influence and give our voice in electing members of the State legislature—members favorable to religious liberty and the rights of conscience. Although the Baptists were not numerous, when there was anything near a division among the other inhabitants in a county, the Baptists, together with their influence, gave a caste to the scale, by which means many a worthy and useful member was lodged in the House of Assembly and answered a valuable purpose there."

Now, this body which met in May, and which had just been elected for one year, was, by its act, made the "House of Delegates" of the first General Assembly under the new Constitution. Hence, while Fristoe is speaking of elections to the Assembly, it is manifest that what he says applies equally to the election in April, which resulted in placing in the Convention, and in the subsequent Assembly, some of the most valiant champions of religious liberty, one of whom was the youthful James Madison, of Orange, and another was French Strother, of Culpeper. The former,

James Madison, needs no further introduction to the reader. His letters to his friend Radford, which have already been given in Chapter II, show that, at the early age of 21, he had espoused the cause of the persecuted Baptists and had imbibed their views on the question of religious liberty. No wonder the Baptists of Orange, and others who sympathized with them, were in favor of putting this young and gifted champion of their cause in that body to which they were going to appeal for redress of grievances.

As to French Strother, the following interesting sketch is given by Rev. Philip Slaughter, D. D., in his History of St. Mark's Parish, Culpeper county, Va., page 170:

"French Strother became a vestryman in 1772, and church warden in 1780. He made himself very popular by releasing a Baptist minister who had been imprisoned by a justice of the peace, by substituting his man Tom in his place and letting him out at night. He represented the county for nearly thirty years in the General Assembly; was a member in 1776, and of the Convention of 1788–'9, and voted against the Constitution and for the famous resolutions of 1798–'9. He was solicited to oppose Mr. Madison for Congress (see Rives' Madison); but Monroe became the candidate, and was badly beaten."

Strother was popular in Culpeper for the same reason that Madison was popular in Orange, and there were doubtless a number of others in that Convention who owed their election to the same influence. It is not a little significant that so many of the changes were in those counties where persecution had raged most fiercely and dissenters had multiplied most rapidly.

Six days after the meeting of the Virginia Convention, Congress met in Philadelphia (May 12), and instructed the colonies to organize independent governments of their own. The war was on. Washington had forced Howe to evacuate Boston, and was now defending New York.

ADDRESS FROM AUGUSTA COUNTY.

The first address presented to the Convention was from
Augusta county—a county noted for its loyalty to the
cause of the Revolution. The Journal of May 10 has
the following notice:

" A representation from the Committee of the county of Augusta
was presented to the Convention and read, setting forth the present
unhappy situation of the country, and, from the ministerial measures
of vengeance now pursuing, representing the necessity of making the
confederacy of the united colonies the most perfect, independent, and
lasting, and of framing an equal, free, and liberal government, that
may bear the test of all future ages."

This was " referred to Committee on State of the Colony."

QUESTION AS TO BAPTIST ADDRESS.

An interesting question is raised, and may be appro-
priately introduced at this point, by the following extract
from an " Oration on the Life, Character, and Services of
James Madison," delivered at Culpeper Courthouse, July
18, 1836, by Hon. John S. Barbour, father of the late
United States Senator of that name:

" He (Madison) well knew, as I am told he often declared, that
the Baptists had been in all his time the fast and firm friends of
liberty; that whilst he was in the Convention of '76, which framed
our State Constitution, they had even then, when hope was sinking
in the despair of our cause, addressed that body. In that address
they declared that the tenets of their religion did not forbid their
fighting for their country, and that the pastors of their flocks would
animate the young of their persuasion to enlist for our battles."

The question raised by this extract is, whether the Baptist address which was presented to the Convention of '75,
and produced such a favorable impression upon that body,
was again read before this Convention of '76 ? That it was
in the custody of the clerk, there can be no doubt; for

even the petitions which were before the House of Burgesses in the spring of '75 were in the custory of the clerk, as appears from an "order" of the Assembly of October 25, 1776, directing the clerk to turn over to the proper committees under the new organization "the several petitions and propositions depending and undetermined before the Assembly in the month of May, 1775." But was that address called for and read to this Convention for the benefit of the twenty-nine new members, and as having an important bearing upon the objects for which the Convention was assembled? It is evident, from Madison's description of it, that it was the same address as the one described in the Journal of August 16, 1775. That there is no reference to it in the Journal of this Convention, may be accounted for on the ground that it was not a new address, but one which had already been received and properly noticed, and also by the further consideration that it was doubtless read in committee of the whole house, of which proceedings no record is made in the Journal, except their report to the House. A number of writers have claimed that that address was read before the Convention of '76 and made a profound impression, and they seem to be sustained by the testimony of Madison, as given by Hon. John S. Barbour.

RESOLUTIONS OF CONVENTION.

On the 15th of May, the Convention adopted the following resolutions:

"*Resolved, unanimously,* That the delegates in General Congress be instructed to propose to that respectable body to declare the united colonies free and independent States, absolved from all allegiance to, or dependence upon, the crown or Parliament of Great Britain; and that they give the assent of this colony to such declaration, and to whatever measures may be thought proper and necessary by the

Congress for forming foreign alliances, and a confederation of the colonies, at such time and in the manner as to them shall seem best; provided, that the power of forming government for and the regulations of the internal concerns of each colony be left to the respective colonial legislatures.

" *Resolved, unanimously*, That a committee be appointed to prepare a Declaration of Rights, and such a plan of government as will be most likely to maintain peace and order in this colony, and secure substantial and equal liberty to the people."

June 12th, the "Declaration of Rights" was adopted, the 16th article of which, as drawn by George Mason, was reported by the committee as follows:

16TH ARTICLE OF BILL OF RIGHTS, AS REPORTED.

" That religion, or the duty we owe to our Creator, and the manner of discharging it, can be directed only by reason and conviction, and not by force or violence ; and, therefore, that all men should enjoy the fullest toleration in the exercise of religion, according to the dictates of conscience, unpunished and unrestrained by the magistrate, unless, under the color of religion, any man disturb the peace, the happiness, or the safety of society; and that it is the mutual duty of all to practise Christian forbearance, love, and charity towards each other."

16TH ARTICLE, AS AMENDED.

On motion of James Madison, this article was amended, in "Committee of the Whole," so as to read:

" That religion, or the duty which we owe to our Creator, and the manner of discharging it, can be directed only by reason and conviction, not by force or violence; and, therefore, all men are equally entitled to the free exercise of religion according to the dictates of conscience; and that it is the mutual duty of all to practise Christian forbearance, love, and charity towards each other."

Between these two there is a radical difference—the difference between toleration and liberty. How came the youthful Madison to understand it?

"Where," asks Dr. John C. Long, "did the stripling learn the distinction between religious freedom and religious toleration? It had not then begun to be recognized in treatises on religion and morals. He did not learn it from Jeremy Taylor or John Locke, but from his Baptist neighbors, whose wrongs he had witnessed, and who persistently taught that the civil magistrate had nothing to do with matters of religion." See address of Memorial Committee of 1873.

The following is from Chambers' Library of Universal Knowledge, IX., 334:

"In the committee, Madison distinguished himself by opposing the use of the following phrase of an article on religion, designed to secure freedom of worship : 'Toleration in the exercise of religion, . . . unpunished and unrestrained by the magistrate, unless under color of religion, any man disturb the peace, the happiness, or the safety of society,' as a dangerous form of guaranty of religious freedom. Toleration, he maintained, belonged to a system where there was an established church, and where it was a thing granted, not of right, but of grace. He feared the power, in the hands of a dominant religion, to construe what 'may disturb the peace, the happiness, or the safety of society,' and he ventured to propose a substitute, which was finally adopted. It marks an era in legislative history, and is believed to be the first provision ever embodied in any constitution or law for the security of absolute equality before the law to all religious opinions."

But why, it may be asked, did not Madison propose the change in the committee room? He was a member of the committee, and so was Patrick Henry. Why did he wait until their report came before the whole house? Was it that he did propose the change in the committee room and it was rejected? Or was it that his own attention was not attracted to the much-needed alteration, or amendment, until the report was under discussion in the "Committee of the Whole," and those Baptist commissioners, Walker, Williams, and Roberts, who had been instructed to be on hand on such occasions, had an opportunity of seeing that obnox-

ious article and making known to him their objection?
Both Howell and Semple say that they were appointed for
this purpose, and while the records of the Convention will
not, of course, indicate the presence of these, or any other
"lobbyists," there is good ground for suspecting their
presence, and tracing to their watchfulness the important
amendment moved by their youthful advocate, James Madison.   Dr. Howell, in his account of the General Association of the Baptists for 1776, which met in August, says:

"Its commissioners to the State Convention, Mr. Walker, Mr.
Williams, and Mr. Roberts, reported, giving a full account of their
mission, and the extraordinary success with which God had crowned
their endeavors. They received the grateful thanks and earnest congratulations of all their brethren." Early Baptists of Virginia,
page 159.

A NEW CLAIM.

It is proper to notice here the recent claim set up in favor
of Patrick Henry as the author of this famous 16th article
of the Bill of Rights.   The basis of that claim is the following extract from "a fragment of Edmund Randolph's
Manuscript History of Virginia":

"The 15th, recommending an adherence and frequent recurrence
to fundamental principles, and the 16th, unfettering the exercise of
religion, were proposed by Mr. Henry. The latter, coming from a
gentleman who was supposed to be a dissenter, caused an appeal to
him whether it was designed as a prelude to an attack on the Establishment, and he disclaimed such an object."

The above is given with the view of letting the reader
judge for himself as to the authorship of that article in its
original form.   All other historians ascribe it to George
Mason.   Rives, in his "Life and Times of Madison," page
138, says that Mason wrote fourteen articles of the Bill of
Rights, and that three were added by the committee.   But

these three did not include the 15th and 16th. Mason's 14th article related to the vital subject of religious liberty, and became the 16th of the bill. He says this article "came before the Convention precisely as it stood in Mason's draft."

But even supposing Randolph's statement to be true, and that Patrick Henry was the author of that article, Randolph's testimony convicts him of being still an undergraduate in the school of religious liberty; for, when challenged by some alert churchman, who had not forgotten the famous "Parsons' Cause," whether this was a prelude to an attack on the Establishment, "he disclaimed such an object." In other words, he was for the broadest toleration towards dissenters, but not in favor of disturbing the Established church, and hence not in full sympathy with the Baptist doctrine of entire separation between Church and State.

BAPTIST MEMORIAL.

The Journal of June 20 has this entry:

"A petition of sundry persons of the Baptist church, in the county of Prince William, whose names are thereunto subscribed, was presented to the Convention and read, setting forth that at a time when this colony, with others, is contending for the civil rights of mankind, against the enslaving schemes of a powerful enemy, they are persuaded the strictest unanimity is necessary among ourselves ; and, that every remaining cause of division may, if possible, be removed, they think it their duty to petition for the following religious privileges, which they have not yet been indulged with in this part of the world—to wit : That they be allowed to worship God in their own way, without interruption ; that they be permitted to maintain their own ministers, and none others ; that they be married, buried, and the like, without paying the clergy of other denominations ; that, these things granted, they will gladly unite with their brethren, and to the utmost of their ability promote the common cause." "Ordered that the said petition be referred to the Committee of Propositions and Grievances ; that they inquire into the allegations thereof, and report the same, with their opinion thereupon, to the Convention."

As the only Baptist church in Prince William county at that time was Occoquon, of which David Thomas was pastor, it would seem that this petition came not from a meeting of the Ketocton Association in Prince William, but from David Thomas' church in that Association. It was the first of those petitions which were being circulated for signatures, and the only one presented to this Convention by any religious body. Like the "sheaf of wheat" "waved before the Lord" at the Passover, it was the "first fruits" of the coming "harvest" of similar petitions that would be gathered together and poured in upon the Assembly in October. And it is worthy of notice, as another illustration of that wisdom that was guiding and directing the campaign, that this, the first petition that struck at the Establishment, was presented to the Convention, not prior to, but *after* the adoption of the Bill of Rights, with the great fundamental principle of Baptists incorporated into the organic law of the now sovereign State, and the State was committed to the cause of independence.

Thus it appears that the Baptists were the only denomination of Christians that addressed either of the Conventions on the subject of going to war with Great Britain, or on the other important subject of the rights of conscience. The Presbyterians are adhering strictly and loyally to the terms of the agreement with Governor Gooch. But the Revolution in Virginia has now freed them from that contract and left them at liberty to act according to their convictions and judgment under the new government. They will be heard from when the Assembly meets in October, and they will be the powerful allies of the Baptists and other dissenters in the war against the Establishment. The cause of religious liberty will receive a strong reinforcement in the person of Thomas Jefferson, who has just won immortal renown as the author of the Declaration of Independence. He will give up his seat in Congress, and refuse all other posts of honor, for the sake of the work of reform in his native State. And when he joins Madison and the other advocates of religious freedom in the first Virginia Legislature, the battle royal will begin. The engagements thus far described have resulted in great gain as to position, but they are only skirmishes as compared with the general engagement which begins in October, 1776, and culminates in the storming of the fortress and the fall of the Establishment in 1779.

CHAPTER V.

Beginning of Struggle in General Assembly, 1776.

THE first republican Legislature assembled at Williamsburg, October 7, 1776, and was immediately flooded with petitions. They began to be presented on the 11th, on which day the House of Delegates appointed "A Committee on Religion, composed of Messrs. Braxton, Harwood, Richard Lee, Bland, Simpson, Starke, Mayo, Hite, Fleming, James Taylor, Watts, Lewis, Adams, Curle, Jefferson, Scott, Page of Spotsylvania, McDowell, and Mr. Treasurer," and with instructions "to meet and adjourn from day to day, and to take under their consideration all matters and things relating to religion and morality, and report," etc. The several petitions, as they were presented to the House and read, were "referred to the Committee on Religion." As some were against the Establishment and some were in its favor, they will be given under these two heads, and in the order in which they were presented.

PETITIONS AGAINST THE ESTABLISHMENT.

I. SUNDRY INHABITANTS OF PRINCE EDWARD.

October 11 : "A petition of sundry inhabitants of the county of Prince Edward, whose names are thereunto subscribed, was presented to the House and read; setting forth that they heartily approve and cheerfully submit themselves to the form of government adopted for this State, and hope that the United American States will long continue free and independent; that they esteem the last article of the Bill of Rights as the rising sun of religious liberty, to relieve them from a long night of ecclesiastical bondage, and do most earnestly request and expect that this House will go on to complete what is so nobly begun ; that is, to raise religious as well as civil liberty to the zenith of glory, and make Virginia an asylum for free inquiry, knowledge, and the virtuous of every denomination ; that justice to themselves and posterity makes it their indispensable duty in particular to entreat that, without delay, all church establishments might be pulled down, and every tax upon conscience and private judgment abolished, and each individual left to rise or sink by his own merit and the general laws of the land."

II. DISSENTERS IN GENERAL.

October 16 : "A petition of dissenters from the ecclesiastical establishment was presented to the House and read ; setting forth that, being delivered from British oppression, in common with the other inhabitants of this Commonwealth, they rejoice in the prospect of having their freedom secured and maintained to them and their posterity inviolate ; that their hopes have been raised and confirmed by the declarations of this House with regard to equal liberty, that invaluable blessing, which, though it be the birthright of every good member of the State, they have been deprived of, in that by taxation their property hath been wrested from them and given to those from whom they receive no equivalent ; that having long groaned under the burden of an ecclesiastical establishment, they pray that this, as well as every other yoke, may be broken, and that the oppressed may go free, that so, every religious denomination being on a level, animosities may cease, and Christian forbearance, love, and charity, practised towards each other, while the Legislature interferes only to support them in their just rights and equal privileges."

III. DISSENTERS IN ALBEMARLE, AMHERST AND BUCKINGHAM.

October 22 : "Two petitions from the dissenters from the Church of England in the counties of Albemarle, Amherst, and Buckingham were presented to the House and read ; setting forth that they have never been upon an equal footing with the good people of this country in respect to religious privileges, having been obliged by law to contribute to the support of the Established church, while at the same time they were moved from a principle of conscience to support the church of which they were members; yet, inasmuch as this was the form of government established when they became dissenters from the Church of England, they submitted to it for the sake of good order, always willing to stand up with the foremost in support of government, and in defence of the just rights and properties of the subject ; that when it became necessary the form of government should be new modelled, in consequence of having thrown off our dependence on the Crown and Parliament of Great Britain, they flattered themselves that form of government would secure equal right to the subject ; that they cannot disguise their real concern to observe that many are still violent for the establishment of the Episcopal church ; and praying that every religious denomination may be put upon an equal footing."

IV. INHABITANTS OF NORTH FARNHAM PARISH.

October 22 : " Also, a petition from the freeholders and other inhabitants of the parish of North Farnham, in the county of Richmond, setting forth that they have been much aggrieved and oppressed by the vestry of said parish, and praying a dissolution thereof."

V. LUTHERANS.

October 22 : "Also, a petition of the German congregation [Lutherans] in the county of Culpeper [now Madison], setting forth that they are oppressed by being obliged to pay parochial charges, as well as to support their own church, and praying that they may be exempted from farther payment of parochial charges, other than to support their own church and poor, and that their ministers may have equal right and privileges with their brethren in Pennsylvania, or the Established church ministers in Virginia, so far as may extend to the members of their church only."

VI. HANOVER PRESBYTERY.

October 24 : "A memorial of the Presbytery of Hanover was presented to the House and read ; setting forth that they are governed by the same sentiments which have inspired the United States of America, and are determined that nothing in their power and influence shall be wanting to give success to the common cause ; that dissenters from the Church of England in this country have ever been desirous to conduct themselves as peaceable members of the civil government, for which reason they have hitherto submitted to several ecclesiastical burthens and restrictions that are inconsistent with equal liberty, but that now, when the many and grievous oppressions of our mother country have laid this continent under the necessity of casting off the yoke of tyranny and of forming independent governments upon equitable and liberal foundations, they flatter themselves they shall be freed from all the encumbrances which a spirit of domination, prejudice, or bigotry hath interwoven with most other political systems; that they are more strongly encouraged to expect this by the declaration of rights, so universally applauded for the dignity, firmness, and precision with which it delineates and asserts the privileges of society and the prerogatives of human nature, and which they embrace as the Magna Charta of the Commonwealth, which can never be violated without endangering the grand superstructure it was destined to support. Therefore, they rely upon this declaration, as well as the justice of the Legislature, to secure to them the free exercise of religion according to the dictates of their consciences; and that they should fall short in their duty to themselves and to the many and numerous congregations under their care, were they upon this occasion to neglect laying before the House a state of the religious grievances under which they have hitherto labored; that they no longer may be continued in the present form of government; that it is well known that in the frontier counties, which are justly supposed to contain a fifth part of the inhabitants of Virginia, the dissenters have borne the heavy burthens of purchasing glebes and supporting the Established clergy, where there are very few Episcopalians either to assist in bearing the expense or to reap the advantage; and that throughout the other parts of the country there are also many thousands of zealous friends and defenders of the State, who, besides the invidious and disadvantageous restrictions to which they have been subjected annually, pay large taxes to support an establishment from which their consciences and principles oblige them to dissent, all which are so many violations of their natural rights, and in their consequences a restraint upon freedom of inquiry and private judgment. In this enlightened age, and in a land where all are united in the most strenuous efforts to be free, they hope and expect that their representatives will cheerfully concur in removing every species of religious as well as civil bondage. That every argument for civil liberty gains additional strength when applied to liberty in the concerns of religion, and that there is no argument in favor of establishing the Christian religion but what may be pleaded for establishing the tenets of Mahomet by those who believe the Alcoran; or, if this be not true, it is at least impossible for the magistrate to adjudge the right of preference among the various sects which profess the Christian faith, without erecting a chair of infallibility, which would lead us back to the Church of Rome. That they beg leave farther to represent that religious establishments are highly injurious to the temporal interests of any community, without insisting upon the ambition and the arbitrary practices of those who are favored by government, or the intriguing, seditious spirit which is commonly excited by this, as well as every other kind of oppression, such establishments greatly retard population, and consequently the progress of arts, sciences, and manufactures. Witness the rapid growth and improvements of the northern provinces, compared with this. That no one can deny the more early settlement and the many superior advantages of our country would have invited multitudes of artificers, mechanics, and other useful members of society to fix their habitation among us, who have either remained in the place of their nativity or preferred worse civil government and a more barren field, where they might enjoy the right of conscience more fully than they had a prospect of doing in this ; from which they infer that Virginia might now have been the capital of America, and a match for the British arms without depending upon others for the necessaries of war, had it not been prevented by her religious establishment. Neither can it be made to appear that the gospel needs any such civil aid ; they rather conceive that, when our blessed Saviour declares his kingdom is not of this world, he renounces all dependence upon State power, and, as his weapons are spiritual, and were only designed to have influence on the judgment and heart of man, they are persuaded that, if mankind were left in the quiet possession of their unalienable religious privileges, Christianity, as in the days of the apostles, would continue to prevail and flourish in the greatest purity by its own native excellence, and under the all-disposing providence of God. That they would also humbly represent that the only proper objects of civil government are the happiness and protection of men in the present state of existence, the security of the life, liberty, and property of the citizens, and to restrain the vicious and encourage the virtuous by wholesome laws, equally extending to every individual ; but that the duty they owe their Creator, and the manner of discharging it, can only be directed by reason and conviction, and is nowhere cognizable but at the tribunal of the Universal Judge ;

and that, therefore, they ask no ecclesiastical establishments for themselves, neither can they approve of them when granted to others, and earnestly entreating that all laws now in force in this Commonwealth which countenance religious dominations may be speedily repealed, that all and every religious sect may be protected in the full exercise of their several modes of worship, and exempted from the payment of all taxes for the support of any church whatever, farther than what may be agreeable to their own private choice, or voluntary obligation.''

VII. DISSENTERS IN GENERAL.

October 25 : ''Two petitions of the dissenters from the Church of England were presented to the House and read ; setting forth that they are exposed to great hardships in being obliged to contribute to the support of the Established church, contrary to the dictates of their conscience, and praying that the ecclesiastical establishment may be suspended, or laid aside.''

ORDER OF HOUSE.

October 25 : ''Ordered, that the several petitions and propositions depending and undetermined before the Assembly in the month of May, 1775, be delivered by the clerk to the several committees before whom the same were depending.''

VIII. DISSENTERS IN ALBEMARLE AND AMHERST.

November 1st: ''A petition from the dissenters from the Church of England in the counties of Albemarle and Amherst was presented to the House and read.'' [For the rest, see dissenters' petition of October 25.]

IX. COMMITTEE OF AUGUSTA.

November 9 : ''A memorial from the Committee for Augusta County was presented to the House and read ; setting forth that there is nothing more necessary in the present struggle for the liberties of America than an union of the minds and strength of its inhabitants, and they conceive themselves and their constituents, who, as well as most of the inhabitants on the western frontiers, are dissenters, to be aggrieved by being obliged to contribute to the support of the Established church, at the same time that they support ministers of their own persuasion ; that they consider this as an unequal burthen, inconsistent with the spirit of taxation, which supposes those on whom impositions are laid to be benefited thereby ; that such partial discriminations tend to embitter the minds of those who are thus imposed upon, and to create discords, ever attendant on such unequal treatment ; and praying such speedy and immediate relief as may best correspond with Christian liberty, and those noble sentiments which should animate every virtuous American.''

This memorial was referred to the ''Committee of the Whole House.''

ORDER OF ASSEMBLY.

''Ordered, that the Committee for Religion be discharged from proceeding on the petitions of several religious societies, and that the same be referred to the Committee of the Whole House upon the state of the country.''

It will be observed that none of the above petitions are from the Baptists as such, although it is freely admitted by the historians of those times that they were not only the first to begin the work, but also the most active in circulating petitions for signatures. Fristoe (page 91) says that the Baptist address was signed by ''about ten thousand,'' including many who were not Baptists. Among the signers were some of all denominations of Christians, and many of no denomination. This explains why the Baptist petition or petitions were from dissenters in general, instead of from Baptist dissenters in particular.

There were some dissenters, however, who acted independently. The reference is not to the Hanover Presbytery, which spoke more especially for the ministry of that denomination, but to certain ''dissenters of Albemarle, Amherst, and Buckingham,'' whose petition was presented to the House on the 22d of October, and is different from a later petition from '' Albemarle and Amherst,'' as well as from those that come from dissenters in general. That petition was certainly not from Baptists, but bears the marks of the Presbyterians. In the first place, it seems to make reference to the agreement with Governor Gooch, where it speaks of their having previously submitted to the Establishment because that was "the form of government established when they became dissenters from the Church of England;" that is, when they moved into Virginia, where the Church of England was the established church.

In the second place, the reference to their having to support their own church, in addition to helping to support the Established church, marks it as of Presbyterian rather than of Baptist origin; for such was the prejudice among the masses against the enforced tax for the support of the clergy of the Establishment that the early Baptist ministers in Virginia not only received little or nothing for their services, that the contrast might be the more marked between them and the "hireling ministry," but they failed to instruct their people in the New Testament duty and rule of giving. It is manifest, therefore, that this petition, and others of the same tenor, were from the Presbyterians, who, for some reason, preferred to act independently of the Baptists.

PETITIONS FOR THE ESTABLISHMENT.

I. METHODIST.

October 28: "A petition of the people commonly called Methodists was presented to the House and read; setting forth that the dissenters are preparing to lay a petition before this House for abolishing the present establishment of the church, and as they may, in the opinion of some, also come under the denomination of dissenters, they beg leave to declare they are a religious society in communion with the Church of England, and do all in their power to strengthen and support the said church; and as they conceive very bad consequences will arise from the abolishing the Establishment, they therefore pray that the Church of England, as it ever hath been, may still continue to be the established church."

II. CLERGY OF THE ESTABLISHED CHURCH.

November 8: "A memorial of a considerable number of the clergy of the Established church of Virginia was presented to the House and read; setting forth that, having understood various petitions have been presented to the Assembly praying the abolition of the Established church in this State, wish to represent that, when they undertook the charge of parishes in Virginia, they depended on the public faith for the receiving that recompense for their services during life or good behavior which the laws of the land promised, a tenure which to them appears of the same sacred nature as that by which every man in the State holds, and has secured to him his private property, and that such of them as are not yet provided for entered into holy orders expecting to receive the several emoluments which such religious establishment offered; that from the nature of their education they are precluded from gaining a tolerable subsistence in any other way of life, and that therefore they think it would be inconsistent with justice either to deprive the present incumbents of parishes of any right or profits they hold or enjoy, or to cut off from such as are now in orders and unbeneficed those expectations which originated from the laws of the land, and which have been the means of disqualifying them for any other profession or way of life; also, that, though they are far from favoring encroachments on the religious rights of any sect or denomination of men, yet they conceive that a religious establishment in a State is conducive to its peace and happiness; they think the opinions of mankind have a very considerable influence over their practice, and that it, therefore, cannot be improper for the legislative body of a State to consider how such opinions as are most consonant to reason and of the best efficacy in human affairs may be propagated and supported; that they are of opinion the doctrines of Christianity have a greater tendency to produce virtue amongst men than any human laws or institutions, and that these can be best taught and preserved in their purity in an established church, which gives encouragement to men to study and acquire a competent knowledge of the scriptures; and they think that, if these great purposes can be answered by a religious establishment, the hardships which such a regulation might impose on individuals, or even bodies of men, ought not to be considered ; also, that, whilst they are fully persuaded of the good effects of religious establishments in general, they are more particularly convinced of the excellency of the religious establishment which has hitherto subsisted in this State; that they ground their conviction on the experience of 150 years, during which period order and internal tranquility, true piety and virtue have more prevailed than in most other parts of the world, and on the mild and tolerating spirit of the church established, which with all Christian charity and benevolence has regarded dissenters of every denomination, and has shown no disposition to restrain them in the exercise of their religion; that it appears to them that the mildness of the church establishment has heretofore been acknowledged by those very dissenters who now aim at its ruin, many of whom emigrated from other countries to settle in this, from motives, as they reasonably suppose, of interest and happiness; that they apprehend many bad consequences from abolishing the church establishment; that they cannot suppose, should all denominations of Christians be placed upon a level, that this equality will continue, or that no attempt will be made by any sect for the superiority, and that they foresee much confusion, probably civil commotions, will attend the contest; that they also dread the ascendancy of that religion which permits its professors to threaten destruction to the Commonwealth, in order to serve their own private ends ; that, though the justice and expediency of continuing the church establishment is a matter of which they themselves have no doubt, yet they wish that the final determination of this House be deferred till the general sentiments of the good people of this Commonwealth can be collected, as they have the best reasons to believe that a majority of them desire to see the church establishment continued; and that, as the sentiments of the people have been attended to in other instances, they submit to the consideration of the House whether some regard should not be paid to their sentiments in a matter which so nearly concerns them as that of religion.''

This completes the list of petitions presented to the Assembly of 1776. They speak for themselves, and give one a pretty fair idea of the differences then prevailing among the several classes in Virginia, and of their respective lines of argument.

The attention of the reader is invited to certain remarkable claims set up, in their memorial by the "Clergy of the Established Church," such as "the mild and tolerant spirit" of said church, and "the Christian charity and benevolence" which "had ever characterized her treatment" of "dissenters of every denomination." The Baptists certainly were not expected to appreciate that part of the memorial, nor does it seem to have been meant for them, but rather for the Presbyterians, of whom the petitioners so bitterly complain for joining the enemies of the church and "aiming at its ruin." To them they had been "mild and tolerant." They had graciously allowed them to settle in Virginia and enjoy their own modes of worship, provided they helped to support the said church with their money and defended the frontier with their lives. And when they saw those same Presbyterians appear before the first Republican Assembly in the army of assailants, they had something of the feeling of him who said: "How sharper than a serpent's tooth to have a thankless child!"

ACTION OF THE ASSEMBLY.

But what response did the Assembly make to these petitions? What action was taken? As already seen, on the 9th of November all of the petitions "were referred to the Committee of the Whole House upon the State of the Country," from which it would appear that the "Committee on Religion" could not agree upon a report. Ten days thereafter, November 19, the following resolutions were adopted in Committee of the Whole House:

RESOLUTIONS OF HOUSE.

1. "*Resolved,* As the opinion of this committee, that all and every act or statute, either of the Parliament of England or of Great Britian, by whatever title known or distinguished, which renders criminal the maintaining any opinions in matters of religion, forbearing to repair to church, or the exercising any mode of worship whatsoever, or which prescribes punishment for the same, ought to be declared henceforth of no validity or force within this Commonwealth."

2. "*Resolved,* That so much of an act of Assembly made in the fourth year of the reign of Queen Anne, intituled, 'An act for the effectual suppression of vice, and restraint and punishment of blasphemous, wicked, and dissolute persons,' as inflicts certain additional penalties on any person or persons convicted a second time of any of the offences described in the first clause of the said act, ought to be repealed."

3. "*Resolved,* That so much of the petitions of the several dissenters from the church established by law within this Commonwealth as desires an exemption from all taxes and contributions whatever towards supporting the said church and the ministers thereof, or towards the support of their respective religious societies in any other way than themselves shall voluntarily agree, is reasonable."

4. "*Resolved,* That, although the maintaining any opinions in matters of religion ought not to be restrained, yet that public assemblies of societies for divine worship ought to be regulated, and that proper provision should be made for continuing the succession of the clergy and superintending their conduct."

5. "*Resolved,* That the several acts of Assembly making provision for the support of the clergy ought to be repealed, securing to the present incumbents all arrears of salary, and to the vestries a power of levying for performance of their contracts."

6. "*Resolved,* That a reservation ought to be made to the use of the said church, in all times coming, of the several tracts of glebe lands already purchased, the churches and chapels already built for the use of the several parishes, and of all plats belonging to or appropriated to the use of the said church, and all arrears of money or tobacco arising from former assessments; and that there should be

reserved to such parishes as have received private donations for the support of the said church and its ministers the perpetual benefit of such donations."

BILL PASSED AND TAX SUSPENDED.

December 5: "An engrossed bill, for exempting the different societies of dissenters from contributing to the support and maintenance of the church as by law established, or its ministers, and for other purposes therein mentioned, was read a third time."

"*Resolved*, That the bill do pass, and that Mr. Starke carry the same to the Senate for their concurrence."

SOME COMMENTS ON THIS STRUGGLE.

THOMAS JEFFERSON.

The following account, from the pen of Jefferson, one of the foremost champions of the cause of liberty, will give some idea of the character of the struggle through which the Legislature has just passed. In Vol. I. of his Works, pages 31, 32, he says:

"The first republican Legislature, which met in 1776, was crowded with petitions to abolish this spiritual tyranny. These brought on the severest contest in which I have ever been engaged. Our great opponents were Mr. Pendleton and Robert Carter Nicholas, honest men, but zealous churchmen. The petitions were referred to a Committee of the Whole House on the State of the Country; and, after desperate contests in the committee almost daily from the 11th of October to the 5th of December, we prevailed so far only as to repeal the laws which rendered criminal the maintenance of any religious opinions (other than those of the Episcopalians), the forbearance of repairing to the (Episcopal) church, or the exercise of any (other than the Episcopal) mode of worship; and to suspend only until the next session levies on the members of that church for the salaries of its own incumbents. For, although the majority of our citizens were dissenters, as has been observed, a majority of the Legislature were churchmen. Among these, however, were some reasonable and liberal men, who enabled us on some points to obtain feeble majorities. But our opponents carried, in the general resolutions of November the 19th, a declaration that religious assemblies ought to be regulated, and that provision ought to be made for continuing the succession of the clergy and superintending their conduct. And in the bill now passed was inserted an express reservation of the question whether a general assessment should not be established by law on every one to the support of the pastor of his choice; or whether all should be left to voluntary contributions ; and on this question, debated at every session from 1776 to 1779 (some of our dissenting allies, having now secured their particular object, going over to the advocates of a general assessment,) we could only obtain a suspension from session to session until 1779, when the question against a general assessment was finally carried, and the establishment of the Anglican church entirely put down."

If the reader should be in doubt as to the identity of those "dissenting allies" who broke ranks in this first engagement, that doubt will be removed by subsequent developments and revelations. One would naturally expect to find them among those dissenters who, instead of falling in with the general movement, sent up separate petitions to the Assembly.

DR. HENRY FOOTE.

There is no better place than this for the following extract from Foote's Sketches, in which (322-3) this candid Presbyterian historian describes the situation in Virginia at the beginning of the Revolution. Referring to the sixteenth article of the Bill of Rights, he says:

"These declarations breathe the spirit of civil and religious liberty, and spoke the true feelings of a majority of the citizens of Virginia. Civil liberty had been discussed with intensity of interest for a long period by the whole community, and its limits and boundaries were comparatively early settled to public satisfaction. Religious liberty had by degrees claimed the public attention, and for a little time excited deep interest ; but its proper meaning was not well understood. While abroad the contest was for the defense of civil liberty against the power of the mother country, at home it was raging for an ill-defined liberty of conscience and the disseverance of religion from the civil power. That something ought to be done for dissenters was evident; but what should actually be done, was the matter of contention. The true principle—the free exercise of religion according to the dictates of conscience—was well expressed in the Bill of Rights, but appears, after all, not to have been well understood by many of the delegates to the Assembly. Many seemed to think that an established religion, with toleration, was freedom enough."

Foote then proceeds to give an account of the struggle in the Assembly, quoting from Jefferson and Semple, but adds no new facts.

Semple and Howell both discuss the action of the Legislature, but give us no additional light.

REV. E. G. ROBINSON, D. D.

In his review of Rives' Life and Times of Madison, *Christian Review* of January, 1860, Dr. Robinson says:

"In October, 1776, the Convention of Delegates which had framed the Constitution became, by the provisions of that instrument, the Lower House of Assembly, and Mr. Madison remained at his post as a member of this first republican Legislature. Scarcely had the session begun, when the House was flooded with petitions for the more perfect establishment of religious freedom. . . They were signed numerously by all classes of the community—excepting alone the Episcopalians and Methodists. . . . Among these petitioners the most active and the most numerous were undoubtedly the Presbyterians and the Baptists. The former argued their petitions on various grounds, and indeed sought for different degrees of religious freedom, while the latter were undeviating and uncompromising in their demands for a total exemption from every kind of legal restraint or interference in matters of religion. For this they were misrepresented and maligned, and treated with every sort of indignity and persecution." . . . "Mr. Jefferson took the lead in behalf of the petitioners, and was promptly supported by Mr. Madison, Colonel Mason, and other influential members."

GENERAL RESULT.

The result of this contest was that another step was taken in the onward march towards absolute religious liberty. The Colonial Convention of 1775 placed dissenting ministers on equality with the clergy of the Establishment *in the army*, while the Convention of 1776 incorporated religious liberty into the organic law of the State. And now the first Legislature, assembled under the new Constitution and Bill of Rights, declares against all laws punishing men for their religious opinions, and exempts dissenters from all taxes for the support of the Establishment. There will be no ground lost in subsequent Legislatures. In spite of the timidity and wavering of some, and the "breaking ranks" on the part of others, the religious liberty army will never sound a retreat, but maintain an aggressive warfare until the last vestige of ecclesiastical tyranny has been removed from the statute books of Virginia.

CHAPTER VI.

Struggle in Legislature Continued.

The struggle which began in the Legislature, or Assembly, of 1776 was continued until December, 1779, before the Establishment was finally put down. All that its adversaries could accomplish in the meantime was to secure a suspension from session to session of the tax levied for its support. In considering the memorials which were presented to the Legislature, it should be borne in mind that there were in those days two sessions each year, one meeting in May and the other in October.

For convenience of reference, the memorials will be presented according to the years to which they belong. In them will be found some very refreshing reading. And one of the principal reasons for copying the Journal notices in full is that the reader may not only have all the evidence or testimony which they contain, but also see the style of argument used both for and against the Establishment, and put himself, as far as possible, in the position of the contestants or memorialists.

1777, SPRING SESSION.

From Cumberland county, favoring Establishment, May 22 :

"A petition of sundry inhabitants of the county of Cumberland, whose names are thereunto subscribed, was presented to the House and read ; setting forth that they are greatly alarmed at the progress which some of the dissenters from the church as by law established are daily making in various parts of this country by persuading the ignorant and unwary to embrace their erroneous tenets, which the petitioners conceive to be not only opposite to the doctrines of true Christianity, but subversive of the morals of the people and destructive of the peace of families, tending to alienate the affection of slaves from their masters, and injurious to the happiness of the public; that while such attempts are making to pull down all the barriers which the wisdom of our ancestors has erected to secure the church from the inroads of the sectaries, it would argue a culpable lukewarmness tamely to sit still and not to make known their sentiments, so contrary to such innovations; that all these bad effects have been already experienced in their country, and the parts adjacent, to be the dismal consequences of the doctrines of these new teachers; that through their means they have seen, with grief, great discontent made between husbands and their wives ; that there have been nightly meetings of slaves to receive the instructions of these teachers, without the consent of their masters, which have produced very bad consequences ; that the petitioners, not actuated by the narrow and blood-thirsty spirit of persecution, wish to see a well-regulated toleration established, by which those conscientious brethren, who, from principle, cannot join with the church, may be permitted to serve God in their own way, without molestation, but that they wish, also, that nightly meetings may be prohibited under severe penalties, and that those only who, after a due examination of their morals, shall be found worthy may be authorized to preach, and that only in such public meeting houses as it may be thought proper to license for the purpose; that they apprehend these purposes may be answered without destroying those gentle and wholesome restraints which the wisdom of ages and the policy of our laws have established ; and praying the church may be maintained in all its legal rights, and that the sectaries may be indulged with such a regulated toleration as shall be thought reasonable, and that the clergy of the Established church may be made accountable for their conduct, and removable for misbehaviour." Consideration of this petition was "referred to the next session of the Assembly."

JOHN LELAND'S COMMENTS.

That the reader may be able to appreciate the true inwardness of the troubles which these dreadful (?) dissenters were causing between masters and slaves, and between husbands and wives, the following extracts are given from "The Virginia Chronicle," published in 1790, by Elder John Leland, one of the ablest Baptist ministers in Virginia during those years of struggling for the rights of conscience for all mankind :

"Liberty of conscience, in matters of religion, is the right of slaves beyond contradiction; and yet many masters and overseers will whip and torture the poor creatures for going to meeting at night, when the labor of the day is over. No longer ago than November, 1788, Mr. ——— made a motion in the Assembly for leave to bring in a bill, not only to prevent the assembling of slaves together, but to fine the masters for allowing of it; but, to his great mortification, it was rejected with contempt." *Virginia Chronicle*, page 8.

Again, on page 44, Leland says :

"The subject of religious liberty has been so canvassed for fourteen years, and has so far prevailed, that in Virginia a politician can no more be popular without the profession of it than a preacher who denies the doctrine of a *new birth;* yet many who make this behave in their families as if they did not believe what they profess. For a man to contend for religious liberty on the court-house green, and deny his wife, children, and servants the liberty of conscience at home, is a paradox not easily reconciled. If a head of a family could answer for all his house in the day of judgment, there would be a degree of justice in his controlling of them in the mode of worship and joining society; but answer for them he cannot; each one must give account of himself to God; and none but cruel tyrants will prevent their wives, children, or servants, either directly or indirectly, from worshipping God according to the dictates of their consciences and joining the society they choose; for as religion does not destroy either civil or domestic government, so neither of them extend their rightful influence into the empire of conscience."

FROM MECKLENBURG COUNTY.

May 29: An address of sundry inhabitants of the county of Mecklenburg, whose names are thereunto subscribed, was presented to the House and read; setting forth that, conscious nothing, in this critical situation of public affairs, when liberty, life, and all are at stake, should engross much of the time of the Legislature, except matters of indispensable obligation, they therefore only beg its attention for a few moments. That the undue means taken to overthrow the Established church, by imposing upon the credulity of the vulgar and engaging infants to sign petitions handed about by dissenters, have, it seems, so far succeeded as to cause a dissolution of her usual mode of support, where they would choose it should rest, in the present exigency of affairs, rather than, by strenuously insisting upon the rectitude of an establishment, throw this State in particular into commotion, and thereby prejudice the common cause, which they are resolved shall receive no detriment from them by any means whatsoever. That if only withholding from a competent number of ministers of the gospel fixed salaries is the most likely means to make men unanimous in the defence of liberty, as hath been urged, they should be sorry, indeed, if there could be one of that reverend order who would repine at the success of the measure; for that even an unwillingness to sacrifice a part of our property to the good of our country, much more an absolute refusal of it, is a poor argument, indeed, of our disinterested zeal for the Commonwealth. Wherefore, they should by no means wish to see churchmen adopt the principles of dissenters, withhold their concurrence in the common cause until their particular requests are granted, for by such a conduct all may be lost. That, notwithstanding they think an established church in any State, under proper limitations and restrictions and founded on the warranty of Holy Scripture, is one of the great bulwarks of liberty, the cement of society, the bond of union, and an asylum for the persecuted to fly to; yet, as this is a controverted point, they are heartily willing it should be debated at a time when there may be nothing of more importance to engage the attention of the Assembly." This address was "referred to Committee on Religion."

BAPTIST ANSWER TO THE ABOVE.

The following extract from Fristoe's History, explaining the Baptist position and their reasons for not waiting until the Revolution was over to press the question of religious liberty, is introduced here as a fitting answer to the insinuations and reflections contained in the above address, which insinuations and reflections come with very poor grace from the representatives of a church which furnished nearly all the *Tories*, whereas the Baptists furnished none. Beginning on page 88, he says :

" The Baptists having labored under oppression for a long time. inclined them to seek redress as soon as a favorable opportunity offered. In the year 1776, they united in a petition to the Assembly of Virginia, stating the several grievances they labored under, requesting a repeal of all such laws as might occasion an odious distinction among citizens. . . . This petition the Baptists were determined to persevere in presenting to the Assembly till such times they were attended to and they were rescued from the hand of oppression, and their just liberties were secured to them. And it appeared at that juncture the most favorable opportunity offered that had ever been—a time when the nation was struggling for civil liberty and casting off British tyranny—a time of aiming to support their independence and relieving of themselves from monarchical usurpation. It became a common saying about this time, ' United we stand, divided we fall.' There was a necessity for an unanimity among all ranks, sects, and denominations of people, when we had to withstand a powerful nation and expel her by force of arms or submit to her arbitrary measures, and the State Legislature became sensible that a division among the people would be fatal to this country ; but the Assembly being chiefly of the Episcopalian order, and being in the habit heretofore of governing with rigor, it was with great reluctance they could pass a law favorable to dissenters and raise them upon a level with themselves. · What inclined dissenters to be more anxiously engaged for their liberty was that, if time passed away and no repeal of those injurious laws, and the nation to which we belonged succeeded in supporting their independence, and our government settled down with these old prejudices in the hearts of those in power, and an establishment of religion survive our revolution, and religious tyranny raise its banner in our infant country, it would leave us to the sore reflection : What have we been struggling for? For what have we spent so much treasure? Why was it that from sentiment we united with our fellow-citizens in the cause of liberty, girded on our sword or took our musket on our shoulder, endured the hardships of a tedious war? Why clash to arms? Why hear the heart-affecting shrieks of the wounded and the awful scene of garments enrolled in blood, together with the entire loss of many of our relations, friends, acquaintances, and fellow-citizens, and, after all this, to be exposed to religious oppression and the deprivation of the rights of conscience in the discharge of the duties of religion, in which we are accountable to God alone, and not to man? The consideration of these things stimulated and excited the Baptists in Virginia to use every effort and adopt every measure embracing that particular crisis as the fittest time to succeed, which, if past by, might never offer again, and they and their posterity remain in perpetual fetters under an ecclesiastical tyranny.''

Subsequent events show the wisdom of their course.

HANOVER PRESBYTERY AGAINST ESTABLISHMENT.

June 3: ''A memorial of the Presbytery of Hanover was presented to the House and read; setting forth that they, together with the religious denomination with which they are connected, are most sincerely attached to the interests of the American States, and are determined that their most fervent prayers and strenuous endeavor shall be united with their fellow-subjects to repel the assaults of tyranny and to maintain their common rights; that nothing has inspired them with greater confidence in the Legislature than the late act of the Assembly declaring equal liberty, as well religious as civil, should be universally extended to the good people of this country, and that all the oppressive acts of Parliament respecting religion which have been formerly enacted in the mother country shall henceforth be of no validity or force in this Commonwealth, and also exempting dissenters from all levies, taxes, and impositions whatsover, towards supporting the Church of England, as it now is, or hereafter may be established; that they wish, therefore, to give the Legislature no farther trouble on the subject, but are sorry to find there yet remains a variety of opinions touching the propriety of a general assessment, or whether every religious society shall be left to the voluntary contributions for the maintenance of our ministers of the gospel of different persuasions. But as this matter is deferred to the discussion and final determination of a future Assembly, they think it their indispensable duty again to repeat part of the prayer of their former memorial, that dissenters, of every denomination, may be exempted from all taxes for the support of any church whatsoever, farther than what may be agreeable to the private choice or voluntary obligation of every individual, while the civil magistrate no otherwise interfere than to protect them all in the full and free exercise of their several modes of worship; and praying the Legislature will never extend to them, or to the congregations under their charge, any assessment for religious purposes." It was "ordered that consideration of this memorial be deferred to the next session of the General Assembly."

FALL SESSION OF 1777.

November 6: "A petition of sundry inhabitants of the county of Cumberland," etc. [This is but a repetition of the petition of May 22 from same county.]

FROM CAROLINE COUNTY, FAVORING ASSESSMENT.

December 5 : "Several petitions of sundry inhabitants of the county of Caroline, whose names are thereunto subscribed, were presented to the House and read ; setting forth that they have seen an act of the last session of the Assembly, by which dissenters from the Church of England are exempted from all levies for the support of the said church and its ministers, and highly approve thereof, as founded on principles of justice and propriety, and favorable to religious liberty ; that, at the same time, they beg leave to suggest that as, in their opinion, public worship is a duty we owe to the Creator and Preserver of mankind, and productive of effects the most beneficial to society, it ought to be enjoined and regulated by the Legislature, so as to preserve public peace, order and decency, without prescribing a mode or form of worship to any ; that in such regulations an expense must unavoidably be incurred, not only for the building and repairing of places of worship, but also for the support of religious teachers or ministers, that they may be freed from the cares of providing for their own and their families' subsistence and attend more constantly and diligently to the cure of souls, which expense they conceive ought to be defrayed by an equal contribution of all men, in proportion to their circumstances, or according to the degree in which they possess that species of property on which the Legislature shall think fit to levy their taxes for public uses; but that equality can never be preserved, if men are left to their voluntary donations, since, while the liberal exceed their proportion, the avaricious and miserly will fall short of theirs, or, perhaps, withhold all contribution; and that at the same time the mode of making and collecting such subscriptions will probably be the source of much contention and ill-will between the minister and his congregation, which circumstance, with the very precarious nature of the provision, must necessarily discourage men of genius and learning from engaging in the ministerial office and bring that order into contempt, and perhaps, in the end, religion itself.

"That upon these, and many other considerations, they are of opinion that it will be most proper to fix on all tithables the payment of one certain annual sum, which may be judged adequate to the decent support of a minister of the gospel and providing places of worship, leaving it to the payer, at the time of giving in his list of tithables, to direct the appropriation of his quota to the use of that church, or its ministers, under such regulations as may be thought best." This was "referred to Committee on Religion."

December 11: Another petition, just like the one of May 29 from Mecklenburg county, was presented from the county of Lunenburg.

1778.

There is a gap then from the end of 1777 to October 9, 1778, when "an address of sundry inhabitants of the county of Westmoreland and parish of Cople was presented," etc. It was essentially the same as the addresses from Mecklenburg and Lunenburg.

The Legislature took no action in reference to these matters except to suspend, from session to session, the church taxes. In the next chapter will be given the memorials of 1779 and the final action of the Assembly in *repealing* all laws levying taxes for the support of the Establishment. That will be followed by a chapter on the several meetings of the Baptists and Presbyterians during these years in which they were striving together against the Established church and in favor of equal liberty for all.

CHAPTER VII.

Fall of the Establishment—1779.

The long and bitter struggle over the Establishment is now drawing to a close. It will be seen from the petitions that come before the Assembly that the friends of the old Establishment are fighting for some sort of compromise on the basis of a general assessment, and that Jefferson's famous "Bill for Religious Freedom" is attracting attention, and exciting both favorable and unfavorable comment. This bill was reported to the House in June, 1779, just after Jefferson was elected governor, to succeed Patrick Henry, and before he took his seat in the governor's chair.

AUGUSTA COUNTY.

"October 20: "A petition of sundry inhabitants of the county of Augusta was presented to the House and read; setting forth that they have seen the plan proposed by the House of Delegates for establishing the privileges of the several denominations of religious societies at the last session of Assembly, and praying that the General Assembly will be pleased to pass the said bill without the least alteration." This was referred to committee to prepare and bring in a bill "concerning religion."

CULPEPER COUNTY.

"October 21: "A petition of sundry inhabitants of the county of Culpeper, whose names are thereunto subscribed, was presented to the House and read; setting forth the evils which they suppose will arise, if the bill for establishing religious freedom, which hath been dispensed among the people, should be passed by the General Assembly, and suggesting such a mode of religious establishment as they suppose will be beneficial to the people, and praying that the aforesaid bill may be unanimously rejected by this House."

ESSEX COUNTY.

October 22: "A petition of sundry inhabitants of the county of Essex, whose names are thereunto subscribed, was presented to the House and read; setting forth that, from the great confusion and disorder which hath arisen on account of religion since the old Establishment hath been interrupted, they are convinced of the necessity of the legislative body's taking this subject into their most serious consideration; that they are much alarmed at the appearance of a bill, entitled 'Religious Freedom,' and praying that the said bill may not take effect, but an establishment adopted under certain regulations."

BAPTIST ASSOCIATION AND MARRIAGE LAW.

October 25: " A petition of the Baptist Association; setting forth that doubts have arisen whether marriages solemnized by dissenting ministers are lawful, and praying that an act may pass to declare such marriages lawful."

JAMES HENRY'S "BILL" CONCERNING RELIGION.

"October 25: "Mr. Henry presented, according to order, a bill 'Concerning Religion,' and the same was received and read the first time, and ordered to be read a second time."

October 26: "A bill 'Concerning Religion' was read the second time. A motion was made, and the motion being put, that the said bill be read a third time on the 1st day of March next, it passed in the negative." It was then "ordered that the bill be committed to the committee of the whole House on Tuesday next." This bill was then put off from day to day, after considering it in committee of the whole House, and finally failed.

AUGUSTA COUNTY, AGAIN.

October 27: " A petition of sundry inhabitants of the county of Augusta, was presented to the House and read; setting forth that they have seen the bill presented to the last Assembly (and published, as they suppose, for the consideration of the people), 'for establishing religious freedom,' which they cordially approve of; and praying that the same may pass into a law." "Ordered, That the said petition be referred to the committee of the whole House on the bill 'Concerning Religion.'"

AMHERST COUNTY.

November 1 : " A petition of sundry inhabitants of the county of Amherst, whose names are thereunto subscribed, was presented to the House, and read; setting forth that they have seen and highly approve the bill which was presented to the last Assembly, 'for establishing religious freedom,' and praying that the same may pass into a law."

LUNENBURG.

November 3: "A petition of sundry inhabitants of the county of Lunenburg, whose names are thereunto subscribed, was presented to the House and read; setting forth that they have seen a bill which they suppose was published by order of the last Assembly, 'for establishing religious freedom,' and are of opinion that the Christian religion, free from the errors of popery, and a general contribution to the support thereof, ought to be established from the principle of public utility; and praying that the reformed Protestant religion, including the different denominations thereof, with a general assessment to support the same, may be established." "Ordered, That the said petition be referred to the committee of the whole House on the bill 'Concerning Religion.'"

November 10, a similar petitition to the above came up from Amherst county, making two petitions from Amherst —one for and one against Jefferson's bill.

BILL TO CUT DOWN ESTABLISHMENT.

November 15: "Ordered, That leave be given to bring in a bill 'for repealing so much of the act of Assembly entitled, 'An Act for the Support of the Clergy,' etc., as relates to the payment of the salaries heretofore given to the clergy of the Church of England; and that Messrs. Mason, Strother, and Randolph do prepare and bring in the same.'"

November 18: "Mr. Mason presented" said bill, and it was ordered to be read a second time. November 19, it was read a second time and committed to a committee of the whole House for the following Monday. It was put off from day to day until December 11, when it was "ordered that the bill be engrossed and read a third time." December 13, it was read a third time and passed. This bill cut the purse-strings of the Establishment, so that the clergy could no longer look for support to taxation. But they still retained possession of the rich glebes, and enjoyed a monopoly, almost, of marriage fees.

Jefferson's bill for "Religious Freedom," while not defeated, has to wait until 1785 before it secures the approval of the legislature. James Henry's bill "Concerning Religion," is defeated in this legislature. The cause of the Revolutionists was not bright at this juncture. The traitor, Arnold, was already plotting to betray his country, and the British had entered the Chesapeake and invaded Virginia during the year. It was no time to alienate the large number of dissenters who were known to be stubbornly opposed to that bill, and so it failed. But it will be revived again after the Revolutionary war is over and independence has been secured, only to receive its final defeat in the same year that witnesses the triumph of the "Bill for Religious Freedom."

AN INTERESTING QUESTION.

But why does Jefferson's bill have to wait so long, when there were votes enough in the Legislature to secure the overthrow of the Establishment? It is manifest that there was not perfect unanimity among the opponents of the Established church, and that some of those who voted to pull down the old Establishment were not prepared to follow Jefferson to the full extent of his radical measure, but rallied to the standard of Patrick Henry, who favored a new and more liberal establishment, which would provide for them all. And, in order that the reader may know who the faithful were and who broke ranks, the following extracts are given from standard authorities.

From Dr. Hawks' "History Protestant Episcopal Church," page 152: "The Baptists were the principal promoters of this work [putting down the Establishment], and in truth aided more than any other denomination in its accomplishment."

Bishop Meade, "Old Churches," etc., I., 52: "They [the Baptists] took the lead in dissent, and were the chief object of persecution by the magistrates, and the most violent and persevering afterward in seeking the downfall of the Establishment."

Campbell, "History of Virginia," 553: "The Baptists, having suffered persecution under the Establishment, were of all others the most inimical to it, and the most active in its subversion."

Tucker's "Life of Jefferson," I., 98: "In the two following years, the question of providing for the ministers of religion by law, or leaving it to individual contributions, was renewed; but the advocates of the latter plan were only able to obtain at each session a suspension of those laws which provided salaries for the clergy— the natural progress in favor of liberal sentiments being counterbalanced by the fact that some of the dissenting sects, with the exception of the Baptists, satisfied with having been relieved from a tax which they felt to be both unjust and degrading, had no objec tion to a general assessment, and on this question voted with the friends of the church. But the advocates of religious freedom finally prevailed, and, after five suspending acts, the laws for the support of the clergy were, at the second session of 1779, unconditionally repealed."

Randall's "Life of Jefferson," I., 222: "This (general assessment) was the best arrangement the Anglican church could now hope for, and most of the dissenters, it would seem (the Baptists being said to be the only exception, as a church), were ready to join the former on this ground and unite in a strenuous effort in favor of the measure."

Rayner's "Life of Jefferson," 141: "This question (general assessment),the last prop of the tottering hierarchy, reduced the struggle to one of pure principle. The particular object of the dissenters being secured, they deserted the volunteer champion of their cause, and went over in troops to the advocates of a general assessment. This step, the natural proclivity of the sectarian mind, showed them incapable of religious liberty upon an expansive scale, or broader than their own interests, as schismatics. But the defection of the dissenters, painful as it was, only stimulated his desire for total abolition, as it developed more palpably the evidence of its necessity. He remained unshaken at his post, and brought on the reserved question at every session from 1776 to 1779, during which time he could only obtain a suspension of the levies from year to year, until the session of 1779, when, by his unwearied exertions, the question was carried definitely against a general assessment, and the establishment of the Anglican church entirely overthrown."

Thus far no Baptist authorities have been quoted. The following are Baptists. The extracts are lengthy ; but our plan is to throw all the light available upon the subject.

Semple's "History of Virginia Baptists," pages 26, 27: "We are not to understand that this important ecclesiastical revolution was effected wholly by the Baptists. They were certainly the most active ; but they were also joined by the other dissenters. Nor was the dissenting interest, all united, by any means, at that time, equal to the accomplishment of such a revolution ; we must turn our eyes to the political state of the country to find adequate causes for such a change.

"The British yoke had now galled to the quick; and the Virginians, as having the most tender necks, were among the first to wince. Republican principles had gained much ground, and were fast advancing to superiority; the leading men on that side viewed the Established clergy and the Established religion as inseparable appendages of monarchy—one of the pillars by which it was supported. The dissenters, at least the Baptists, were Republicans from interest as well as principle; it was known that their influence was great among the common people; and the common people of every country are, more or less, Republicans. To resist British oppressions effectually, it was necessary to soothe the minds of the people by every species of policy. The dissenters were too powerful to be slighted, and they were too watchful to be cheated by an ineffectual sacrifice. There had been a time when they would have been satisfied to have paid their tithes, if they could have had liberty of conscience; but now the crisis was such that nothing less than a total overthrow of all ecclesiastical distinctions would satisfy their sanguine hopes. Having started the decaying edifice, every dissenter put to his shoulder to push it into irretrievable ruin. The revolutionary party found that the sacrifice must be made, and they made it.

"It is said, however, and probably not without truth, that many of the Episcopalians who voted for abolishing the Establishment did it upon an expectation that it would be succeeded by a general assessment; and, considering that most of the men of wealth were on that side, they supposed that their funds would be lessened very little. This, it appeared in the sequel, was a vain expectation. The people, having once shaken off their fetters, would not again permit themselves to be bound. Moreover, the war now rising to its height, they were in too much need of funds to permit any of their resources to be devoted to any other purpose during that period; and we shall see that when it was attempted, a few years after the expiration of the war, the people set their faces against it.

Howell's "Early Baptists of Virginia," page 165: "Meantime, a new theory of a State religious establishment was devised, and began, in private circles, to be warmly discussed. This theory had its origin with the Presbyterians, and was in their subsequent memorials tenaciously and elaborately advocated. It proposed, not the abrogation of the State religious establishment, the measure demanded by the Baptists, but that the State, instead of selecting one denomination, as the Episcopal, and establishing that as the religion of the State, and giving to that alone its support, should establish all the denominations—Presbyterians, Methodists, and Baptists, as well as Episcopalians—and make them all equally and alike the religion of the State and to be supported by the State. How this could be done we shall hereafter see fully explained in some of the Presbyterian memorials. Of this plan of reconciling and harmonizing all parties Patrick Henry was the ablest and most eloquent advocate. It had the merit of British precedent, since Episcopalianism in England and Presbyterianism in Scotlond were alike the established religion of the empire."

It is evident from the above testimony that those "dissenting allies" who deserted Jefferson in the crisis of the struggle for absolute religious freedom were not Baptists. That they were, in the main, Presbyterians is evident from the fact that they were at that time the only other denomination of dissenters of any strength in Virginia. Whether, as Dr. Howell says, the "new theory of a religious establishment" had its origin among the Presbyterians we may not know with certainty. It may have originated with them, or it may have originated with the more liberal Episcopalians, who were willing to adopt any compromise measure that would save their own church establishment; or it may have been born of the two denominations jointly— of an effort on the part of their leaders to secure harmony. It is worthy of note that the first petition presented to the Legislature in favor of this "new theory of an establishment" came from Caroline, a county in which Presbyterians, as well as Episcopalians, were strong. It is worthy of note, also, that Patrick Henry, the reputed political father of the scheme for the new order of establishment, while claimed by Bishop Meade and Dr. Hawks as an Episcopalian, was allied to the Presbyterians through his Presbyterian wife, and by the further fact that he caught his first inspiration under the ministry of the great Samuel Davies, whose preaching stirred the slumbering genius of the awkward and uncouth young man, and started him on his career as the "Orator of the Revolution." It is true that the Hanover Presbytery, as a body, expressed itself, at first, as opposed to any general assessment. It is also true, as will hereafter be shown, that the Presbytery subsequently yielded its opposition, and agreed to an assessment on a "plan" proposed by themselves, and that never, until August, 1785, when all hope of a general assessment was gone, did any presbytery or convention of Presbyterians endorse Jefferson's bill for establishing religious freedom in Virginia. That bill was proposed in the spring of 1779, and was bidding for popular favor until the fall of 1785 before becoming a law. It is significant that the Presbyterians, as a body, waited for more than five years before giving that important measure their approval. These are facts.

CHAPTER VIII.

Baptist and Presbyterian Meetings During Struggle Just Closed—1776-1779.

FOR the sake of unity, we deem it best to make a separate chapter of the meetings and doings of the Baptists and Presbyterians during the struggle for the overthrow of the Establishment.

BAPTIST ASSOCIATION OF AUGUST, 1776.

According to Semple (62), there was a meeting of the Baptist General Association in August, 1776, at Thompson's meeting-house, Louisa county, in which seventy-four churches were represented. The letters from the churches brought "mournful tidings of coldness and declension," attributed by some to "too much concern in political matters, being about the commencement of the Revolution." Jeremiah Walker was moderator of this meeting, and John Williams, clerk, their names being signed to a complimentary address which was adopted by this body and sent to Patrick Henry, who had been recently elected Governor of the State. The address, together with Governor Henry's response, is found in the *Virginia Gazette* of August 23, 1776. Of this address Semple strangely makes no mention. But Dr. Howell, in his account of this meeting, page 159, says: "Its commissioners to the State Convention, Mr. Walker, Mr. Williams and Mr. Roberts, reported, giving a full account of their mission and the extraordinary success with which God had crowned their endeavors." He adds: "An address to the Legislature soon to convene was reported, considered, and adopted. This paper I have been unable to find.'' It is not improbable that the address here referred to is the one which was sent to Governor Henry, and published in the *Gazette*.

BAPTIST ASSOCIATIONS OF 1777.

Semple tells of a proposed division of the General Association into four districts, two south and two north of the James river; but, as the division was not perfected, he ignores it, and treats the whole under one view. He then mentions two meetings on the Southside—one at ''Falls Church meeting-house, Halifax county, first Saturday in November, 1776, of which he could get no account, and the other at Williams' Sandy Creek meeting-house, the last Saturday in April, 1777.'' Of this latter meeting Semple could give no regular account; but Howell gives valuable information concerning what he calls ''the session of the General Association for 1777,'' and which was evidently this meeting in April, at a church which was planted by Walker, within the bounds of the old Meherrin church, and of which Williams was then pastor. Here is Howell's account of the meeting (164):

''A committee was appointed, charged with the duty of examining the laws of the Commonwealth and designating all such as were justly considered offensive; of recommending the method to be pursued to obtain their removal from the statute book; to propose in form such laws, to be laid before the Legislature, as should firmly establish and maintain 'religious freedom' in all its extent and bearings, and to report at the earliest moment practicable.''

He then proceeds to describe their report as follows:

''In that report numerous laws were designated as offensive, prominent among which was the law which required all marriages to be performed by Episcopal clergymen, with the ceremonies of the

Established church, and made all otherwise performed illegal and void; and all the laws establishing the Episcopal church as the religion of the State, and providing for its support from the public purse. As the best method to procure their removal from the statute book, continued agitation among the people and petitions to the Legislature were recommended; and, as expressive of such government action as was desired, a law was drawn up in form and reported, entitled, ' An Act for the E-tablishment of Religious Freedom,' to be presented to the Legislature, with an earnest petition that it might be adopted as a law of the State.''

And he adds:

''This report was received, amply discussed, and adopted. An address was prepared, embodying all the suggestions of the report, especially the proposed law to establish religious liberty; commissioners were appointed, to whose fidelity it was confided, and they were instructed to remain with the Legislature and give their attention to these interests during the approaching session.''

HANOVER PRESBYTERY, IN 1777.

According to Dr. Foote (327), the Hanover Presbytery, in a meeting at Timber Ridge, in April, 1777, adopted a '' Memorial to the General Assembly of Virginia,'' drafted by '' Rev. Messrs. Stanhope Smith and Daniel Rice, bearing date of April 25th,'' and signed by Richard Sankey, moderator. This memorial was presented to the Assembly on the 3d of June following, the Journal notice of which has already been given. It is a '' remonstrance against a general assessment.'' [See Appendix.]

At a subsequent meeting, at Concord, Bedford county, June 19, 1777, '' The Presbytery, considering it as probable that our General Assembly may come to a final determination concerning church establishments at their next session, which may make it of importance for this Presbytery further to concern themselves in the case before our next stated meeting, we, therefore, appoint the Rev. Messrs. Sankey, Todd, Rice, Wallace, and Smith, or any of them, a committee to meet at Hampden Sidney on the 26th of September, or sooner, if any two of them shall judge it necessary, to do and act in behalf of this Presbytery in that case."

GENERAL ASSOCIATION OF MAY, 1778.

Returning now to Semple, we find mention (63) of a meeting in May, 1778, at Anderson's meeting-house, in Buckingham county, of which he says:

"A committee was appointed to inquire whether any grievances existed in the civil laws that were oppressive to the Baptists. In their report they represent the marriage law as being partial and oppressive, . . . upon which it was agreed to present to the next General Assembly a memorial praying for a law affording equal privileges to all ordained ministers of every denomination."

William Webber was moderator, and John Williams, clerk.

GENERAL ASSOCIATION OF OCTOBER, 1778.

Continuing (64), he says:

"They appointed their next Association at Dupuy's meeting-house, Powhatan county, second Saturday in October, 1778. They met, according to appointment, and chose Samuel Harris, moderator, and John Williams, clerk. A committee of seven members were appointed to take into consideration the civil grievances of the Baptists, and report.

"1. They reported on Monday that, should a general assessment take place, that it would be injurious to the dissenters in general.

"2. That the clergy of the former Established church suppose themselves to have the exclusive right of officiating in marriages, which has subjected dissenters to great inconveniences.

" 3. They, therefore, recommended that two persons be appointed to wait on the next General Assembly and lay these grievances before them.

"Jeremiah Walker and Elijah Craig (and, in case of the failure of either, John Williams) were appointed to attend the General Assembly."

Howell also gives an account of this meeting on pages 166-7. That he does not confound it with the meeting already described as having met and acted in 1777, is evident. He gives a full account of the meeting in 1778, at which the "committee of seven" was appointed on "civil grievances," and "Walker, Craig, and Williams" were appointed commissioners. The explanation seems to be this: That the movement looking to a revision of the marriage and order laws was initiated by those eminent leaders, Walker and Williams, at Williams' Sandy Creek meeting-house, of which Semple could get no account, probably because it was only a meeting of one of the proposed divisions of the General Association, and that the movement was subsequently made general by the action of the whole body in the two meetings of 1778, mentioned above by Semple.

It should be borne in mind that Williams was appointed, with John Leland, to write the history of Virginia Baptists. Before the work could be completed, Leland returned to Massachusetts, and the work was committed to Williams alone. His health failed, and then Robert B. Semple was appointed in his place. Semple tells us in his preface that, while he was compelled to select out of the mass of materials gathered such as seemed most reliable and most important, there was much that he could not get, owing to the "unaccountable backwardness of many to furnish in any way the information possessed." Dr. Howell, a much later writer, seems to have gathered valuable facts not recorded by Semple—facts which he collected during his missionary labors on the south side of the James, and during his pastorate in the city of Richmond, where he had ample opportunity for such work. It should be noted that Howell ignores the fact that there were two meetings of the General Association each year, just as he does as to the two sessions of the General Assembly. We have already seen that he treats of everything that was presented to the Conventions of 1775 and 1776 and the Assembly of 1776 as though they were one and the same body, although he must have known that they were not. This makes him commit the mistake (150) of representing the Presbyterians, Methodists, and Episcopalians as addressing "*the Convention*," when, as a matter of fact, these did not appear until the *Assembly* met in October, 1776. All of this is explained by the fact that Howell's book was, in its original form, an "*Address*," delivered before the American Baptist Historical Society in 1856, and which was subsequently expanded into a book.

There be some who will question the accuracy of Howell's account of the origin of the "Bill for Establishing Religious Freedom." Howell says that the Baptists took the initiative at the April meeting in 1777. Jefferson, in the account already given from his own pen, says that he drafted the "bill" in the year 1777, as part of his great work of revision of Virginia's laws, but that it was not reported to the Assembly until 1779. We will see how both statements may be true.

GENERAL ASSOCIATION OF 1779.

Semple (65) mentions a meeting at Dover meeting-house, Goochland county, on the second Saturday in May,

1779, but he could get no account of its doings. Of the next meeting, in October, he says :

"On the second Saturday in October, 1779, the Association met at Nottoway meeting-house, Amelia county—Samuel Harris, moderator ; Jeremiah Walker, clerk. The report by Jeremiah Walker, as delegate to the General Assembly, was highly gratifying, upon which the following entry was unanimously agreed to be made : ' On consideration of the bill establishing religious freedom, agreed : That the said bill, in our opinion, puts religious freedom upon its proper basis, prescribes the just limits of the power of the State with regard to religion, and properly guards against partiality towards any religious denomination. We, therefore, heartily approve of the same, and wish it to pass into a law.'

" ' Ordered, That this, our approbation of the said bill, be transmitted to the public printers, to be inserted in the Gazettes.' "

Howell, in his account, page 167, says :

"When the General Association assembled in 1779, Mr. Walker, after having reported the proceedings of the commissioners at the Capitol, made to the body a most important communication. Two years before (1777), a committee had reported to that body the project of a law for ' the establishment of religious liberty.' This form had been embodied in its memorial and submitted to the Legislature. The General Assembly, as we have seen, was then in no temper to act favorably on this or any similar subject. The form submitted had, however, attracted the attention of several members of the Legislature, and especially of Mr. Jefferson and Mr. Madison, and had led to various private interviews between them and the commissioners on the subject. Mr. Jefferson had kindly undertaken to prepare the law, make it accord with their wishes, render it as perfect as possible, and at the earliest practicable day secure its adoption by the General Assembly as a law of the State. This form, as thus prepared, was now laid before the General Association by Mr. Walker for its consideration, advice, and approval. The paper was read carefully, and prayerfully considered, and the following proceedings unanimously adopted." He then gives the " resolutions " already quoted from Semple.

It appears from these accounts of Baptist and Presbyterian meetings that both denominations were anxiously watching the proceedings of the Assembly, and were seeking, not only by means of petitions, but also through their own chosen commissioners, to guard and further their interests before that body. The Journal of the House makes no mention of their presence, of course, but only of such petitions and addresses as are from time to time presented to that body. But it is evident that these commissioners were on hand at the proper time and that they did some effective "lobbying."

HOWISON ON THE BAPTISTS.

There is no more appropriate place than this to introduce the testimony of this historian as to the character and influence of the Baptists. If it be asked why the Baptist Association ordered their opinions and doings to be published in the Gazettes, the answer will be found in their growing influence, and in their policy of throwing that influence, in elections, in favor of the candidate who was favorable to religious liberty. Of two Churchmen, for example, who were candidates for the Legislature, the Baptists would unite on the one who was pledged to the doctrine of equal rights for all. And that the Baptist influence counted, even in those days, Mr. Howison testifies in his History of Virginia, Vol. II., page 170 :

" The influence of the denomination (Baptists) was strong among the common people, and was beginning to be felt in high places. In two points they were distinguished. First, in their love of freedom. No class of the people of America were more devoted advocates of the principles of the Revolution ; none were more willing to give their money and goods to their country ; none more prompt to march to the field of battle, and none more heroic in actual combat than the Baptists of Virginia. Secondly, in their hatred of the church Establishment. They hated not its ministers, but its principles."

HOWELL AS AN AUTHORITY.

The attempt has been made to discredit Howell's book as an authority. He claims "too much for the Baptists" to suit some writers, and hence he is set down as "a later and not so accurate a writer" as Semple, and even characterized as "unreliable." It is meet, therefore, that something should be said at this point about the man and his work.

Dr. R. B. C. Howell was born in Wayne county, N. C., March 10, 1801; baptized February 6, 1821; attended Columbian College; and, at the earnest request of Dr. Robert B. Semple, president of the Board of the General Association of Virginia, accepted an appointment as missionary in the Portsmouth Association. He had thirty-two preaching places. Became pastor of Cumberland Street church, Norfolk, in 1828, where he remained eight years; went to Nashville in 1835; was called to the Second Baptist church, Richmond, in 1850, which church he served for seven years, and then returned to Nashville. He was imprisoned by Governor Andrew Johnson, June 18, 1862, and died in 1868. Hence he was cotemporary with William Fristoe, who died in 1828; of Robert B. Semple, who died in 1831; of Thomas Jefferson, who died July 4, 1826, and of James Madison, who died in 1836.

In his book he makes *twenty-five references* to Semple's History, which may be divided into three classes.

The first class comprises those cases (four in number) in which Howell refers to Semple as authority for his statements, but without quoting his words. These are found on pages 70, 91, 94, and 240, and all are correct, except that on page 70 the reference to ''Semple, page 4, *et seq.*,'' should be ''page 41, *et seq.*,'' where Semple begins his account of the General Association.

The second class comprises those cases in which Howell *quotes* from Semple, introducing the quotation by some such words as ''Semple says.'' There are six such references, found on pages 73, 97, 133, 137, 142, and 178, and all correct.

The third class comprises those cases in which Howell quotes from original sources, such as journals, minutes of associations, memorials, addresses, etc., and then refers the reader to the page in Semple's History which gives *his* account of the same matter. Of this class there are fifteen cases, found on pages 91, 95, 96, 105, 106, 110, 114, 125, 145, 150, 168, 174, 184, 199, and 225, all of which are correct, except that in four cases the reference is to the wrong page. On page 91 the reference should be ''Semple, page 57,'' instead of 55; on page 95 it should be 68, 69, instead of 59, 60; on page 105 it should be 56, instead of 50, and on page 150 it should be 435, instead of 345.

Semple had '' materials,'' which he used very sparingly, and others which, owing to the ''narrow limits '' of his work, he did not use at all. On page 246 he suggests that an interesting and useful ''volume '' might be made up of ''circular letters'' which he had, but could not use in his ''sketch.''

In the first chapter of Howell's work, he says that '' the history of the Baptists of Virginia remains unwritten '' ; that ''ample materials for a full and faithful history are accessible '' ; and he then goes on to tell where they may be found. His work was not designed to be such a history, but was only '' an enlargement of an address delivered by

him in New York, in 1856, before the American Baptist
Historical Society," and published, in its present form,
after the author's death. His son, Hon. Morton B. Howell,
of Nashville, in a private letter, says that some of his
father's materials were obtained from Semple, but that
"the bulk was procured in the State Library," and that he,
the son, aided him in procuring them. "From my personal
knowledge," he writes, "of the manner in which the materials were gathered, I will risk my life that every statement of
fact is made with scrupulous accuracy and careful precision."

Mr. Howell sends the following interesting note, written,
by his father on the fly-leaf of "a first draft" of the
proposed book:

"PRIVATE NOTE."

"The following pages are a first draft of the work proposed.
The facts and authorities are, however, all verified, and may be re-
lied upon. The whole must be rewritten and perfected. Should I
not live to do this, I desire my nephew, Rev. C. H. Toy, of Norfolk,
Va., to do it for me.   R. B. C. HOWELL."

"The above was written when I was thrown into prison by the
Federal Government in 1862."

His son adds that "the rewriting" was done by his
father "during the enforced leisure of 1864–'5;" that
soon after his death, April 5, 1868, he sent the manuscript
to Dr. Toy, who, as the preface shows, published it just
"as the author left it."

Dr. Howell, as missionary among the churches on the
south side of the James, and as pastor in the city of Richmond, had the best opportunities for gathering information
which Semple did not have and "could not get," and he
who would discredit his work must impeach the character
of the author. There is no discrepancy or conflict between
him and Semple.

CHAPTER IX.

Desultory Engagement, or Lull Before the Final Struggle—1780-1783.

THIS period, from 1780 to 1783, begins with the darkest hour of the Revolution and closes with the signing of the treaty of peace between Great Britian and the United States. The "Continental currency" had become worthless. "It took $150 of it to buy a bushel of corn, and an ordinary suit of clothes cost $2,000." The greatest distress prevailed in the army and throughout the country. Congress was weak through its inability to tax the people for the support of the war. It was in this period of darkness and gloom (1780) that the whole country was startled and alarmed by the treachery and desertion of General Arnold, who sought to sell the cause of independence for British gold. But his accomplice, Major Andre, had scarcely been executed when the star of hope rose in the South, in the important victory at King's Mountain, October 7, followed, January 17, 1781, by another signal victory at the Cowpens. This was followed by the march of Cornwallis northward to Guilford Courthouse, whence, after a severe engagement with General Greene, he marched through lower Virginia to Yorktown, where he was finally cooped up by the French and Americans, and forced to surrender, October 19, 1781. This practically ended the war. November 30, 1782, a provisional treaty of peace was signed; on the 30th of April, 1783, General Washington proclaimed a cessation of hostilities, and the final treaty of peace between Great Britain and the United States was signed at Paris, September 3, 1783.

During all this period, the General Assembly does very little either for or against the cause of religious liberty. The old Establishment is down, but some of its relics remain, and, while there is desire and effort on the part of many to complete the work, there are others who are waiting for a favorable opportunity to set up a new establishment on a broader and more liberal basis. The doings of the several denominations are here presented in their order, together with the Journal notices of their memorials and the action of the Assembly.

HANOVER PRESBYTERY, APRIL, 1780.

According to Dr. Foote (page 332), the Presbytery of Hanover met in April, 1780, at Tinkling Spring congregation, in Augusta county; present, Rev. Messrs. Todd, Brown, Waddel, Rice, Irvin, Smith, and Crawford. On the 28th of the month, being at Mr. Waddel's, " A memorial to the Assembly of Virginia, from this Presbytery—to abstain from interfering in the government of the church—was prepared, and, being read in Presbytery, is appointed and directed to be transmitted to the House."

"The Presbytery do request Colonel McDowell and Captain Johnson to present their memorial to the Assembly, and to second it by their influence; and Mr. Waddel and Mr. Graham are appointed to inform these gentlemen of the request of Presbytery."

PETITION FROM AMELIA.

May 12, 1780: "A petition of sundry inhabitants of the county of Amelia, whose names are thereunto subscribed, was presented to the House and read; setting forth that they conceive the present constitution of parish vestries is a public grievance; that doubts have arisen as to the validity of marriages solemnized by dissenting ministers, and praying that the vestries in the several parishes may be dissolved, and elected hereafter by the free choice of the people, and that marriages solemnized by dissenting ministers may be declared lawful." "Referred to Committee on Religion."

ORDER OF ASSEMBLY.

June 4, 1780 : "Ordered, That leave be given to bring in a bill 'for saving the property of the church heretofore by law established," and that the committee appointed to prepare and bring in a bill 'for religious freedom' do prepare and bring in the same."

BAPTIST PETITION.

June 5, 1780 : "A petition of the society of people called Baptists was presented to the House and read; setting forth that doubts have arisen whether marriages solemnized by dissenting ministers are valid, and praying that an act may pass to declare such marriages lawful." "Referred to Committee on Religion."

BILL FOR RELIGIOUS FREEDOM ADVANCING.

June 14, 1780: "A bill 'for establishing religious freedom' was read a second time." It was then resolved by the House to defer the third reading of the said bill till the 1st day of August. At the same time it was resolved that the bill "for saving the property of the church heretofore by law established" be read a second time on the 1st day of August. But the House adjourned, June 26, till the first Monday in October.

SOME VESTRIES DISSOLVED.

July 5, 1780: "An engrossed bill 'for dissolving several vestries and electing overseers of the poor' was read the third time and passed."

GENERAL ASSOCIATION OF 1780.

According to Semple (page 66), the Baptist General Association met at Waller's meeting-house, Spotsylvania county, the second Saturday in May, 1780, but "no account could be obtained of the proceedings of this session." The next meeting was at Sandy Creek meeting-house,

Charlotte county, the second Saturday in October; Samuel Harris, moderator, and John Williams, clerk.

"From the minutes it appears that some jealousy was still entertained respecting the power of the associations. In consequence of which, an entry is made disavowing any authority over the churches."

"A letter was received from a committee of the Regular Baptists, requesting that a similar committee should be appointed by this Association to consider national grievances in conjunction. This was done accordingly, and Reuben Ford, John Williams, and E. Craig were appointed."

"The third Thursday in November following was appointed a day of fasting and prayer, in consequence of the alarming and distressing times."

BAPTIST PETITION.

November 8, 1780: "A memorial of the Baptist Association was presented to the House and read; setting forth that they consider the present vestry law as a restriction on their religious liberties, and that marriages solemnized by dissenting ministers, not being confirmed and sanctioned by law, they also consider as a grievance; and praying relief."

PRINCE EDWARD COUNTY.

November 10, 1780: "A petition of sundry inhabitants of the county of Prince Edward, whose names are thereunto subscribed, was presented to the House and read; setting forth that they consider it as unwise to extend the privileges granted to well-affected citizens to those who refuse to give assurance of fidelity to the State; that dangerous consequences may ensue by admitting the exercise of any of the learned professions to non-jurors; and praying that all non-juring clergymen, of whatever denomination, may be silenced, and such as have them deprived of their benefices; that those who refuse to give assurance of allegiance to the State may be prohibited the exercise of either of the professions of law or physic; and that double taxes be imposed on all non-jurors."

November 23, several petitions from Cumberland county to the same effect were presented to the House. There was another from Buckingham county, November 7, exactly like the above.

By "non-jurors" is meant those inhabitants of Virginia who, after the colony had thrown off allegiance to Great Britian and set up a new government, had failed to take the oath of allegiance to Virginia. The Revolution was still in progress and its issue uncertain. The object of the above petitions was to throw out of employment, especially in the professions, all who failed to swear allegiance.

BISHOP MEADE.

The following from Meade's "Old Churches," etc. (Vol. 2, page 445), seems to fix the responsibility for this movement on the Presbyterians:

"November, 1780: Petition and counter-petition of the inhabitants of Cumberland. The Presbyterians pray the Assembly to declare all non-juring clergymen incapable of preaching. The Episcopalians indignantly declare the Presbyterians 'disorderly and turbulent, desirous of giving laws to all societies,' and fond of noise and violence. The real object of their (the Presbyterians') petition, the memorialists say, is to ruin the Rev. Christopher MacRae, who, although prevented by conscientious scruples from taking the oath, is a most benevolent man, a pattern of piety, and one who wishes liberty and happiness to all mankind. The ruin of the church in Cumberland is declared to be the ultimate object of the Presbyterians."

On the same page (445), Bishop Meade gives the following from the Journal of the House:

"November 22, 1781: Sundry inhabitants of Prince Edward county pray that all the old vestries may be dissolved by act of Assembly and new ones elected by the body of the community at large, dissenters to be equally competent with conformists to the post of vestrymen, and the sole *proviso* to be 'attachment to the present form of government.' Referred to next Assembly, and, June 9, 1782, rejected."

Had this movement prevailed as to "non-jurors" and

as to elections of vestrymen, the houses of worship belonging to the Establishment and the "glebes" would, in many cases, have fallen into the hands of dissenters. It does not appear that the Baptists took any part in this attempt at "reconstruction." The incident is recorded here as explaining, in part at least, the enmity which existed between the Presbyterian and Episcopal clergy, and which will appear later on as one of the obstacles in the way of the success of the "General Assessment Bill."

RESOLUTIONS OF ASSEMBLY.

November 21, 1780: "Mr. Carrington reported from the Committee for Religion that the committee had, according to order, had under their consideration the memorial of the Baptist Association, to them referred, and had come to several resolutions thereupon, which he read in his place, and afterwards delivered in at the clerk's table, when the same were again read, and are as followeth:

Resolved, That it is the opinion of this committee that such parts of the said memorial as pray that marriages solemnized by dissenting ministers may be declared lawful is reasonable.

Resolved, That it is the opinion of this committee that such other parts of the said memorial as pray that the vestries in the several parishes throughout this State may be dissolved is reasonable."

The first resolution was read a second time and agreed to by the House. The second was read a second time and ordered to lie on the table.

NEW MARRIAGE LAW.

"An act declaring what shall be a lawful marriage" was passed by the Legislature during this fall session of 1780; but it was so clogged by "*provisoes*" as to materially abate the satisfaction with which it was received by the people. These objectionable restrictions were all removed by the Legislature of 1784, and the ministers of all denominations placed upon an equal footing, as they are to this day. Foote says (331): "This act, clogged as it was, to be in full force from the 1st of January, 1781, was an advance in religious liberty. The solemn vows to live as husband and wife might be uttered in words and with forms agreeable to the tastes and consciences of the parties concerned."

GENERAL ASSOCIATION OF 1781.

Semple (page 66) says: "The next Association was appointed at Anderson's meeting-house, Buckingham county, second Saturday in May, 1781. They met according to appointment. About this time, the British, under Lord Cornwallis, were marching through Virginia from the South, and were now at no great distance from the place of the Association. On this account, there were but sixteen churches corresponded. They chose William Webber moderator, and J. Williams, clerk. After making some few arrangements, and appointing the next Association at Dover meeting-house, Goochland county, the second Saturday in October, 1782, they adjourned."

GENERAL ASSOCIATION OF 1782.

Semple (page 67): "They met at Dover meeting-house, agreeable to appointment. Letters from thirty-two corresponding churches were read. William Webber, moderator; John Williams, clerk. Jeremiah Walker was appointed a delegate to attend the next General Assembly, with a memorial and petitions against ecclesiastical oppression. Robert Stockton attended this Association as a delegate from the Strawberry Association. The large number of churches, and the great distance which many of their delegates had to travel, rendered a General Association in Virginia extremely inconvenient; so that they would probably long before this date have divided into districts, if they had not been holden together by apprehensions of oppression from civil government. They could not make head against their powerful and numerous opponents with any hope of success unless they were united among themselves. 'In order to be all of one mind, it was necessary they should all assemble around one council board. For these reasons, the General Association was kept up as long as it was. Finding it, however, considerably wearisome to collect so many from such distant parts, and having already secured their most important civil rights, they determined to hold only one more General Association, and then, dividing into districts, to form some plan to keep a standing sentinel for political purposes." . . . "They then proceeded to appoint the Association at Dupuy's meeting-house, Powhatan county, second Saturday in October, 1783." . . . "The first Wednesday in November was appointed a day of fasting and prayer, on account of the prospects of famine, and to avert the judgments of God on account of the increasing wickedness of the land."

BAPTIST MEMORIALS.

May 30, 1783 : "A memorial of the ministers and messengers of the Baptist Association was presented to the House and read ; setting forth that, while they rejoice at the prospect of liberty and independence which the return of peace has produced, they conceive themselves oppressed by the operation of the laws respecting vestries and marriages ; and praying that said laws may be revised and amended."

June 1, 1783 : "An address of the ministers and messengers of the Baptist Association was presented to the House and read ; setting forth that, notwithstanding the joy which is diffused amongst them on the return of peace and the happy establishment of our independence, they think they have some reason to complain, as the laws respecting vestries and marriages are peculiarly oppressive upon them ; and praying that the said laws may be revised and amended."

LAST MEETING OF GENERAL ASSOCIATION.

"Second Saturday in October, 1783, they met in General Association, according to appointment, and for the last time. Thirty-seven delegates, including most of the active preachers in Virginia, were present. William Webber, moderator ; John Williams, clerk. The following business was transacted in this Association :

"*Resolved*, That our General or Annual Association cease, and that a general committee be instituted, composed of not more than four delegates from each district association, to meet annually, to consider matters that may be for the good of the whole society, and that the present Association be divided into four districts—Upper and Lower District, on each side of James river."

" Reuben Ford and John Waller were appointed delegates to wait on the General Assembly with a memorial. Then dissolved." Semple, pages 68, 69.

HOWELL'S TESTIMONY.

Dr. Howell (173) adds little to Semple, except in the matter of details. He says:

"The meetings of the General Association for 1782 and for 1783 had a full attendance. The remaining laws of the State regarded by them as unequal and oppressive received their elaborate attention. Prominent among these were 'the vestry and glebe laws.' The project, before mentioned, of incorporating, or establishing as the religion of the State, all the prevailing denominations, and assessing taxes upon the people to support the ministers of all alike, was now warmly advocated by Presbyterians, Episcopalians and Methodists, and becoming quite popular. To this scheme the Baptists still gave the most determined opposition, and sent up against it the most vigorous remonstrances. They also continued to petition for the adoption of the proposed 'Act to Establish Religious Freedom.' To bear these addresses to the Legislature and to superintend them before that body, Jeremiah Walker was appointed by the former meeting, and by the latter, Reuben Ford and John Waller. The extraordinary state of the country, however, prevented, on the part of the government, any important action on these subjects."

JOURNAL OF NOVEMBER 6, 1783.

"A petition of the ministers and messengers of the several Baptist churches was presented to the House and read ; setting forth that several oppressive distinctions between dissenters and the Church of England still exist in the vestry law and marriage act, in favor of the latter ; and praying that all such distinctions may be done away, and religious freedom established. Referred."

November 8, 1783 : "A petition of sundry inhabitants of the county of Lunenburg, whose names are thereunto subscribed, was presented to the House and read ; setting forth that they conceive it would greatly tend to promote religion and the propagation of the gospel if a general and equal contribution for the support of the clergy were established ; and praying that an act may pass to that effect."

November 27, 1783: Similar petition from Amherst county.

This closes the second period of the struggle for religious liberty—the period of the Revolution. The independence of the colonies has been acknowledged by Great Britain, as well as by other nations, and the infant republic has entered upon a perilous struggle for separate existence. But, while threatened by difficulties within and foes without, there is hope of its future in the fact that the leaven of religious liberty has been cast into the lump—a principle which is destined to leaven the whole mass.

CHAPTER X.

Struggle Renewed—General Incorporation and Assessment Bills.

THE period immediately succeeding the Revolution was marked by a renewal of the struggle between the friends and the opponents of absolute religious freedom. The Baptists continued to present an unbroken front against every vestige of union between Church and State; the Episcopalians, on the other hand, sought to recover lost ground under a new and more liberal form of church establishment; while the Presbyterians occupied a sort of middle ground, which caused confusion in their own ranks and compromised them in the estimation of others.

The petitions are presented here in the order in which they were presented to the House of Delegates.

FOR GENERAL ASSESSMENT.

May 15, 1784: "A petition of sundry inhabitants of the county of Warwick, whose names are thereunto subscribed, was presented to the House and read; setting forth that, in the present neglected state of religion and morality, they conceive a general assessment would greatly contribute to restore and propagate the holy Christian religion; and praying that an act may pass for the assessment upon all titheables for the support of religion."

BAPTIST MEMORIAL.

May 26, 1784: "A memorial of the Baptist Association was presented to the House and read; setting forth that the distinctions established by law in favor of the Episcopal church are injurious to the religions of all other denominations, and that they consider the present vestry and marriage acts as unequal and oppressive ; and praying that perfect and equal religious freedom may be established."

PRESBYTERIAN CLERGY.

"Also, a memorial of the united clergy of the Presbyterian church in Virginia ; setting forth that they consider the present existing laws in favor of the Episcopal church as creating invidious and exclusive distinctions, dangerous to religious freedom ; that, in particular, the several acts which recognize that as the established church enable it to acquire and possess property for ecclesiastical purposes, to celebrate marriages throughout the State *ex officio*, and that the laws concerning vestries are unjust, unequal, and oppressive ; and praying that the Legislature will do away with all such distinctions and secure their future and religious freedom upon the broad basis of perfect political equality." [See Appendix for memorial.]

Both these petitions were referred to the Committee on Religion.

RESOLUTION FAVORING ASSESSMENT.

May 27, 1784 : "*Resolved*, That it is the opinion of this committee, that the petition of sundry inhabitants of the county of Warwick, whose names are thereunto subscribed, praying that an act may pass for a general assessment upon all titheables of this Commonwealth for the support of the Christian religion within the same, is reasonable."

This was from the Committee on Religion and was referred to the Committee of the Whole House.

PRESBYTERIANS WANT LAND.

June 1, 1784 : "Also, a petition of the president and trustees of Hampden-Sidney College ; setting forth that the funds of the said College are inadequate to its support and the erection of the necessary buildings ; and praying that the Legislature will aid their funds by a grant of 400 acres of confiscated land, late the property of Spiers & Company, in the neighborhood of the said College."

June 4, 1784 : "*Resolved*, That it is the opinion of this committee that the petition of the president and trustees of Hampden-Sidney College, praying that a tract of land containing about 400 acres, which is now vested in the Commonwealth by the laws of escheat and forfeiture, and which adjoins the said College, may be vested in the president and trustees thereof, is reasonable."

EPISCOPALIAN PETITION.

June 4, 1784 : "A petition of the Protestant Episcopal church was presented to the House and read ; setting forth that their church labors under many inconveniences and restraints by the operation of sundry laws now in force, which direct modes of worship and enjoin the observance of certain days, and otherwise produce embarrassment and difficulty ; and praying that all acts which direct modes of faith and worship and enjoin the observance of certain days may be repealed ; that the present vestry laws may be repealed or amended ; that the churches, glebe lands, donations, and all other property heretofore belonging to the Established church, may be forever secured to them by law ; that an act may pass to incorporate the Protestant Episcopal church in Virginia, to enable them to regulate all the spiritual concerns of that church after its form of worship, and constitute such canons, by-laws, and rules for the government and good order thereof as are suited to their religious principles ; and, in general, that the Legislature will aid and patronize the Christian religion."

RESOLUTIONS.

June 8, 1784 : "*Resolved*, That it is the opinion of this committee that the memorial of the clergy of the Protestant Episcopal church of Virginia, praying that the laws within this Commonwealth, which restrain the said church from the like powers of self-government as is enjoyed by all other religious societies, and which prescribe the mode of appointing vestries and the qualifications of vestrymen, may be changed ; and that the churches, glebe lands, donations, and all other property belonging to the said church, may forever be secured to them, is reasonable."

"*Resolved*, That it is the opinion of this committee that so much of the memorials from the united clergy of the Presbyterian church in Virginia and the Baptist Association as prays that the laws regulating the celebration of marriage and relating to the constitution of vestries, may be altered ; and that in general all legal distinctions in favor of any particular religious society may be abolished, is reasonable."

"*Resolved*, That it is the opinion of this committee that so much of the memorials from the clergy of the Protestant Episcopal church in Virginia and the united clergy of the Presbyterian church in Virginia as relates to an incorporation of their societies is reasonable; and that a like incorporation ought to be extended to all other religious societies within the Commonwealth which may apply for the same."

PRESBYTERIANS GET LAND.

June 10, 1784: "An engrossed bill, 'giving certain lands to Hampden-Sidney College, in the county of Prince Edward,' was read the third time. *Resolved*, That the bill do pass, and that the title be 'An Act Giving Certain Lands to Hampden-Sidney College, in the County of Prince Edward.'"

BILL TO INCORPORATE EPISCOPAL CHURCH REPORTED.

June 16, 1784: "Mr. Jones, of King George, reported from the Committee for Religion, according to order, a bill 'for incorporating the Protestant Episcopal church, and for other purposes'; and the same was received and read the first time, and ordered to be read a second time."

FOR GENERAL ASSESSMENT.

November 4, 1784: "A petition of sundry inhabitants of the county of Isle of Wight, whose names are thereunto subscribed, was presented to the House and read ; setting forth that they are much concerned to see the countenance of the civil power wholly withdrawn from religion, and the people left without the smallest coercion to contribute to its support ; that they consider it as the duty of a wise Legislature to encourage its progress and diffuse its influence ; that, being thoroughly convinced that the prosperity and happiness of this country essentially depends on the progress of religion, they beg leave to call the attention of the Legislatnre to a principle, old as society itself, that whatever is to conduce equally to the advantage of all should be borne equally by all ; and praying that an act may pass to compel every one to contribute something, in proportion to his property, to the support of religion."

BAPTIST GENERAL COMMITTEE.

November 11, 1784: "A memorial of a committee of sundry Baptist associations, assembled at Dover meeting-house, was presented to the House and read; setting forth that they have still reason to complain of several acts now in force, which they conceive are oppressive and repugnant to the equal rights of religious liberty, particularly the marriage and vestry laws; and praying that the same may be amended."

The marriage law was so amended at this session as to be acceptable to all dissenters.

LOOKING TO A GENERAL ASSESSMENT.

On the same day, November 11, it was resolved in Committee of the Whole—

"That the people of this Commonwealth, according to their respective abilities, ought to pay a moderate tax or contribution annually for the support of the Christian religion, or of some Christian church, denomination, or communion of Christians, or of some form of Christian worship."

PRESBYTERIAN CLERGY GO OVER.

November 12, 1784: "A memorial of the united clergy of the Presbyterian church; setting forth that they feel much uneasiness at the continuance of their grievances, which they complained of in a memorial presented to the last session of Assembly, increased by the prospect of an addition to them by certain exceptionable measures said to be proposed to the Legislature; that they disapprove of all acts for incorporating the clergy of any society independent of theirs, or any interference of the Legislature in the spiritual concerns of religion; and that a general assessment for its support ought, they think, to be extended to those who profess the public worship of the Deity, and are comprised within the Declaration of Rights." [See Appendix for memorial.]

PRESBYTERIAN PLAN OF ASSESSMENT.

Dr. Foote, on pages 336–338, gives this memorial in full, and adds:

"There was a strong impression that some kind of assessment would be demanded by a majority of the citizens of the State. And it appears that for a time there was a leaning that way in some, at least, of the members of Presbytery; for at the same session of Presbytery in which the foregoing memorial was prepared (October 27, 1784) the following 'plan was also introduced, agreeably to which alone Presbytery are willing to admit a general assessment for the support of religion by law, the leading principles of which are as follows : (1st) Religion as a spiritual system is not to be considered as an object of human legislation, but may in a civil view, as preserving the existence and promoting the happiness of society ; (2d) that public worship and public periodical instruction to the people be maintained in this view by a general assessment for this purpose ; (3d) that every man, as a good citizen, be obliged to declare himself attached to some religious community, publicly known to express the belief of one God, his righteous providence, our accountableness to him, and a future state of rewards and punishments ; (4th) that every citizen should have liberty annually to direct his assessed proportion to such community as he chooses; (5th) that twelve tithe-ables, or more, to the amount of one hundred and fifty families, as near as local circumstances will admit, shall be incorporated, and exclusively direct the application of the money contributed for their support. Messrs. Todd, Graham, Smith, and Montgomery are appointed to present the memorial and attend the Assembly with the plan of an assessment.' "

It thus appears that the Presbyterian clergy were willing to have a general assessment for the support of religion, provided they could have it on their own plan—a plan broad and liberal enough for those who believe in a union of Church and State, but not for those who hold to the absolute freedom of the conscience from all control of civil or ecclesiastical authority.

ORDER OF ASSEMBLY.

November 13, 1784: "Ordered, That the Committee for Religion be discharged from further proceeding on the memorials of the committee of the Baptist associations, and that the same be referred

to the Committee of the Whole House on the State of the Commonwealth."

RESOLUTIONS IN COMMITTEE OF THE WHOLE.

November 17, 1784 : "*Resolved*, That it is the opinion of this
committee that so much of the petition of the Presbytery of Hanover and of the Baptist Association as prays that the laws regulating
the celebration of marriage and relating to the construction of the
vestries may be altered, is reasonable."

"*Resolved*, That it is the opinion of this committee that acts
ought to pass for the incorporation of all societies of the Christian
religion which may apply for the same."

Baptists, at least, could not *apply* for incorporation
without stultifying themselves, and the members of Assembly ought to have known that they could not.

These resolutions were reported to the House, and, on
being read the second time, were agreed to. The latter
resolution was adopted by a vote of 62 ayes, including
Patrick Henry, the author of the bill, against 23 noes,
including James Madison, Zacharia Johnston, French
Strother, and Wilson Carey Nicholas.

FOR INCORPORATION OF EPISCOPAL CLERGY.

On the same day, November 17, it was "Ordered,
That leave be given to bring in a bill to incorporate the
clergy of the Protestant Episcopal church, and that Messrs.
Carter Henry Harrison, Henry, Thomas Smith, William
Anderson, and Tazewell, do prepare and bring in the
same."

On the same day, Patrick Henry was again elected
Governor of the State.

CHARACTER OF THIS BILL OF INCORPORATION.

As the Journal gives only the title of the bill proposed,
and which failed to become a law, we must look to other

sources for information as to its character.   The following is James Madison's description, as given by Rives, in his "Life and Times of Madison," Vol. I., page 562:

"The Episcopal clergy introduced a notable project for re-establishing their independence of the laity.   The foundation of it was that the whole body should be legally incorporated, invested with the present property of the church, made capable of acquiring indefinitely, empowered to make canon and by-laws not contrary to the laws of the land ; and incumbents, when once chosen by the vestries, to be irremovable otherwise than by sentence of the convocation. Extraordinary as such a project was, it was preserved from a dishonorable death by the talents of Mr. Henry.   It lies over for another session."

GENERAL ASSESSMENT BILL.

The "Bill Establishing a Provision for Teachers of Religion," otherwise known as the "General Assessment Bill," which was complementary to the General Incorporation Bill, was reported December 3, 1784.   The preamble was as follows:

"Whereas the general diffusion of Christian knowledge hath a natural tendency to correct the morals of men, restrain their vices, and preserve the peace of society, which cannot be effected without a competent provision for learned teachers, who may be thereby enabled to devote their time and attention to the duty of instructing such citizens as from their circumstances and want of education cannot otherwise attain such knowledge ; and it is judged such provision may be made by the Legislature, without counteracting the liberal principle heretofore adopted and intended to be preserved, by abolishing all distinctions of pre-eminence amongst the different societies or communities of Christians."

MADISON WRITES FROM SCENE OF ACTION.

In a letter to James Monroe, dated Richmond, November 27, 1784, Madison says:

"The bill for a religious assessment has not been yet brought in. Mr. Henry, the father of the scheme, is gone up to his seat for his family, and will no more sit in the House of Delegates—a circumstance very inauspicious to his offspring."

To same party he writes again, December 4:

"The bill for the religious assessment was reported yesterday, and will be taken up in a committee of the whole next week. Its friends are much disheartened at the loss of Mr. Henry." Writings of Madison, I., 111, 113.

This bill had passed to its third reading, when its progress was arrested and it was postponed until the fourth Thursday in November, 1785. It was ordered to be printed and distributed among the people, who were requested to signify their opinion respecting it.

MADISON AGAIN.

In a letter to James Monroe, April 12, 1785, he says:

"The only proceeding of the late session of Assembly which makes a noise through the country is that which relates to a general assessment. The Episcopal people are generally for it, though I think the zeal of some of them has cooled. The laity of the other sects are generally unanimous on the other side. So are all the clergy, except the Presbyterian, who seem as ready to set up an establishment which is to take them in as they were to pull down that which shut them out. I do not know a more shameful contrast than might be found between their memorials on the latter and former occasions." Rives, I., 630.

RIVES ON THE SAME.

In his "Life and Times of Madison," I., 602, Mr. Rives says:

"What is especially remarkable is that, in a memorial presented by the united clergy of the Presbyterian church—a body which had hitherto distinguished itself by its zeal in favor of the principles of unlimited religious freedom—an opinion was now expressed, as cited in the Journal of the House of Delegates, that 'a general assessment for the support of religion ought to be extended to those who profess the public worship of the Deity.' . . . It is, perhaps, not to be wondered at that, among a people accustomed from their earliest times to see religion lean for support on the arm of secular power, an apprehension should have been felt of its decline upon the withdrawal of that support."

DR. FOOTE'S APOLOGY FOR HIS BRETHREN.

Dr. Foote does not try to conceal or evade the fact that there was wavering among the Presbyterian clergy in this fight over the assessment; he only seeks to account for their action and to explain it as an acceptance of the lesser of two evils. In his sketch of Rev. William Graham, he says:

"When the bill for a general assessment was brought forward, with such an advocate as Patrick Henry, and with the Episcopal church to support it, it was generally supposed that it would certainly become a law. To those who had been paying to support their own church and another, foreign to it, this bill proposed relief; they were to pay only for the support of the church of their choice. As it was a relief from their former burdens, and as the Presbyterian congregations would not be called on to pay more for the support of their own ministers than they would cheerfully give by voluntary subscription, Mr. Graham was agreed with his brethren to send up the memorial which gives their sentiments on the subject of the support of religion, disclaiming all legislative interference, and, under the conviction that the law would in some form pass, proposing the least offensive form in which the assessment could be levied." Sketches of Virginia, page 455.

BAPTISTS STAND FIRM.

The Baptists, through their General Committee, had, in the meeting of October 9, 1784, "resolved to oppose the law for a general assessment, and that for the incorporation of religious societies, which were now in agitation." Granted that the proposed incorporation bill would take them in, as well as the Presbyterians, Methodists and Episcopalians, they were irreconcilably opposed to any sort of union between Church and State. Granted that the proposed assessment bill would allow them to designate their own ministers as the beneficiaries of their part of the tax, they believed in a voluntary religion and in free-will offerings for its support, and hence could not consistently favor a measure which looked to the support of the ministry by means of a compulsory tax, levied and collected by civil authority. Granted that the great " Orator of the Revolution " was the father and advocate of these measures, they could resist the charm of his siren voice, when that voice was raised in advocacy of what they believed to be an unholy cause. We close this chapter with a statement by Rev. William Fristoe of the reasons why the Baptists " considered themselves under the necessity of appearing again on the public theatre and express their disapprobation to the above proposition, and use their influence to prevent its passing into a law."

WILLIAM FRISTOE ON BAPTIST POSITION.

On page 92 of his History of the Ketocton Association, he says:

" First, it was contrary to their principles and avowed sentiments, the making provision for the support of religion by law; that the distinction between civil and ecclesiastical governments ought to be kept up without blending them together; that Christ Jesus hath given laws for the government of his kingdom and direction of his subjects, and gave instruction concerning collections for the various purposes of religion, and therefore needs not legislative interference.

"Secondly, should a legislative body undertake to pass laws for the government of the church, for them to say what doctrines shall be believed, in what mode worship shall be performed, and what the sum collected shall be, what a dreadful precedent it would establish; for when such a right is claimed by a legislature, and given up by the people, by the same rule that they decide in one instance they may in every instance. Religion in this is like the press; if government limits the press, and says this shall be printed and that shall not, in the event it will destroy the freedom of the press; so when legislatures undertake to pass laws about religion, religion loses its form, and Christianity is reduced to a system of worldly policy.

"Thirdly, it has been believed by us that that Almighty Power that instituted religion will support his own cause; that in the course of divine Providence events will be overruled, and the influence of grace on the hearts of the Lord's people will incline them to afford and contribute what is necessary for the support of religion, and therefore there is no need for compulsory measures.

"Fourthly, it would give an opportunity to the party that were numerous (and, of course, possessed the ruling power) to use their influence and exercise their art and cunning, and multiply signers to their own favorite party.   And, last, the most deserving, the faithful preacher, who in a pointed manner reproved sin and bore testimony against every species of vice and dissipation, would, in all probability, have been profited very little by such a law, while men-pleasers, the gay and fashionable, who can wink at sin and daub his hearers with untempered mortar, saying, 'Peace, peace,' when there is no peace, who can lay out his oratory in dealing out smooth things mingled with deception, the wicked, it is clear, would like to have it so; and it follows the irreligious and carnal part of the people would richly reward them for their flattery, and the undeserving go off with the gain."

CHAPTER XI.

Decisive Victory for Religious Liberty.

WHEN the Legislature of 1784 adjourned, the Baptists of Virginia stood alone, as a denomination, in opposing the general assessment and kindred bills, and the outlook was not bright for the triumph of their principles. The only hope of the opponents of the assessment was in an appeal to the people, as a majority of the Legislature were churchmen. Hence, immediately after they succeeded, by a vote of 43 ayes to 38 noes, in having the third reading of the bill postponed till the fourth Thursday in November, 1785, they offered the following resolution, which was adopted:

"*Resolved*, That the engrossed bill, establishing a provision for the teachers of the Christian religion, together with the names of the ayes and noes on the question of postponing the third reading of the said bill to the fourth Thursday in November next, be published in hand-bills, and twelve copies thereof delivered to each member of the General Assembly, to be distributed in their respective counties ; and that the people thereof be requested to signify their opinion respecting the adoption of such a bill to the next session of Assembly." Semple, page 33.

Semple adds:

"The above resolution drew forth a number of able and animated memorials from religious societies of different denominations against the general assessment. Among a great variety of compositions, possessing different degrees of merit, a paper drawn up by Colonel James Madison, intituled, 'A Memorial and Remonstrance,' will ever hold a most distinguished place. For elegance of style, strength of reasoning, and purity of principle, it has, perhaps, seldom been equalled, certainly never surpassed, by anything in the English language." Page 33. [See Appendix for remonstrance.]

Of this " memorial and remonstrance," Dr. George B. Taylor says: " It may certainly be called a Baptist document this far, that they only, *as a people*, held its views, and pressed those views without wavering." Memorial Series, No. IV., page 19.

Dr. E. G. Robinson writes to the same effect in the January, 1860, number of the *Christian Review*, of which he was editor:

" In a word, the great idea which he [Madison] put forth was identical with that which had always been devoutly cherished by our Baptist fathers, alike in the old world and the new, and which precisely a century and a half before had been perfectly expressed in the celebrated letter of Roger Williams to the people of his own settlement, and by him incorporated into the fundamental law of the colony of Rhode Island. By Mr. Madison it was elaborated with arguments and wrought into the generalizations of statesmanship, but the essential idea is precisely the same with the ' soul liberty' so earnestly contended for by the Baptists of every age."

ASSESSMENT BILL LOSING GROUND.

As the masses of the people became acquainted with the provisions and the true character of the assessment bill, there was developed a decided change in public sentiment. In a letter to James Monroe, May 29, 1785, Madison writes:

" The adversaries to the assessment begin to think the prospect here flattering to their wishes. The printed bill has excited great discussion, and is likely to prove the sense of the community to be in favor of the liberty now enjoyed. I have heard of several counties where the representatives have been laid aside for voting for the bill, and not a single one where the reverse has happened. The Presbyterian clergy, too, who were in general friends of the scheme, are already in another tone, either compelled by the laity of that sect or alarmed at the probability of farther interference of the Legislature, if they begin to dictate in matters of religion." Rives, I., 630.

PRESBYTERY RECONSIDERS.

On the 19th of May, 1785, just a few days before the date of the above letter, the Presbytery of Hanover met at Bethel, in Augusta county.

"Present, Rev. Messrs. John Todd, John Brown, William Graham, Archibald Scott, Edward Crawford, John B. Smith, William Ervin, Moses Hoge, Samuel Houston, Samuel Carrick, and Samuel Shannon, with Elders James Henry, William McKee, John Tate, James Hogshead, William Yool, and Andrew Settington." "A petition was presented to the Presbytery from the session of Augusta congregation, requesting an explication of the word '*liberal*,' as used in the Presbytery's memorial of last fall; and, also, the motives and end of the Presbytery in sending it to the Assembly. Messrs. Hoge and Carrick are appointed a committee to prepare an answer to the above petition, and report to Presbytery."

"On motion, the opinion of Presbytery was taken—whether they do approve of any kind of an assessment by the General Assembly for the support of religion. *Presbytery are unanimously against such a measure*." Foote, page 341.

And yet only a few months before this same body had memorialized the Legislature in favor of an assessment.

Dr. Foote, their historian, adds:

"The question from Augusta congregation referred to that part of the memorial of the preceding fall which says: 'Should it be thought necessary at present for the Assembly to exact this right of supporting religion in general by an assessment on all the people, we would wish it to be done on the most liberal plan.' Did this mean that they approved of an assessment, or that they acquiesced, or merely submitted; that they wished a large assessment, or one that favored all equally, without any distinction of sect? Whatever may have been the private opinions of any of the members in 1784 and previous, or the influence of that popular champion, Patrick Henry, over their judgments when first contemplating a subject of which he was the advocate—now, when the whole subject was thrown before the people, and the principles to govern the connection of Church and State to be settled by a popular vote, the Presbytery, in full session, declared themselves unanimously against all assessments by the Legislature for the support of religion.'' Page 341.

PRESBYTERIAN CONVENTION AT BETHEL.

Before the Presbytery adjourned, it was resolved to call a convention of the whole Presbyterian body to meet at the same place, on the 10th day of August, at which a paper, prepared by Rev. William Graham, was submitted and adopted, which, Dr. Foote says, ''expresses the true feeling of the Presbyterian church, after much private and public discussion.'' Page 341. [See Appendix for memorial.]

It is worthy of note, as a link in the chain of evidence, that this paper was the first and only Presbyterian memorial that asked for the passage of Jefferson's ''Bill for Establishing Religious Freedom,'' although that bill had been before the Legislature and the people ever since June, 1779.

BAPTIST GENERAL COMMITTEE.

This body met for the second time at Dupuy's meeting-house, in Powhatan, August 13, 1785. It was the business of this committee to consider all the political grievances of the whole Baptist society in Virginia and to take such action as was best calculated to secure redress. Four associations were represented by delegates in this meeting, of which Semple gives the following account, beginning at page 71:

''Reuben Ford reported that, according to the directions given him, he presented a memorial and petition to the honorable General Assembly; that they met with a favorable reception; that certain amendments were made to the marriage law, which he thought satisfactory.

"To this report the General Committee concurred.

"They were further informed that, at the last session of the General Assembly, a bill for a general assessment was introduced, and had almost passed into a law; but when at that stage in which it is called an engrossed bill, a motion was made and carried that it should be referred to the next Assembly, in order to give the people an opportunity to consider it."

"The General Committee, as guardians of the rights of Virginia Baptists, of course, took up the subject, and came to the following resolution:

"'*Resolved*, That it be recommended to those counties which have not yet prepared petitions to be presented to the General Assembly against the engrossed bill for a general assessment for the support of the teachers of the Christian religion, to proceed thereon as soon as possible; that it is believed to be repugnant to the spirit of the gospel for the Legislature thus to proceed in matters of religion; that no human laws ought to be established for this purpose, but that every person ought to be left entirely free in respect to matters of religion; that the Holy Author of our religion needs no such compulsive measures for the promotion of his cause; that the gospel wants not the feeble arm of man for its support; that it has made, and will again through divine power make, its way against all opposition; and that, should the Legislature assume the right of taxing the people for the support of the gospel, it will be destructive to religious liberty.'

"Therefore, this committee agrees, unanimously, that it will be expedient to appoint a delegate to wait on the General Assembly, with a remonstrance and petition against such assessment.

"Accordingly the Rev. Reuben Ford was appointed."

Thus the Presbyterians and Baptists are again standing together in opposition to an assessment for religious purposes. But whether they were actuated by the same motives and same considerations, each reader will judge for himself. The following is the opinion of Mr. Madison.

MADISON WRITES AGAIN.

From his home in Orange, August 20, he writes thus to Mr. Jefferson:

"The opposition to the general assessment gains ground. . . . .
The Presbyterian clergy have at length espoused the side of the opposition, being moved either by a fear of their laity or a jealousy of
the Episcopalians. The mutual hatred of these sects has been much
inflamed by the late act incorporating the latter. I am far from
being sorry for it, as a coalition between them could alone endanger
our religious rights, and a tendency to such an event has been suspected." Writings of Madison, I., 175.

ASSESSMENT BILL DIES IN COMMITTEE.

The General Assembly met on the 17th of October,
1785, and was flooded with petitions and memorials from all
parts of the State, some for and some against the pending
bill. Petitions against the bill came up from Cumberland,
Rockingham, Caroline, Buckingham, Henry, Pittsylvania,
Nansemond, Bedford, Richmond (county), Campbell,
Charlotte, Accomac, Isle of Wight, Albemarle, Amherst,
Louisa, Goochland, Westmoreland, Essex, Culpeper,
Prince Edward, Fairfax, Orange, King & Queen, Pittsyl-
vania, Mecklenburg, Amelia and Brunswick; Middlesex,
Chesterfield, Fairfax, Montgomery, Hanover, Princess
Anne, Amelia, Henrico, Brunswick, Dinwiddie, Northum-
berland, Prince George, Powhatan, Richmond (county),
Spotsylvania, Botetourt, Fauquier, Southampton, Lunen-
burg, Loudoun, Stafford, Henrico; also, "a memorial and
remonstrance of the ministers and lay representatives of the
Presbyterian church in Virginia, assembled in convention;"
"a petition and remonstrance of the committee of sundry
Baptist associations;" also, petitions from "members of
Presbyterian church near Peaks of Otter, Bedford county;"
"several petitions of members of sundry Presbyterian
societies," from "the Quakers," from "several Baptist
churches, assembled by their representatives in general
association in the county of Orange, on the 17th of Sep-

tember," and from "sundry citizens of the Commonwealth."

Petitions in favor of the bill came up from Mecklenburg,
Westmoreland, Essex, Richmond (county), Pittsylvania,
Lunenburg, Surry, and Amelia.

The people were found to be overwhelmingly against the
bill, and, after a brief consideration in Committee of the
Whole House, it was given up forever. Dr. Foote, page
431, says that it was lost by a majority of only three votes,
which plainly indicates that, but for this appeal to the people, the obnoxious measure would have been fastened upon
Virginia.

JEFFERSON'S BILL TRIUMPHS.

As the assessment bill was buried under the weight of
numerous petitions and memorials, Madison took advantage
of the favorable opportunity thus presented to bring forward Mr. Jefferson's "Bill for Establishing Religious
Freedom." He advocated it with an able speech, and it
was reported to the House, by which body it was adopted,
December 17, 1785, by a vote of 67 ayes against 20 noes.
January 16, 1786, certain amendments which were reported
from the Senate were agreed to by the House, and Mr.
Madison was directed to inform the Senate. The enrolled
bill was signed by the Speaker, January 19, 1786.

Of this bill, Dr. Foote wrote as follows, in 1850:

"After an experiment of more than half a century, the bill for
religious freedom holds its place among the fundamental laws of the
Virginia statute book. Religion and morals have not suffered.
Four colleges, two theological seminaries, and the University have
been added to the public institutions for instruction. Authorized
ministers of the gospel have increased about tenfold, and professors
of the religion of the gospel in the same proportion. Churches,
academies, and school-houses are multiplying throughout the ex-

tended State. All parties agree that 'the mind is free;' that even prisoners, slaves, and convicts enjoy freedom of conscience." Sketches of Virginia, page 348.

And yet there were many in that day who looked upon Jefferson's bill as dangerous to the cause of Christianity. Dr. Hawks says:

"There is reason in his [Jefferson's] case, therefore, to believe that, under cover of an attack upon a religious establishment, a blow was aimed at Christianity itself. Be this as it may, it is certain that an act was passed by the Legislature of 1785, which was viewed by many as utterly subversive in its declarations of the Christian religion, and called forth at the time the severe animadversions of some who still reverenced the faith of the apostles. This was the 'Act for Establishing Religious Freedom,' drawn by Mr. Jefferson, and preceded by a memorial from the pen of Mr. Madison, which is supposed to have led to the passage of the law." History Protestant Episcopal Church of Virginia, page 173.

The world—even the Christian world—was slow to understand and to lay hold of the true principle of soul liberty —a principle which had always been fundamental with the Baptists, and which, in the providence of God, they were destined to teach to their fellows.

CHAPTER XII.

Following Up Victory.

ALTHOUGH the assessment bill was dead and the "Act for Establishing Religious Freedom" had become law in Virginia, still there remained vestiges of establishment. The act incorporating the Protestant Episcopal church had been passed by the Legislature (signed by speaker January 5, 1785), and the glebes were still the property of that church. The Baptists, at least, deemed it unwise to leave any roots of the old establishment in the laws of the State, and so they kept up the war until 1802, when the glebes were sold and all religious societies were placed on an equal footing before the law.

THE GLEBES.

In order that the general reader may understand what the glebes were, and why the Baptists insisted on their sale, we give the following extract from Fristoe, page 94:

"The reader is to understand that in every parish there was a tract of land purchased and commodious buildings erected on it fit for the accommodation of a family, and all at the expense of the people within the parish. When a minister was inducted into the parish by the vestry he was possessed with said plantation, called glebe land. Now, inasmuch as these glebe lands were purchased with money extorted from the people by an arbitrary law under a kingly government, it has been thought unreasonable, after a revolution has taken place, the shackles of monarchical government burst asunder, and republicanism set up, religious establishments abolished in part, and equal liberty secured to the different citizens, that this property should not return to the right owners—these original purchasers or their representatives.

"And that it was a shameful partiality exercised by the government in favor of one particular sect, so incompatible with republican principles ; moreover, we were left to fear it would be made use of in a future day and the Established church have it to say there was a reserve of property to them, in preference to all other sects, and that establishment was only in part abolished, and this cockatrice egg produce in time a fiery, flying serpent."

GENERAL COMMITTEE.

Hence, in their meeting of August 5, 1786, the General Committee, acting for all the Baptists—

"*Resolved,* That petitions ought to be drawn and circulated in the different counties, and presented to the next General Assembly, praying for a repeal of the incorporating act, and that the public property which is by that act vested in the Protestant Episcopal church be sold and the money applied to public use ; and that Reuben Ford and John Leland attend the next Assembly as agents in behalf of the General Committee." Semple, 73.

UNION OF BAPTISTS.

It is worthy of note that it was at this meeting that the Regular Baptists of the Ketocton Association sent delegates to the General Committee, and were received on equal footing with those from the other associations. This gave rise to the following resolution :

" It is recommended to the different associations to appoint delegates to attend the next General Committee, for the purpose of forming an union with the Regular Baptists." Semple, 73.

That union was perfected at the next meeting of the General Committee, August 10, 1787, when all of the associations in the State, six in number, were represented by delegates. Thus it was that the discordant elements of the Baptist denomination in Virginia were brought into closer fellowship and harmony in the long and bitter struggle for religious liberty.

ACT OF INCORPORATION REPEALED.

At this meeting, August 10, 1787, Rev. Messrs. Ford and Leland

"*Reported*, That, according to their instructions, they presented a memorial praying for a repeal of the incorporating act; that the memorial was received by the honorable house, and that that part of the said act which respected the incorporation of the Protestant Episcopal church as a religious society, and marking out the rules of their procedure, was repealed, but that that part which respected the glebes, etc., remained as it was."

"Whereupon," says Semple (page 74), "the question was put whether the General Committee viewed the glebes, etc., as public property. . . . By a majority of one they decided that they were."

"That vote," says Dr. Hawks, "decided the fate of the glebes."

PRESBYTERIAN CO-OPERATION.

The Presbyterians co-operated with the Baptists in 1786 by memorializing the General Assembly to repeal the act of incorporation, but never afterwards took any action as a body. Of their action in this respect, Dr. Hawks says:

"Scarcely had the church begun to reap the benefits resulting from its incorporation by the Legislature before it was again assailed. The Presbytery of Hanover, in the same year in which the act of incorporation was passed, presented a memorial to the Legislature complaining of the peculiar privileges which the church was said thereby to obtain. . . . It will scarcely be thought strange that this manifestation of a willingness to forego what they themselves owned to be a benefit, because obliged to share it with Episcopalians, should have been construed, as it was, into a settled determination, if possible, to destroy the Episcopal church." History Protestant Episcopal Church in Virginia, Vol. I., page 172.

FINAL ACTION OF LEGISLATURE.

The Bapti-ts continued to memorialize the Legislature from year to year, and in 1799 that body passed an act entitled "An Act to Repeal Certain Acts, and to Declare the Construction of the Bill of Rights and the Constitution Concerning Religion," which act declared that no religious establishment had legally existed since the Commonwealth took the place of the regal government, repealed all laws giving to the Protestant Episcopal church any special privileges, and declared that "the act establishing religious freedom" contains the true construction of the Bill of Rights and of the Constitution; but no order was given for the sale of the glebes. True to their principles, the Baptists persevered in the fight, until at last, in January, 1802, the Legislature passed a law for the sale of the glebes and the proper appropriation of the proceeds. See Fristoe, page 95, and Semple, page 74 and following.

COMMENT OF DR. HAWKS.

Speaking of the protracted struggle for the overthrow of the Establishment, Dr. Hawks says:

"The Baptists were the principal promoters of this work, and in truth aided more than any other denomination in its accomplishment. Their historian (Semple) boasts that they alone were uniform in their efforts to destroy the system of an assessment and introduce the plan of voluntary contribution; that in the other denominations there was much division of sentiment between ministers and people, and that remonstrance came at last from none but Baptists. Whether this be so or not, it is very certain that in the associations of that sect held from year to year a prominent subject of discussion always was as to the best mode of carrying on the war against the former Establishment. After their final success in this matter of voluntary contribution, their next efforts were to procure a sale of the church lands. This, however, it seems, was not undertaken without some misgivings of its propriety; for when the question was put in their

'General Committee' whether the glebes were public property, it was settled in the affirmative by a majority of but one vote. That one vote sealed the fate of the church lands; for the efforts of the Baptists never ceased until, as we shall see hereafter, the glebes were sold." History Protestant Episcopal Church in Virginia, Vol. I., page 152.

EFFECT ON EPISCOPAL CHURCH.

While the effect of these acts was to destroy the Establishment and to temporarily embarrass the Protestant Episcopal church, by forcing them to seek pecuniary support, like other sects, from voluntary contributions, the final result was most salutary. Says Bishop Meade:

"Nothing could have been more injurious to the cause of true religion in the Episcopal church, or to its growth in any way, than the continuance of either stipend or glebes. Many clergymen of the most unworthy character would have been continued among us, and such a revival as we have seen have never taken place. As it was, together with the glebes and salaries, evil ministers disappeared and made room for a new and different kind." Old Churches and Families of Virginia, Vol. I., page 49.

SLAVERY QUESTION.

In the meeting of the General Committee, March 7, 1788, the following question was considered and referred to next session:

"Whether a petition should be offered to the General Assembly, praying that the yoke of slavery may be made more tolerable."

And in their meeting of August 8, 1789, in Richmond, the following resolution, offered by John Leland, was adopted:

"*Resolved*, That slavery is a violent deprivation of the rights of nature and inconsistent with a republican government, and, therefore, recommend it to our brethren to make use of every legal measure to extirpate this horrid evil from the land ; and pray Almighty

God that our honorable Legislature may have it in their power to proclaim the great jubilee, consistent with the principles of good policy." Semple, pages 77 and 79.

This action reflects no little credit upon the motives of the Baptists in their long and arduous struggle for liberty. They had sought religious liberty, not for themselves only, but for all mankind ; and as they breathed the atmosphere of both civil and religious freedom, they placed themselves on record as opposed to the perpetuation of human slavery in a free country.

REVIVAL OF RELIGION.

It is an important and significant fact that the period covered by this chapter—the period following the great and decisive victory for religious liberty—was a period of great religious revival. It began in the very year of the defeat of the Assessment Bill and the triumph of the "Act for Establishing Religious Freedom." Moreover, it began among the Baptists, the people who began the struggle, and who never wavered or faltered until the victory was complete. The following extracts from Semple, beginning on page 35, are worthy of note:

"The war, though very propitious to the liberty of the Baptists, had an opposite effect upon the life of religion among them. As if persecution was more favorable to vital piety than unrestrained liberty, they seem to have abated in their zeal upon being unshackled from their manacles." And then, after discussing the several causes of this declension, he says, on page 35 : "This chill to their religious affections might have subsided with the war, or perhaps sooner, if there had not been subsequent occurrences which tended to keep them down. The opening a free trade by peace served as a powerful bait to entrap professors who were in any great degree inclined to the pursuit of wealth. Nothing is more common than for the increase of riches to produce a decrease of piety. Speculators seldom make warm Christians. Kentucky and the Western country took off many of the preachers who had once been exceeding successful in the ministry.   From whatever cause, certain it is that they suffered a very wintry season.   With some few exceptions, the declension was general throughout the State.   .   .   .   The long and great declension induced many to fear that the times of refreshing would never come, but that God had wholly forsaken them.   .   .   .   The set time to favor Zion at length arrived, and, as the declension had been general, so also was the revival.   It may be considered as having begun in 1785, on James river.   It spread as fire among stubble. Continuing for several years in different parts, very few churches were without the blessing.   How great the change!"   Page 36. This revival "continued spreading until 1791 or 1792.   Thousands were converted and baptized, besides many who joined the Methodists and Presbyterians.   The Protestant Episcopalians, although much dejected by the loss of the Establishment, had, nevertheless, continued their public worship, and were attended by respectable congregations; but after this revival their society fell fast into dissolution." Page 38.

The Episcopal church, or Church of England, had already suffered a loss in another way.   Up to the year 1784, the Methodists had continued in the fellowship and communion of the mother church, Wesley himself styling them "converted societies in an unconverted church." But when the Revolutionary War was over and the independence of the colonies was recognized by Great Britian, it was deemed best for the cause of Methodism in America that their societies should be independent and separate from the Church of England.   Hence, in 1784, in the city of Baltimore, the Methodist Episcopal church was organized. The revival began the year following among the Baptists, and two years later (1787) among the Presbyterians on the south side of the James.   When the revival closed, the old Church of England was in ruins.   But out of the ruins of the old there sprang up a new church—the Protestant Episcopal church of Virginia.   The demolition

of the Establishment had driven out the *hireling* ministry
and made way for the introduction of men of piety and
consecration; so that the loss of the support of the civil
arm was a real and permanent gain, and the war which
the Baptists so "relentlessly" waged proved to be, in
truth, a "holy war." It marked the beginning of a new
era in the religious life of Virginia. All denominations
shared in the fruits of this revival; but the Baptists, as
being the recognized leaders, seem to have prospered most.
"They were much more numerous," says Semple (page
39), "and, of course, in the eyes of the world, more
respectable. Besides, they were joined by persons of much
greater weight in civil society. Their congregations
became more numerous than those of any other Christian
sect; and, in short, they might be considered, from this
period, as taking the lead in matters of religion in many
places of the State." God honors most those who most
honor him.

CHAPTER XIII.

Struggle Over The Constitution.

THIS narrative would not be complete without some account of the agency of the Baptists of Virginia in engrafting the principle of religious liberty upon the Constitution of the United States by means of the famous first amendment; and, in order to appreciate properly the part performed by them, it is necessary that we consider, not only what they did towards securing that first amendment, but also their attitude towards the Constitution and its ratification. The reader will, therefore, pardon a somewhat fuller and more circumstantial account of the struggle over the Constitution than would naturally be expected here, the object being to throw all the light possible upon this important subject.

After the independence of the colonies had been established, it soon became apparent that the old "Articles of Confederation" were too weak, that they did not give to Congress sufficient power to secure coöperation at home or respect abroad. Hence a movement was set on foot by James Madison to revise those "Articles" and give additional power to Congress—a movement which culminated in the calling of the Philadelphia Convention of 1787. Virginia selected as her representatives a number of her best men, including Washington, Madison, and Henry. Mr. Henry, however, declined to serve, and his refusal excited criticism and caused apprehension. Says Madison, in a letter to Randolph, March 25, 1787: "The refusal of Mr. Henry to join in the task of revising the Confederation is ominous." Madison Papers, Vol. II., page 627. And in another letter to Jefferson, March 19, he attributes Mr. Henry's refusal to attend the Convention to "the policy of keeping himself free to combat or espouse the result of the Mississippi business."

But the attempt to patch up the old Articles was vain, and so a new paper was prepared—the Constitution of the United States, of which James Madison was the father. It was the result of compromises, each section yielding something in the effort to secure unity and strength. It was submitted to the several States for ratification, with a *proviso* that when ratified by nine States the new government should be organized. Eight States—viz., Delaware, Pennsylvania, New Jersey, Connecticut, Massachusetts, Georgia, Maryland, and South Carolina — had passed articles of ratification when the Virginia Convention met on the 2d day of June, 1788. Patrick Henry and George Mason were there to oppose ratification without *previous* amendments, while Madison led the forces which favored immediate ratification and *subsequent* amendments. It was a "battle of giants," which culminated, June 25, in a victory for ratification by a majority of ten.

ATTITUDE OF BAPTISTS.

When the Constitution first appeared, in the fall of 1787, the impression made upon the Baptists was unfavorable. It did not seem to make sufficient provision for religious liberty. And when the General Committee met at Williams' meeting-house, Goochland county, March 7, 1788, this was one of the questions considered: "Whether the new Federal Constitution, which had now lately made its appearance in public, made sufficient provision for the secure enjoyment of religious liberty; on which it was agreed unanimously that, in the opinion of the General Committee, it did not." Semple, page 76.

The only provision in the Constitution touching religion was in the sixth article, and in these words: "No religious test shall ever be required as a qualification to any office or public trust under the United States." This was virtually a declaration in favor of the most absolute religious liberty, in that it published to all the world that this government, at least, would not allow a man's religion to bar his way to the highest office in the gift of the people. But the Baptists were not satisfied. They had been great sufferers in the past, and, having just emerged from a long and arduous struggle for their rights, they were apprehensive that, if they entered into this new and stronger union with States that still had religious establishments, there might be a reaction disastrous to their liberties. Hence they resolved to oppose ratification, and Elder John Leland, the most popular Baptist minister in Virginia, was nominated as a delegate from Orange county to the Convention. This was done while Madison was yet in the North, where he remained some months after the Constitution was framed and published, engaged, with Jay and Hamilton, in writing articles in explanation of the new scheme of government— articles since known as "The Federalist." Patrick Henry, who was strenuously opposed to the Constitution on other grounds, and especially as having "a squint towards monarchy," was quick to take advantage of this prejudice of the Baptists to enlist them on the side of the opposition.

MADISON ON THE SITUATION.

The situation in Virginia before Madison's return is well set forth in his letter to Jefferson, December 9, 1787:

"The body of the people in Virginia, particularly in the upper and lower country and in the Northern Neck, are, as far as I can gather, much disposed to adopt the new Constitution. The middle country and the south side of James river are principally in the opposition to it. As yet a large majority of the people are under the first description ; as yet, also, are a majority of the Assembly. What change may be produced by the united influence and exertions of Mr. Henry, Mr. Mason, and the Governor, with some pretty able auxiliaries, is uncertain. My information leads me to suppose there must be three parties in Virginia. The first, for adopting without attempting amendments. This includes General Washington and the other deputies who signed the Constitution, Mr. Pendleton (Mr. Marshall, I believe), Mr. Nicholas, Mr. Corbin, Mr. Zachary Johnson, Colonel Innes (Mr. Randolph, as I understand), Mr. Harvey, Mr. Gabriel Jones, Dr. Jones, etc., etc. At the head of the second party, which urges amendments, are the Governor and Mr. Mason. These do not object to the substance of the government, but contend for a few additional guards in favor of the rights of the States and of the people. I am not able to enumerate the characters which fall in with their ideas, as distinguished from those of the third class, at the head of which is Mr. Henry. This class concurs at present with the patrons of amendments, but will probably contend for such as strike at the essence of the system, and must lead to an adherence to the principle of the existing Confederation, which most thinking men are convinced is a visionary one, or to a partition of the union into several confederacies." And he adds, a little later : "Mr. Henry is the great adversary who will render the event precarious. *He is*, I find, *with his usual address, working up every possible interest into a spirit of opposition.*" (Italics mine.)

REV. JOHN BLAIR SMITH ON HENRY'S METHODS.

It has already been stated that Mr. Henry was quick to take advantage of the apprehensions of the Baptists on the subject of religious liberty to array them against the Constitution. Although he had been opposed to them in their war against the Establishment and in their fight against the assessment, he now poses as their champion in opposition to the Constitution, and seeks to array them against their old leader, James Madison. His methods are severely criticised by Rev. John Blair Smith, president of Hampden-Sidney College, in a letter to Mr. Madison, June 12, 1788:

"Before the Constitution appeared," he writes, "the minds of the people were artfully prepared against it; so that all opposition [to Mr. Henry]. at the election of delegates to consider it, was in vain. That gentleman has descended to lower artifices and management on the occasion than I thought him capable of. . . . If Mr. Innes has shown you a speech of Mr. Henry to his constituents, which I sent him, you will see something of the method he has taken to diffuse his poison. . . . It grieves me to see such great natural talents abused to such purposes. He has written letters repeatedly to Kentucky, and, as the people there are alarmed with an apprehension of their interests being about to be sacrificed by the Northern States, I am convinced that it has been owing to a story which I have heard Mr. Henry tell, respecting the measure proposed in Congress for a perpetual relinquishment of the navigation of the Mississippi to the Spaniards. He has found means to make some of the best people here believe that a religious establishment was in contemplation under the new government. He forgets that the Northern States are more decided friends to the voluntary support of Christian ministers than the author, or at least warm abettor, of the assessment bill in this State." Rives, II., 544.

MADISON WINS BAPTIST SUPPORT.

As already stated, Elder John Leland was made the candidate of the opposition in Orange, and was pitted against James Madison. But on the day of election Leland withdrew in favor of Madison, who was thus easily elected. That act of his put into the Convention the man who, above all others in Virginia, understood the new scheme of government and was best prepared to defend it against its enemies. It has been claimed that, had Madison been defeated, the Virginia Convention would have failed to ratify, and that, had Virginia refused to ratify, the whole scheme would have failed. Hence it was that Hon. J. S. Barbour, in a eulogy upon the character of Mr. Madison, referred to this incident and gave Elder Leland the credit for the ratification of the Constitution by Virginia and the triumph of the new system of government.

LELAND'S ACCOUNT OF THE MATTER.

This matter is of such importance as to justify the introduction of the somewhat lengthy account given by Leland himself. It is found in Sprague's "Annals of the American Baptist Pulpit," beginning at page 179, and contained in a letter of Hon. G. N. Briggs, LL. D., Governor of Massachusetts, who received it from Leland's own lips. Governor Briggs was an intimate friend of Leland after the latter's return to Massachusetts, and, when he read Mr. Barbour's reference to him, he paid him a visit and asked him about it. Leland replied that Barbour gave him too much credit, and then told the story as follows:

"Soon after the Convention which framed the Constitution of the United States had finished their work and submitted it to the people for their action, two strong and active parties were formed in the State of Virginia on the subject of its adoption. The State was nearly equally divided. One party was opposed to its adoption, unless certain amendments, which they maintained that the safety of the people required, should be incorporated into it before it was ratified by them. At the head of this great party stood Patrick Henry, the orator of the Revolution, and one of Virginia's favorite sons. The other party agreed with what their opponents said as to the character and necessity of the amendments proposed, but they contended that the people would have the power and could as well incorporate those amendments into their Constitution after its adoption as before ; that it was a great crisis in the affairs of the country, and if the Constitution then presented to the people by the Convention should be rejected by them, such would be the state of the public mind that there was little or no reason to believe that another would be agreed upon by a future convention ; and, in such an event —so much to be dreaded—the hopes of constitutional liberty and a confederated and free republic would be lost. At the head of this party stood James Madison. The strength of the two parties was to be tested by the election of county delegates to the State Convention. That Convention would have to adopt or reject the Constitution. Mr. Madison was named as the candidate in favor of its adoption for the county of Orange, in which he resided. Elder Leland, also, at that time lived in the county of Orange, and his sympathies, he said, were with Henry and his party. He was named as the candidate opposed to the adoption, and in opposition to Mr. Madison. Orange was a strong Baptist county, and his friends had an undoubting confidence in his election. Though reluctant to be a candidate, he yielded to the solicitations of the opponents of the Constitution and accepted the nomination. For three months after the members of the Convention at Philadelphia had completed their labors and returned to their homes, Mr. Madison, with John Jay and Alexander Hamilton, had remained in that city for the purpose of preparing those political articles that now constitute 'The Federalist.' This gave the party opposed to Madison, with Henry at their head, the start of him in canvassing the State in his absence. At length, when Mr. Madison was about ready to return to Virginia, a public meeting was appointed in the county of Orange, at which the candidates for the Convention—Madison on the one side, and Leland on the other—were to address the people from the stump. Up to that time he had but a partial personal acquaintance with Mr. Madison, but he had a high respect for his talents, his candour, and the uprightness and purity of his private character. On his way home from Philadelphia, Mr. Madison went some distance out of his direct road to call upon him. After the ordinary salutations, Mr. Madison began to apologize for troubling him with a call at that time, but he assured Mr. Madison that no apology was necessary. 'I know your errand here,' said he ; 'it is to talk with me about the Constitution. I am glad to see you, and to have an opportunity of learning your views on the subject.' Mr. Madison spent half a day with him, and fully and unreservedly communicated to him his opinions upon the great matters which were then agitating the people of the State and the Confederacy. They then separated to meet again very soon, as opposing candidates before the electors, on the stump. The day came and they met, and with them nearly all the voters in the county of Orange, to hear their candidates respectively discuss the important questions upon which the people of Virginia were so soon to act. 'Mr. Madison,' said the venerable man, 'first took the stump, which was a hogshead of tobacco standing on one end. For two hours he addressed his fellow-citizens in a calm, candid, and statesmanlike manner, arguing his side of the case, and fairly meeting and replying to the arguments which had been put forth by his opponents in the general canvass of the State. Though Mr. Madison was not particularly a pleasing or eloquent speaker, the people listened with respectful attention. He left the hogshead, and my friends called for me. I took it—and went in for Mr. Madison, and he was elected without difficulty. This,' said he, 'is, I suppose, what Mr. Barbour alluded to.' A noble, Christian patriot! That single act, with the motives which prompted it and the consequences which followed it, entitle him to the respect of mankind."

But how are we to explain Madison's call upon his opponent? It was a very unusual, if not unprecedented, proceeding, and it is to be accounted for only on the ground of the former relations of Madison to the Baptists in their struggle for religious liberty. He had, while yet a young man, shown his warm sympathy for them in their persecutions; he had incorporated their cherished principle of religious liberty into the Bill of Rights ; he had been the true yoke-fellow of Mr Jefferson in his great work in pulling down the establishment; and then, when Jefferson was representing his country at a foreign court, he had taken his place as the political leader of the Baptists and their allies in their fight against the general assessment. And knowing, as he did, the chief ground of opposition to the Constitution, he felt that he could afford to approach their leading representative in Orange with the view of explaining that paper which he himself had framed, and relieving their apprehensions as to its bearing upon the question of religious liberty.   Thus were Leland and the Baptists of Orange won over to the side of Madison, and Madison was sent to the Convention to meet and defeat Mr. Henry.

CHAPTER XIV.

First Amendment to Constitution.

THE Constitution having been ratified by a sufficient number of States, the next step was to organize under the new government. George Washington was elected President, and Thomas Jefferson was made Secretary of State. What post should be filled by the "Father of the Constitution?" Surely he will not be left out! And yet that is just what the Virginia Assembly sought to do. The situation in Virginia was different from that of any of the other ratifying States, in that "the politics of the legislature were at variance with the sense of the people, expressed by their representatives in convention." The Legislature, being dominated by Henry and opposed to the Constitution, was hostile to Madison, and when he was nominated by his friends for the United States Senate, he was defeated. Mr. Rives, commenting on this, says:

"Mr. Henry, as we learn from contemporary testimony, not only took the unusual liberty of nominating both of the candidates of his party (for the United States Senate), but animadverted with freedom and unreserve on the political principles and conduct of Mr. Madison, then absent in the discharge of his public duties as one of the delegates of the State in the Congress at New York. He particularly alleged, notwithstanding the declarations to the contrary which had been made by Mr. Madison in the Convention of Virginia, that he was wholly opposed to amendments of the Constitution. The skilful orator well calculated the effect of this assertion on an Assembly already committed by its acts to the pursuit of amendments at every cost." Rives, Vol. II., page 652.

This left Mr. Madison to run for a seat in the House of Representatives, which he preferred.

"But here again," says Mr. Rives, "unceasing efforts were made by the Anti-Federal leaders in the Legislature to bar against him every avenue to success. In laying off the State into districts for the election of representatives, ingenious and artificial combinations were resorted to for the purpose of insuring his defeat. The county in which he resided was thrown into association with seven others, five of which, through their delegates in the Convention, had given an undivided vote against the acceptance of the Constitution; another had divided its vote; and only one, besides the county in which he lived, had given an undivided vote for the ratification. At the same time a restriction unknown to the Constitution, and supposed to be specially aimed at him, was enacted, which required that the representative should be a resident of the district for which he was chosen. The candidate to oppose him seems also to have been selected under the counsel and direction of a controlling junto in the legislature." Rives, Vol. II., page 653.

MADISON ON THE SITUATION.

In a letter to Mr. Jefferson, dated Philadelphia, December 8, 1788, Madison expresses himself freely in reference to the machinations against him and his chances for success:

"I shall leave this place in a day or two for Virginia, where my friends, who wish me to coöperate in putting our political machine into activity as a member of the House of Representatives, press me to attend. They made me a candidate for the Senate, for which I had not allotted my pretensions. The attempt was defeated by Mr. Henry, who is omnipotent in the present Legislature, and who added to the expedients common on such occasions a public philippic against my Federal principles. He has taken equal pains, in forming the counties into districts for the election of representatives, to associate with Orange such as are most devoted to his politics and most likely to be swayed by the prejudice excited against me. From the best information I have of the prevailing temper of the district, I conclude that my going to Virginia will answer no other purpose than to satisfy the opinions and entreaties of my friends." Writings of Madison, Vol. I.

It is evident from this letter that Madison expected defeat. His district was composed of the counties of Orange, Amherst, Albemarle, Louisa, Culpeper, Spottsylvania, Goochland, and Fluvanna, of which only Albemarle and Orange, the counties, respectively, of Jefferson and Madison, had given an undivided vote for the Constitution. Louisa had divided her vote, one delegate voting for and the other against ratification; while Culpeper, Spottsylvania, Goochland, Amherst, and Fluvanna had voted soldily against ratification. In all these counties there was a strong Baptist sentiment, and in most of them the Baptist element was large enough to hold the balance of power. I have before me a table, made up from Semple's History, showing the number of churches in each county the year of this election. According to this table, allowing one-half of a church to each of the two counties on the boundary line between which it was located, Culpeper had 6½ churches; Spottsylvania, 5½; Goochland, 3½; Albemarle, 4; Louisa, 2½; Orange, 2; Amherst, 2, and Fluvanna, 1. These numbers do not look large to us, who are familiar with counties having from twenty to forty churches. But we must consider difference in conditions. Then population was sparser, and churches were more potent factors than they are now. They were not multiplied at every cross-roads and in every little community, but they embraced large sections of country. John Leland said that Orange was a "strong Baptist county," with only two churches, and yet all of the other counties of the district had more than Orange, except Amherst, which had the same number, and Fluvanna, which had only one. It should be also considered that the membership of these churches was not "mixed," as is too much the case now, but was composed of men and women of stalwart convictions. Only three years before (1785), they had fought and won the battle against the assessment, and they were still engaged in the war against the glebes. It was this large and influential element in those counties that Patrick Henry and his lieutenants had counted on to defeat Madison, when they arranged his district. And when it is remembered that the Baptist General Committee had unanimously decided that the Constitution did not make religious liberty secure, and that they had already commenced a correspondence with the Baptists of the North with the view of securing an amendment, the prospect for Madison's election to Congress, with James Monroe pitted against him, was not bright. Granted that he had been elected to the Convention from the "strong Baptist connty" of Orange, that victory was due to Leland, and did not extend to the other counties. As has already been shown, Madison himself was not sanguine. In a letter to Washington, dated Orange, January 14, 1789, he says:

"The event of our [his and Monroe's] competition will probably depend on the part to be taken by two or three descriptions of people, whose decision is not known, if not yet to be ultimately formed. I have pursued my pretentions much farther than I had premeditated, having not only made great use of epistolary means, but actually visited two counties, Culpeper and Louisa, and publicly contradicted the erroneous reports propagated against me. It has been industriously inculcated that I am dogmatically attached to the Constitution in every clause, syllable, and letter, and, therefore, not a single amendment will be promoted by my vote, either from conviction or from a spirit of accommodation. This is the report most likely to affect the election, and most difficult to be combatted with success within the limited period." Writings of Madison, Vol. I., page 449.

BAPTISTS SAVE MADISON AGAIN.

Here, again, Madison's former relations to the Baptists as one of the leading advocates of their cause, and their confidence in his honesty and integrity, served him a good turn; for he was enabled to correct the false impressions made upon their minds by his political enemies, relieve their apprehensions as to any change in his principles, and assure them of his readiness to aid in securing a proper amendment to the Constitution on the subject of religious liberty. And as, in the case of his candidacy for a seat in the Convention, John Leland and his Baptist following turned the scale in Madison's favor in Orange, so now, when running for Congress, it was the large Baptist element in his district which turned prospective defeat into victory and secured his triumph over all opposing forces.

CULPEPER THE CRITICAL COUNTY.

It seems that the result hinged on Culpeper, the strongest Baptist county in the district. Just after the election, Madison writes (March 1) to Edmund Randolph as follows:

"I am persuaded, however, that my appearance in the district was more necessary to my election than you then calculated. In truth, it has been evinced by the experiment that my absence would have left a room for the calumnies of Anti-Federal partisans, which would have defeated much better pretensions than mine. In Culpeper, which was the critical county, a continued attention was necessary to repel the multiplied falsehoods which circulated." Writings of Madison, I., 450.

In this stronghold of the Baptists, made such largely by the fiery persecutions through which they had passed before the Revolution, the fight waxed hottest, and the grossest misrepresentations were used against their old friend and champion, as if he had deserted their cause. But by his personal visit and the free use of "epistolary means," he succeeded in allaying the apprehensions of all honest men and convincing the lovers of liberty that their interests would be safe in the hands of the man who had substituted *liberty* for *toleration* in the Virginia Bill of Rights, and was the author of the "Memorial and Remonstrance Against the General Assessment."

MADISON MOVES THE FIRST AMENDMENT.

And one of the very first things Madison did, after the First Congress was organized, in 1789, was to propose, June 8, certain amendments to the Constitution, the first of which says:

"Congress shall make no law respecting an establishment of religion, or prohibiting the free exercise thereof; or abridging the freedom of speech, or of the press; or the right of the people peaceably to assemble and to petition the Government for a redress of grievances."

MADISON'S MOTIVES.

It is claimed by some modern writers, who have been industriously engaged in rewriting the history of the struggle for religious liberty, that Madison proposed this amendment in compliance with an "enforced promise" made in the famous debate over ratification and in obedience to the mandate of the Convention, which, after ratifying the Constitution, "recommended to the consideration of Congress" a "bill of rights," containing twenty articles, and also twenty "amendments," making forty in all.   To this we reply, first, that no such promise was extorted from Madison.   The debates clearly show that he wrenched victory from the hands of Mr. Henry, not by promising to do what he had hitherto been unwilling to do (that is, aid in securing *subsequent* amendments), but by an unanswerable and invulnerable array of facts and arguments.   In the language of Hon. William Wirt, ''he met, on this topic, fought hand to hand, and finally vanquished that boasted prodigy of nature, Patrick Henry.''

But we answer, secondly, that if this contention proves anything, it proves too much; for, if he was acting under an enforced promise and under the mandate of the Convention, he should have proposed the whole batch of forty amendments, instead of the small number of ten. The amendments themselves, both as to number and character, and the speech with which he introduced them, plainly indicate that, while prompted by a sense of obligation to his constituents, he was not executing the will of the Virginia Convention, which had proposed forty amendments; nor yet of the Virginia Legislature, which had done all in its power to keep him out of Congress and thus prevent his proposing any amendments at all.

But let us hear from Madison himself. The following extracts are taken from the speech which he delivered on the 8th day of June, 1789, on the subject of amendments:

''I will state my reasons why I think it proper to propose amendments, and state the amendments themselves, so far as I think they ought to be proposed. If I thought I could fulfill the duty which I owe to myself and my constituents, to let the subject pass over in silence, I most certainly should not trespass on the indulgence of this House. But I cannot do this, and am, therefore, compelled to beg a patient hearing to what I have to lay before you. . . . It appears to me that this House is bound by every motive of prudence not to let the first session pass over without proposing to the State Legislatures some things to be incorporated into the Constitution that will render it as acceptable to the whole people of the United States as it has been found acceptable to a majority of them. I wish, among other reasons why something should be done, that those who have been friendly to the adoption of the Constitution may have the opportunity of proving to those who were opposed to it that they were as sincerely devoted to liberty and a republican government as those who charged them with wishing the adoption of this Constitution in order to lay the foundation of an aristocracy or despotism. It will be a desirable thing to extinguish from the bosom of every member of the community any apprehensions that there are those among his countrymen who wish to deprive them of the liberty for which they valiantly fought and honorably bled. And if there are amendments desired of such a nature as will not injure the Constitution, and they can be engrafted so as to give satisfaction to the doubting part of our fellow-citizens, the friends of the Federal Government will evince that spirit of deference and concession for which they have been hitherto distinguished. . . . It cannot be a secret to the gentlemen in this House that, notwithstanding the ratification of this system of government by eleven of the thirteen United States, in some cases unanimously, in others by large majorities, yet still there is a great number of our constituents who are dissatisfied with it, among whom are many respectable for their talents and patriotism, and respectable for the jealousy they have for their liberty, which, though mistaken in its object, is laudable in its motive. *There is a great body of the people falling under this description, who at present feel much inclined to join their support to the cause of Federalism, if they were satisfied on this one point.* [Italics mine.] . . . But perhaps there is a stronger motive than this for one going into a consideration of the subject. It is to provide those securities for liberty which are required by a part of the community. I allude in a particular manner to those two States [Rhode Island and North Carolina] that have not thought fit to throw themselves into the bosom of the confederacy. It is a desirable thing, on our part as well as theirs, that a reunion should take place as soon as possible. . . . But I will candidly acknowledge that, over and above all these considerations, I do conceive that the Constitution may be amended ; that is to say, if all power is subject to abuse, that then it is possible the abuse of the powers of the general Government may be guarded against in a more secure manner than is now done, while no one advantage arising from the exercise of that power shall be damaged or endangered by it. We have in this way something to gain; and, if we proceed with caution, nothing to lose." Annals of Congress, Vol. I., pages 431–2.

This language is not that of a man acting under whip

and spur, but of one who, conscious of his own integrity and strength, and of the fact that he owed his seat in that first Congress to the suffrages of a people who were jealous of their liberty, was now ready to conciliate and to make all reasonable concessions to the doubting and distrustful. And if we are right in taking the "*one point,*" in the sentence which we have italicized above, as referring to *religious liberty,* the chief subject of the first amendment, then the "great body of people" to whom he refers must have been the Baptists. Of all the denominations in Virginia, they were the only ones that had expressed any dissatisfaction with the Constitution on this point, or that had taken any action looking to an amendment. The Baptist General Committee had opened correspondence with the Baptists of other States, especially in Massachusetts, Rhode Island, and New York, with Elder John Leland at the head of the committee, the object being to secure coöperation in the matter of obtaining an amendment to the Constitution. The same General Committee, in its session in the city of Richmond, August 8, 1789, two months after the date of Madison's speech in Congress, addressed a patriotic letter to President Washington, invoking his aid in the movement which they had set on foot. This letter, together with Washington's reply, will appear in the next chapter.

Dr. Cathcart, on page 109 of his "Centennial Offering," says:

"Denominationally, no community asked for this change in the Constitution but the Baptists. The Quakers would probably have petitioned for it, if they had thought of it, but they did not. John Adams and the Congregationalists did not desire it; the Episcopalians did not wish for it; it went too far for most Presbyterians in Revolutionary times, or in our own days, when we hear so much about putting the divine name in the Constitution. The Baptists asked it through Washington; the request commended itself to his judgment and to the generous soul of Madison; and to the Baptists, beyond a doubt, belongs the glory of engrafting its best article on the noblest Constitution ever framed for the government of mankind."

But let it not be supposed that it was an easy task to secure this amendment. There was opposition to any amendments at this first session of Congress. Says Mr. Rives:

"Nothing short of the high standing of Mr. Madison in the public councils, and the deference accorded to his opinions and his virtues, could have secured a favorable reception for propositions so counter to the prepossessions of the body to which they were addressed." Rives, Vol. III., page 40.

In the light of this statement, we have all the higher appreciation of the services of the Baptists, in that they not only brought to bear upon Congress their influence in favor of a religious liberty amendment, but that they also helped to place in that Congress the man who, above all others, was able to secure for the measure a favorable consideration. The amendment was adopted on the 25th of September, 1789, and there it stands as a beacon-light to the world, and as a monument to Baptist watchfulness and unswerving loyalty to liberty.

CHAPTER XV.

Correspondence.

THE documentary evidence is now all in, with the exception of certain letters which passed between the Baptists and the leading statesmen of the country, and which throw some light upon the questions involved. We have deemed it best to present these letters in a separate chapter and in the order of their dates, beginning with the correspondence between the Baptist General Association of Virginia and her first republican Governor, Patrick Henry. This correspondence is found in the *Virginia Gazette* of August 23, 1776.

"*To His Excellency, Patrick Henry, Jun., Esq., Governor of the Commonwealth of Virginia :*

"The humble address of the ministers and delegates of the Baptist churches, met in Association in Louisa, August 12, 1776, in behalf of their brethren.

"May it please Your Excellency, as your advancement to the honorable and important station of Governor of this Commonwealth affords us unspeakable pleasure, we beg leave to present Your Excellency with our most cordial congratulations.

"Your public virtues are such that we are under no temptation to flatter you. Virginia has done honor to her judgment in appointing Your Excellency to hold the reins of government at this truly critical conjuncture, as you have always distinguished yourself by your zeal and activity for her welfare, in whatever department has been assigned you. As a religious community, we have nothing to request of you. Your constant attachment to the glorious cause of liberty leaves us no room to doubt of Your Excellency's favorable regards, while we worthily demean ourselves.

"May God Almighty continue you long, very long, a public blessing to this your native country; and, after a life of usefulness here, crown you with immortal felicity in the world to come.

"Signed by order.

"JEREMIAH WALKER, Moderator.

"JOHN WILLIAMS, Clerk."

GOVERNOR HENRY'S REPLY.

"*To the Ministers and Delegates of the Baptist Churches, and the Members of that Communion:*

"Gentlemen—I am exceedingly obliged to you for your very kind address, and the favorable sentiments you are pleased to entertain respecting my conduct, and the principles which have directed it. My constant endeavor shall be to guard the rights of all my fellow-citizens from every encroachment.

"I am happy to find a catholic spirit prevailing in our country, and that those religious distinctions which formerly produced some heats are now forgotten. Happy must every friend to virtue and America feel himself to perceive that the only contest among us, at this most critical and important period, is, who shall be foremost to preserve our religious and civil liberties.

"My most earnest wish is that Christian charity, forbearance, and love may unite all our different persuasions, as brethren who must perish or triumph together, and I trust that the time is not far distant when we shall greet each other as the peaceable possessors of that just and equal system of liberty adopted by the last Convention, and in support of which may God crown our arms with success.

"I am, gentlemen, your most obedient and very humble servant,

P. HENRY, JUN.

"August 13, 1776."

It should be rembered that Mr. Henry had endeared himself to the Baptists by volunteering to defend them when arraigned before the courts for preaching the gospel.

CORRESPONDENCE WITH WASHINGTON.

The following is the address of the Baptist General Committee to President Washington, referred to in the preceding chapter. It was prepared by John Leland, and is found, with the answer thereto, in Bitting's "Notes on the Century History of the Strawberry Association," and also in Leland's Works, 52-54:

"Address of the Committee of the United Baptist Churches of Virginia, assembled in the city of Richmond, August 8, 1789, to the President of the United States of America:

"Sir—Among the many shouts of congratulation that you receive from cities, societies, States, and the whole world, we wish to take an active part in the universal chorus, in expressing our great satisfaction in your appointment to the first office in the nation. When America, on a former occasion, was reduced to the necessity of appealing to arms to defend her natural and civil rights, a Washington was found fully adequate to the exigencies of the dangerous attempt; who, by the philanthropy of his heart and the prudence of his head, led forth her untutored troops into the field of battle, and, by the skilfulness of his hands, baffled the projects of the insulting foe and pointed out the road to independence, even at a time when the energy of the Cabinet was not sufficient to bring into action the natural aid of the confederation, from its respective sources.

"The grand object being obtained, the independence of the States acknowledged, free from ambition, devoid of thirst of blood, our hero returned, with those he commanded, and laid down the sword at the feet of those who gave it him. 'Such an example to the world is new.' Like other nations, we experience that it requires as great valor and wisdom to make an advantage of a conquest as to gain one.

"The want of efficacy in the confederation, the redundancy of laws, and their partial administration in the States, called aloud for a new arrangement in our systems. The wisdom of the States for that purpose was collected in a grand convention, over which you, sir, had the honor to preside. A national government, in all its parts, was recommended as the only preservation of the Union, which plan of government is now in actual operation.

"When the constitution first made its appearance in Virginia, we, as a society, had unusual strugglings of mind, fearing that the liberty of conscience, dearer to us than property or life, was not sufficiently secured. Perhaps our jealousies were heightened by the usage we received in Virginia under the regal government, when mobs, fines, bonds and prisons were our frequent repast.

"Convinced, on the one hand, that without an effective national government the States would fall into disunion and all the consequent evils, and on the other hand, fearing that we should be accessory to some religious oppression, should any one society in the Union preponderate over the rest; amidst all these inquietudes of mind our consolation arose from this consideration—viz., the plan must be good, for it has the signature of a tried, trusty friend, and if religious liberty is rather insecure in the Constitution, 'the Administration will certainly prevent all oppressions, for a WASHINGTON will preside.' According to our wishes, the unanimous voice of the Union has called you, sir, from your beloved retreat, to launch forth again into the faithless seas of human affairs, to guide the helm of the States. May that divine munificence which covered your head in battle make you a yet greater blessing to your admiring country in time of peace! Should the horrid evils that have been so pestiferous in Asia and Europe—faction, ambition, war, perfidy, fraud, and persecution for conscience sake, ever approach the borders of our happy nation, may the name and administration of our beloved President, like the radiant source of day, scatter all those dark clouds from the American hemisphere.

"And, while we speak freely the language of our hearts, we are satisfied that we express the sentiments of our brethren whom we represent. The very name of Washington is music in our ears, and, although the great evil in the States is the want of mutual confidence between rulers and people, yet we all have the utmost confidence in the President of the States, and it is our fervent prayer to Almighty God that the Federal Government, and the governments of the respective States, without rivalship, may so co-operate together as to make the numerous people over whom you preside the happiest nation on earth, and you, sir, the happiest man, in seeing the people whom, by the smiles of Providence, you saved from vassalage by your valor and made wise by your maxims, sitting securely under their vines and fig trees, enjoying the perfection of human felicity. May God long preserve your life and health for a blessing to the world in general, and the United States in particular; and when, like the sun, you have finished your course of great and unparalleled services, and go the way of all the earth, may the Divine Being, who will reward every man according to his works, grant unto you a glorious admission into his everlasting kingdom, through Jesus Christ. This, sir, is the prayer of your happy admirers.

"By order of the Committee.

"SAMUEL HARRIS, Chairman.
"REUBEN FORD, Clerk."

WASHINGTON'S REPLY.

"*To the General Committee, Representing the United Baptist Churches in Virginia:*

"Gentlemen—I request that you will accept my best acknowledgments for your congratulations on my appointment to the first office in the nation. The kind manner in which you mention my past conduct equally claims the expression of my gratitude.

"After we had, by the smiles of Divine Providence on our exertions, obtained the object for which we contended, I retired at the conclusion of the war, with an idea that my country could have no further occasion for my services, and with the intention of never again entering public life. But when the exigencies of my country seemed to require me once more to engage in public affairs, an honest conviction of duty superseded my former resolution, and became my apology for deviating from the happy plan which I had adopted.

"If I could have entertained the slightest apprehension that the Constitution framed by the Convention, where I had the honor to preside, might possibly endanger the religious rights of any ecclesiastical society, certainly I would never have placed my signature to it; and if I could now conceive that the general government might be so administered as to render the liberty of conscience insecure, I beg you will be persuaded that none would be more zealous than myself to establish effective barriers against the horrors of spiritual tyranny and every species of religious persecution; for you doubtless remember I have often expressed my sentiments, that any man, conducting himself as a good citizen, and being accountable to God alone for his religious opinions, ought to be protected in worshipping the Deity according to the dictates of his own conscience.

"While I recollect with satisfaction that the religious society of which you are members have been, throughout America, uniformly

and almost unanimously the firm friends to civil liberty, and the persevering promoters of our glorious revolution, I cannot hesitate to
believe that they will be the faithful supporters of a free, yet efficient,
general government.   Under this pleasing expectation, I rejoice to
assure them that *they may rely upon my best wishes and endeavors to promote their prosperity.*

" In the meantime, be assured, gentlemen, that I entertain a
proper sense of your fervent supplications to God for my temporal
and eternal happiness.

"I am, gentlemen, your most obedient servant,

"GEORGE WASHINGTON."

Sparks' Writings of Washington, Vol. XII., page 154.

JEFFERSON'S LETTERS.

It seems that, after Jefferson was inaugurated President,
in 1801, the Baptists from all parts of the country
addressed letters to him at different times expressive of
their appreciation of him as the friend of liberty and their
confidence in his administration.   They did this the more
because of the direful predictions of disaster to religion and
morals, made by the pharisees of New England and other
parts, if Thomas Jefferson should be placed at the head of
government.   Those letters are not preserved, but his
answers are, and will be found below.   The important
parts only are given.

"JANUARY 1ST, 1802.

" *To Messrs. ———, a Committee of the Danbury Baptist Association,
in the State of Connecticut:*

"The affectionate sentiments of esteem and approbation which
you are so good to express towards me, on behalf of the Danbury
Baptist Association, give me the highest satisfaction. . . .

"Believing with you that religion is a matter which lies solely
between man and his God, that he owes account to none other for his
faith or his worship, that the legislative powers of government reach
actions only, and not opinions, I contemplate with sovereign reverence that act of the whole American people which declared that

their legislature should 'make no law respecting an establishment of religion, or prohibiting the free exercise thereof,' thus building a wall of separation between Church and State. . . .

"I reciprocate your kind prayers for the protection and blessing of the Common Father and Creator of man, and tender you, for yourselves and your religious association, assurances of my high respect and esteem." Jefferson's Works, Vol. VIII., page 113.

"NOVEMBER 18TH, 1807.

"To Captain John Thomas:

"Sir—I received, on the 14th instant, your favor of August 31st, and I beg you to assure my fellow-citizens of the Baptist church of Newhope meeting-house that I learn with great satisfaction their approbation of the principles which have guided the present administration of the government. . . .

". . . Among the most inestimable of our blessings, also, is that you so justly particularize, of liberty to worship our Creator in the way we think most agreeable to his will—a liberty deemed in other countries incompatible with good government, and yet proved by our experience to be its best support. Your confidence in my dispositions to befriend every human right is highly grateful to me, and is rendered the more so by a consciousness that these dispositions have been sincerely entertained and pursued. I am thankful for the kindness expressed towards me personally, and pray you to return to the society in whose name you have addressed me my best wishes for their happiness and prosperity, and to accept for yourself assurances of my great esteem and respect." Jefferson's Works, Vol. VIII., page 119.

And on page 124 is a similar letter, dated December 21, 1807, in response to an "Address of October 21st" from the "Appomattox Association," of Virginia, forwarded by Abner Watkins and Bernard Todd.

"OCTOBER 17, 1808.

"To the Members of the Baltimore Baptist Association:

"I receive with pleasure the friendly address of Baltimore Baptist Association, and am sensible how much I am indebted to the kind dispositions which dictated it.

" In our early struggles for liberty, religious freedom could not fail to become a primary object. All men felt the right, and a just animation to obtain it was exhibited by all. I was only one among the many who befriended its establishment, and am entitled but in common with others to a portion of that approbation which follows the fulfilment of a duty." Vol. VIII., page 137.

"OCTOBER 18, 1808.

" *To the Members of the Ketocton Baptist Association:*

[First sentence as above.] " In our early struggles for liberty, religious freedom could not fail to become a primary object. All men felt the right, and a just animation to obtain it was excited in all. And, although your favor selected me as the organ of your petition to abolish the religious domination of a privileged church, yet I was but one of the many," etc., etc. (Concludes as above.) Vol. VIII., page 138.

"NOVEMBER 21, 1808.

" *To the General Meeting of Correspondence of the Six Baptist Associa-tions Represented at Chesterfield, Va.:*

"In reviewing the history of the times through which we have past, no portion of it gives greater satisfaction, on reflection, than that which presents the efforts of the friends of religious freedom and the success with which they were crowned. We have solved, by fair experiment, the great and interesting question whether free-dom of religion is compatible with order in government and obe-dience to the laws; and we have experienced the quiet, as well as the comfort, which results from leaving every one to profess freely and openly those principles of religion which are the inductions of his own reason and the serious convictions of his own inquiries." Vol. VIII., page 139.

"APRIL 13, 1808.

"*To the Members of the Baptist Church of Buck Mountain, in Albemarle:*

[This letter was in answer to their congratulations on his return home.] " Your approbation of my conduct is the more valued as you have best known me, and is an ample reward for any services I may have rendered. We have acted together from the origin to the end of a memorable revolution, and we have contributed, each in the line allotted us, our endeavors to render its issue a permanent bless-ing to our country." Vol. III., page 169.

PRESIDENT MADISON'S LETTER.

"JUNE 3, 1811.

"*To the Baptist Churches on Neal's Creek and on Black Creek, North Carolina:*

"I have received, fellow-citizens, your address approving my objection to the bill containing a grant of public land to the Baptist church at Salem meeting-house, Mississippi Territory. Having always regarded the practical distinction between religion and civil government as essential to the purity of both, and as guaranteed by the Constitution of the United States, I could not have otherwise discharged my duty on the occasion which presented itself. Among the various religious societies in our country, none has been more vigilant or constant in maintaining that distinction than the society of which you make a part; and it is an honorable proof of your sincerity and integrity that you are ready to do so in a case favoring the interest of your brethren, as in other cases. It is but just, at the same time, to the Baptist church at Salem meeting-house to remark that their application to the national legislature does not appear to have contemplated a grant of the land in question, but on terms that might be equitable to the public as well as to themselves."

If such men as Madison filled the presidential office in these later days there would be no grants of land or money by the government for sectarian or religious purposes.

CONCLUSION.

As a fitting conclusion of this series of letters, and of this mass of evidence in reference to the struggle for religious liberty in Virginia, we give the following extract from a letter of Madison to Robert Walsh, dated Montpelier, March 2, 1819, nearly thirty-four years after the enactment of Jefferson's bill for establishing religious freedom:

"It was the universal opinion of the century preceding the last that civil government could not stand without the prop of a religious establishment, and that the Christian religion itself would perish, if not supported by a legal provision for its clergy. The experience of Virginia conspicuously corroborates the disproof of both opinions. The civil Government, though bereft of everything like an associated hierarchy, possesses the requisite stability and performs its functions with complete success; whilst the number, the industry, and the morality of the priesthood, and the devotion of the people, have been manifestly increased by the total separation of the Church from the State."

CHAPTER XVI.

Summary and Argument.

HAVING laid before the student of history all of the evidence which we have been able to collect concerning the struggle for religious liberty in Virginia, we now proceed to sum up that evidence, with the view of showing to the general reader what is proven. Our object is to establish the truth, and to settle forever some questions which have arisen since the close of the struggle, at the end of the eighteenth century.

It will be seen that from the planting of the colony at Jamestown down to the year 1699 the Church of England was the only denomination of Christians recognized and supported by law. In that year, the Act of Toleration, which had been passed by the British Parliament in 1689, began to obtain recognition in Virginia, when Francis Makemie, a Presbyterian minister of Accomac county, obtained license to preach at two places on his own property. This begins the period of toleration, which extends to the year 1768, when *legal persecutions* began against the Baptists. In 1770, the Baptists petitioned the House of Burgesses against the hardships to which their ministers were exposed in being required to do military duty, and also against their not being allowed to preach at any other places than those which where specifically mentioned in their licenses. These petitions came from the Regular Baptists, who, with few exceptions, were the only Baptists who condescended to ask the civil authorities for permission to preach the gospel. But this petition for relief was rejected.

In February, 1772, the Baptists of Lunenburg, Mecklenburg, Sussex, and Amelia counties petitioned the House for their rights as Protestant dissenters under the English Act of Toleration, and asked that they be treated with the same indulgence as Presbyterians, Quakers, and other Protestant dissenters enjoyed.   In response to these petitions, a new bill, known as the "Toleration Bill," was reported to the House and put upon its passage.   But, instead of being a measure of relief, it was more restrictive and burdensome in its provisions than the English Act of Toleration, and it called forth earnest protests from the persecuted Baptists against whom it was aimed.   But, while aimed at the Baptists, it struck the Presbyterians also, and aroused them to opposition and protest.   The bill would doubtless have been passed, in spite of this opposition, but for the strife which arose at that time between the Burgesses and Governor Botetourt, who prorogued the House until March, 1773.   When the Burgesses met again they were prorogued by Governor Dunmore, who had succeeded Lord Botetourt.   He continued to prorogue the House until May, 1774.   On the 12th of May the persecuted Baptists appeared before the House with a petition against the unjust restrictions of the Toleration Bill. The Hanover Presbytery had taken no action as yet, except to appoint two of their number to attend the Assembly and act in the premises "as their prudence might direct and the nature of the case might require."

But a petition was presented at this session of the Assembly (May 17) from the Presbyterians of Bedford county, *complaining of the voluntary method of supporting the ministry by subscriptions*, and asking for such legislative act as would enable them "to take and hold lands and slaves for such use."   [Italics mine.]

In November, 1774, the Hanover Presbytery took a decided stand against the Toleration Bill, and their first memorial was presented to the Assembly on the 5th day of June, 1775, supported by another Baptist petition, June 13. Nothing was sought in any of these petitions against the new bill more than to defend the rights of the petitioners under the English Act of Toleration, and to secure, if possible, more liberal concessions from the local government. But such was the intolerance of the clergy of the Established church towards the aggressive and rapidly growing sect of Baptists that the Assembly, which was composed chiefly of churchmen, would have been driven to the passage of the obnoxious "bill" but for the political exigencies of the times. The storm of the American Revolution had already burst upon the country, and there was imperative need of peace and harmony at home. The services of the despised Baptists, as well as of the Presbyterians, were needed in the defence of the colony against British oppression, and hence the "Toleration Bill" was dropped and allowed to "wait until the clouds rolled by."

We wish to emphasize the fact that up to this time—the date of the American Revolution—no petition had been presented to the Assembly asking that the Establishment be abolished, or that no tax should be levied for the support of religion, or that the State should cease to concern itself about religion save only to protect all its citizens in the enjoyment of their equal and inalienable rights of conscience. Whatever opinions were entertained at that time by the dissenting sects, *religious liberty*, as distinguished from *religious toleration*, was not contemplated in their petitions to the House of Burgesses before the Revolution.

A most labored effort has been made by the Presbyterians, under the lead of the Hon. William Wirt Henry, to make it appear that they "anticipated the Baptists in their memorials asking for religious liberty." To support this contention Mr. Henry produces the memorial of the Hanover Presbytery of November, 1774, and represents it as a plea for religious liberty, instead of toleration, and as "the advance guard of that army of remonstrances which so vigorously attacked the establishment," etc. In this "the wish is father to the thought." It does not take a very careful reading of that document, which is given in full in Chapter II., to satisfy any candid and unbiased mind that such a claim is preposterous. The memorial makes no attack whatever upon the Establishment, but professes loyalty to King George, and also to the Establishment itself, which they were bound by their contract with Governor Gooch to support so long as they were allowed their rights under the Act of Toleration. It is not the first time that eminent legal talent has been pressed into service "to make the worse the better cause appear." [For fuller discussion, see Appendix.]

THE FIRST ORGANIZED EFFORT FOR RELIGIOUS LIBERTY.

The first organized action towards securing religious liberty in Virginia was taken by the Baptists in their General Association at Dupuy's, August, 1775. Governor Dunmore had fallen out with the House of Burgesses and taken refuge on a "man-of-war," and the Burgesses had declared his place vacant and had met in Richmond July 17 as a convention. The Baptists saw their opportunity and were not slow to take advantage of it. As "when rogues fall out honest men get their dues," so now, when

oppressors fall out, there is presented a favorable opportu-
tunity for the oppressed lovers of soul liberty to strike for
their rights. Hence the Baptists did two notable things in
their meeting at Dupuy's. First, they resolved to circulate petitions throughout the State for signatures, petitioning the Assembly to abolish the Establishment, leave
religion to stand on its own merits, put all denominations on the same legal footing and protect all in the
peaceable enjoyment of their own religious principles and
modes of worship. Secondly, they resolved to send a patriotic address to the Convention then in session declaring
their sympathy with the colonists in their struggle against
British oppression, offering the services of their young
men as soldiers and asking for their ministers the privilege of preaching to the soldiers in the army. The Baptist address was gratefully received and their request
granted by those who had but recently been throwing
their ministers into prison for preaching the gospel ; and
thus, as Dr. Hawks well says, " the first step was made
towards placing the clergy of all denominations upon an
equal footing in Virginia."

On the 5th of May, 1776, a newly elected Convention
met in Williamsburg. This body, however, contained
only twenty-nine members who were not in the Convention
of July and August, 1775. One of the new members
was the youthful James Madison, of Orange county,
whose sympathies had been aroused in behalf of his persecuted Baptist neighbors, and who rendered his name
immortal by his famous amendment to the sixteenth article of the Bill of Rights, striking out *toleration* and in-
serting *liberty* in its stead. No sooner had this Convention
instructed the Virginia delegates to the General Congress
in Philadelphia to vote for independence of Great Britain

than there was presented a petition from the Baptists of
Prince William county, asking "that they be allowed
to worship God in their own way without interruption ;
that they be permitted to maintain their own ministers
and none others ; that they be married, buried, and the
like, without paying the clergy of other denominations ;
that, these things granted, they will gladly unite with
their brethren, and to the utmost of their ability promote
the common cause."

Thus two important conventions have been held since
the battle of Lexington and the failure of the Toleration
Bill, and yet the Baptists are the only denomination of
Christians that has addressed either body on the subject of
war with Great Britain, or on the all-important subject of
religious liberty.

When the first republican Legislature met, in October,
1776, petitions came pouring in from all denominations—
from Episcopalians and Methodists in favor of maintaining
the existing church establishment, and from Baptists,
Presbyterians, and other dissenters, in favor of disestablishment and for putting all on equal footing before the
law. The Baptist petition was signed by about 10,000.
The memorial of the Hanover Presbytery was the first of
its kind from the Presbyterians, and it reflected great
credit on its author, or authors, being, perhaps, the most
scholarly paper presented to the Assembly during the entire
struggle. These memorials brought on a desperate struggle between the friends and the foes of the Establishment,
in which the latter were led by Thomas Jefferson, supported by James Madison, George Mason, and other influential members. The result was a partial victory for liberty.
The Legislature repealed the laws which subjected dissenters to punishment for dissenting from the Established

church and which taxed them for its support, and it also
suspended until the next session levies on the members of
that church for the salaries of its own incumbents. But
the same body declared that public assemblies of societies
for divine worship ought to be regulated, and that proper
provision should be made for continuing the succession of
the clergy and superintending their conduct. The question
whether a general assessment should be established by law
on every one to the support of the pastor of his choice, or
whether all should be left to voluntary contributions, was
expressly reserved for future decision, and was not settled
until 1779, when the establishment of the Anglican church
was put down.

THE PRESBYTERIANS WERE THE "DISSENTING ALLIES."

Mr. Jefferson explains the failure to settle this question
earlier in these words: "Some of our dissenting allies,
having now secured their particular object, went over to
the advocates of a general assessment." And the evidence
is conclusive that these "dissenting allies" were the Presbyterians, who, having secured exemption from taxation
for the support of the Anglican church, were ready to join
the members of that church in support of a broader and
more liberal scheme for the support of all denominations
by means of a general assessment. It has hitherto been
supposed by many that this break in the ranks of the
Presbyterians took place only in the final struggle over the
assessment bill, in 1784–5; but the evidence adduced in
Chapter V. shows that it occurred first in the Legislature
of 1776, in the very beginning of the struggle. It is not
charged that the Hanover Presbytery or that the Presbyterians throughout the State went over in a body to the
new scheme, but that enough of their representatives in

the Legislature broke ranks with Jefferson and his supporters to accomplish a partial and temporary defeat of their
efforts. That this action of "some of the dissenting allies"
did not meet with the approval of the Presbyterians generally is evidenced by the fact that the next memorial of
the Hanover Presbytery, which was presented to the House
on the 3d of June, 1777, opposed the scheme of a general
assessment.

In June, 1779, Jefferson's bill "for establishing religious
freedom" was reported to the House and passed to its
second reading. When the Legislature met, the following
October, petitions were presented, some for and some
against Jefferson's bill, but not one from the Hanover
Presbytery, or from the Presbyterians as such. There
were, however, two antagonistic petitions from Augusta
county, whose population was decidedly Presbyterian.
According to Semple's tables, there was not a Baptist
church in the county at that time. One of these petitions,
which was presented on the 20th of October, referred to
"the plan proposed by the House of Delegates for establishing the privileges of the several denominations of
religious societies at the last session of Assembly," and
asked for its passage without the least amendment. It was
referred to the committee to prepare and bring in a bill
"concerning religion;" and on the 25th of October James
Henry, a Presbyterian elder of Accomac, presented,
according to order, a bill "concerning religion." As this
bill did not become a law, its provisions are not definitely
known, save that it was antagonistic to Jefferson's bill, and
was the formulated plan for a general assessment, which
had been under discussion since the beginning of the struggle in 1776.

The second of these petitions from Augusta county was presented on the 27th of October, and favored Jefferson's bill. And, as it is practically certain that the petitioners in both cases were largely, if not altogether, Presbyterians, the two petitions show division of sentiment among them with reference to Jefferson's bill, and with reference, also, to the general assessment.

While action on Jefferson's bill was delayed, for want of union among dissenters, the Legislature at this session repealed "so much of the act of Assembly entitled, 'An Act for the Support of the Clergy, &c.,' as relates to the payment of the salaries heretofore given to the clergy of the Church of England." This act cut the purse strings of the Establishment, but it left the clergy in possession of the glebes and with a monopoly of marriage fees.

In 1780, the Assembly responded to the petitions of the Baptists and others by passing a new marriage law, which made it lawful for marriages to be solemnized by ministers whom the contracting parties preferred. It went into effect January 1, 1781, and gave great relief to dissenters, although it was clogged by restrictions. In 1784, it was so amended as to remove all objections, and thus another victory was scored in the battle for equal rights, and another forward step taken in the cause of religious freedom.

During the same year (1780), the Presbyterians petitioned the Assembly to declare all "non-juring" clergymen incapable of preaching. This aroused the indignation of the Episcopalians, at whom it was aimed, and Bishop Meade is severe in his denunciation of this abortive attempt to stop the mouth of an Episcopal minister because of his political sentiments.

THE POST-REVOLUTION STRUGGLE.

No sooner had the Revolution ended and the independence of the colonies been declared than the struggle over religious liberty was renewed. Many of those who had voted for disestablishment and against the scheme for a general assessment had done so from patriotic motives, and for the sake of unity and coöperation as against Great Britain. But now, that they are no longer deterred by the fear of a common danger from abroad, they begin anew the discussion of questions of Church and State. The Episcopalians, on the one hand, seek to recover lost ground under a new and more liberal form of church establishment, which would take in all denominations; the Baptists, on the other hand, presented, as they had always done, an unbroken front against any and every form of church establishment, and continued to memorialize the Assembly against the inequalities of the marriage and vestry laws; while the Presbyterians were divided, some being in favor of and some against the new scheme. The wavering in their course is to be explained only on the ground that there was division of sentiment among them—that they were not agreed on the principle of religious liberty.

During the first session of the Assembly in 1784, when petitions were coming in both for and against the new scheme of a general assessment, there was presented, June 1, a "petition of the president and trustees of Hampden-Sidney College, setting forth that the funds of the said college are inadequate to its support and the erection of the necessary buildings, and praying that the Legislature will aid their funds by a grant of 400 acres of confiscated land, late the property of Spiers & Company, in the neighborhood of the said college." Their petition was granted, and a bill was passed on the 10th of June making the grant. And it is not a little significant that on the 16th of June, only six days afterwards, the committee " for religion " reported a bill " for incorporating the Protestant Episcopal Church and for other purposes," which was passed at the next session, in October. On the 11th of November, a resolution was adopted looking to a general assessment for religious purposes, and on the following day there was presented a memorial of the " united clergy of the Presbyterian church," favoring the general assessment, provided it was based upon the plan which they therewith submitted, and which, as has already been shown (Chapter X), was not in accord with the principles of religious liberty. It does look as if the Presbyterians and Episcopalians were getting together as against the Baptists. The General Assembly, which was composed largely of churchmen, makes a grant of 400 acres of public land to the Presbyterians, and the Presbyterians, in return, aid the Episcopalians in their effort to secure the incorporation of their church and in the establishment of a general assessment for religious purposes. No wonder that James Madison and others of his day suspected a tendency towards a coalition between the clergy of these two denominations—a coalition which, he said, would endanger the cause of liberty.

THE PRESBYTERIAN LAITY.

But, while the Presbyterian *clergy* favored the assessment, their *laity* were largely opposed to it, especially in Augusta county, and this division in their ranks paralyzed their efforts either for or against the bill; and, but for the united and strenuous opposition of the Baptists, this new scheme would have prevailed and a religious establishment would have been again fastened upon Virginia. On this point, Dr. Semple, at page 72, has the following: "The inhibition of the general assessment may, in a considerable degree, be ascribed to the opposition made to it by the Baptists; for it is stated by those who were conversant with the proceedings of those times that the reference made to the people, after the bill was engrossed, was done with a design to give the different religious societies an opportunity of expressing their wishes. The Baptists, we believe, were the only sect who plainly remonstrated. Of some others it is said that the laity and ministry were at variance on the subject, so as to paralyze their exertions either for or against the bill. These remarks, by-the-by, apply only to religious societies acting as such. Individuals of all sects and parties joined in the opposition."

Dr. Foote's apology for the going over of the Presbyterian clergy to the general assessment is unsatisfactory, even to the Presbyterians, as is evident from the fact that they have been making strenuous efforts to rewrite the history of that struggle, and to correct their "foresight" by their "back-sight." Foote says that they were led to believe that some such scheme would surely be adopted by the Assembly, and that they went over in order to secure as liberal a measure as possible. But this explanation reflects upon Presbyterian character for steadfastness in holding to and even suffering for their convictions. It is according to the dictates of worldly policy, and not according to the teachings of Christianity, to compromise with error. And, had the Presbyterians of Virginia believed in the principle of religious liberty as fully and unequivocally as did the Baptists, they would doubtless have held out with the Baptists, steadfast unto the end. But they did not believe in it. In spite of their memorials of 1776

and 1777, we affirm, and will undertake to prove, that
their memorial of 1784, favoring the assessment, was in
accord with, and not out of harmony with, their principles
and their previous record.

It will be freely admitted that the Presbyterians had
been, from their origin at Geneva, the advocates of the
union of the Church and the State, and of the use of the
civil power to punish heresy. It will not be denied that
the "Solemn League and Covenant," which was "forced
on the Scotch nation by the pains of excommunication,"
bound its signers to persecute Prelatists and Papists, and
was designed to establish a national church. And it was
this attempt to force the Presbyterian doctrine and discipline on England that made Milton speak of "saving free
conscience from the paw of the Presbyterian wolf;" and
again, that "New Presbyter" was only "Old Priest writ
large." It is matter of history that the Presbyterians of
Scotland and England of the seventeenth century did not
believe even in *toleration*. The writings of such leaders as
Richard Baxter show plainly that they "abhorred toleration." The president of the Scotch Parliament wrote to
the Parliament of England, February 3, 1645, as follows:
" It was expected the honorable houses would add their
civil sanction to what the pious and learned assembly have
advised; and I am commanded by the Parliament of this
kingdom to demand it, and I do in their names demand it.
And the Parliament of this kingdom is persuaded that the
piety and wisdom of the honorable houses will never admit
toleration of any sects or schisms contrary to our Solemn
League and Covenant." See Cramp's History, page 308.

It is not to be wondered at, then, that, when Presbyterians emigrated to America, they should have brought
with them the views and practices which had prevailed

among them in the Old World. The early history of
Massachusetts, at least, shows that they remained un-
changed; for, at the very time when Presbyterians and
other dissenters in Virginia were obliged to pay taxes for
the support of Episcopal clergymen, Baptists and other
dissenters were being taxed in Massachusetts to support
Presbyterian ministers. And if their ministers were not
supported in the same way in Virginia, it was not because
of any natural or constitutional aversion to this way, but
because the Anglican, or Episcopal, church had preoccu-
pied the ground.

If we turn now to their *creed*, we find that our contention is supported by the Westminster Confession. That
celebrated Confession "declares that persons maintaining
or publishing erroneous opinions destructive to the peace
and order of the church 'may be lawfully called to account
and proceeded against by the censures of the church and
by the power of the civil magistrate.'" It further declares
that the magistrate "hath authority and it is his duty to
take order that unity and peace be preserved in the church,
that the truth of God be kept pure and entire, that all
blasphemies and heresies be suppressed, all corruptions and
abuses in worship and discipline prevented or reformed,
and all the ordinances of God duly settled, administered,
and observed." See "The Denominations and Religious
Liberty," by Professor John Pollard, D. D. This document manifestly aimed at conformity in faith and practice,
and at the putting down of non-conformists, or dissenters.

NOT BETTER THAN ITS CREED.

As a stream does not rise higher than its source, so a
denomination is not better than its creed. There may be,
and doubtless are, in all denominations individuals who do

not hold to all the principles or teachings of their respective creeds. These individuals, however, are to be found chiefly, if not almost wholly, among the laity. The clergy, as a rule, adhere to their creed. Hence it was but natural that the Presbyterian clergy of Virginia, who had been brought up on the Westminster Confession and the writings of their fathers, and who had before them the example of their brethren both in the Old World and in the New, should not appear in the Revolution as the bold and consistent advocates of religious liberty. It could not have been expected of them, for they did not really and truly believe in religious liberty, and one cannot be expected to be very brave and self-sacrificing and persistent in fighting for a cause which is no part of his creed, and in which he does not fully and heartily believe.

But, it will be asked, does not their celebrated memorial of October, 1776, prove that they did believe in religious liberty? Well, it does read that way, and if we were to judge them by the light of that paper alone, we should answer in the affirmative. But, unfortunately, their previous and subsequent history does not admit of our accepting that paper as all-sufficient and incontrovertible evidence in the case. Bishop McTyeire, in his "History of Methodism" (page 25), writes thus of the times immediately succeeding the execution of Charles I., of England: "The House of Commons was now the government. The Presbyterians were paramount in it, and proceeded to remodel the church on the plan of the Westminster Assembly of Divines. It was ordered that the Solemn League and Covenant should be taken by all persons above the age of eighteen; and, as this instrument bound all who received it to endeavor to extirpate Episcopal church government, its enforcement led to the ejection of 1,600 bene-

ficed clergymen from their livings. . . . *There was,
indeed, scarcely any part of ecclesiastical polity, except prelacy, against which Puritans had inveighed when in subjection that they did not adopt and practice when in power.
. . . . Those who had pleaded so earnestly for
liberty of conscience, and who had deprecated the interference of the civil powers in matters purely religious, now,
that they were at the helm of affairs, were of another mind.*"
[Italics mine.]   "It is far easier," writes Dr. Albert
Henry Newman in his review of "Muller's History of
the Anabaptists of Bern," "to be eloquent in advocating
liberty of conscience when one is in the minority and his
freedom is imperilled than to bestow it upon a weak and despised party," etc. What a man says when he is down and is
trying to get up is not an infallible index to the true state
of his mind nor prophecy of what he will do if he once
gets up. So with denominations and parties. Professions
made when out of office and out of power are not always
indications of real sentiments and beliefs; and the wise
and prudent will wait to see how the party behaves in the
hour of triumph before accepting for their face value the
enunciation of principles made in the party platform.
Now, the Presbyterian memorial of 1776 was prepared
when they (the Presbyterians) were down and the Episcopalians were at the helm in Virginia, just as they had been
in England at the time of which Bishop McTyeire writes.
It was their first deliverance of the kind, and in it they join
hands with the Baptists in their attack upon the Establishment.   It was a powerful plea for religious liberty, and if
it faithfully represented the views of the Presbyterians at
that time, then there must have been a sudden and decided
conversion from previous belief and practice. But had
there been any such conversion, or was that memorial

a true exponent of Presbyterian faith ? Does their subsequent course sustain or justify such a view? We think not. When we see how they broke ranks in the very first engagement ; how they sought to have Episcopal ministers ejected from their livings and prohibited from preaching the gospel because they had not sworn allegiance to the new government ; how the new theory of establishment found favor among them and a prominent Presbyterian elder presented to the Assembly the first bill "concerning religion" embodying that idea ; how that, so soon as the Revolutionary war was over and the friends of church establishment began a new and final struggle, the Presbyterian clergy were found advocating the new scheme ; how the same year which witnessed their joining hands with their whilom rivals and enemies in support of this new scheme witnessed also their asking and receiving at the hands of the Legislature a grant of 400 acres of land for denominational uses ; and how Jefferson's bill for "establishing religious freedom," which was proposed in 1779, and was delayed for want of adequate support until December, 1785, never received any recognition at the hands of the Hanover Presbytery, or any other body of Presbyterians until August, 1785, when all hope of the success of the "general assessment" had gone down before the rising tide of opposition—when we consider all these things we are forced to the conclusion that whatever change the Revolution and other causes were working in them, the Presbyterians had not departed materially from the principles of the Westminster Confession and that their great memorial of 1776 was a weapon of *de*-struction, but not of *re*-construction—the plea of a minority for the destruction of the old establishment, but not a rule to live by when the minority should become the majority ; for it was James Madison, the "father of the Constitution" and the fourth President of the United States, who said of the Presbyterian clergy, in the midst of the fight over the assessment, that they "seemed as ready to set up an establishment which was to take them in as they had been to pull down that which shut them out."

The only theory which is creditable to the Presbyterians as a denomination is that which treats the entire struggle in Virginia as a period of transition—of transition from the old to the new order of things. No one at all conversant with their previous history can believe that they were wanting in the stuff of which martyrs are made. And yet to suppose, as some maintain, that at the date of the Revolution they stood as squarely and unequivocally for religious liberty as did the Baptists, is to make them out recreants and cowards for not standing heroically and fearlessly with the Baptists in the subsequent struggle. Had they fully understood the doctrine of religious liberty and been fully committed to it, they would doubtless have stood by it without wavering. But it was no part of their creed, and, while they were learning from their persecuted Baptist brethren and fellow-citizens, they had not learned the difference between *toleration* and *liberty*. And it is to be feared that some distinguished Presbyterians of our own times have yet to learn it. When a Presbyterian Governor and leading Presbyterian ministers propose to a Virginia Legislature a *penitentiary religious establishment*, we feel that they need some Baptist Aquila or Priscilla to teach them the way more perfectly.

We have said that the Presbyterians were, during the struggle for religious liberty in Virginia, in a transition state ; it should be added that in 1788, the year the Constitution of the United States was ratified, "the

United Synod of Philadelphia and New York, catching the American spirit, made such modifications of the Westminster Confession of Faith as removed all intolerance from that famous creed and put it in harmony with freedom of conscience." Dr. Pollard's Tract, page 12.

POINTS ESTABLISHED.

What does this evidence prove? It proves that the Baptists were the first and only religious denomination that struck for independence from Great Britian, and the first and only one that made a move for religious liberty before independence was declared.

It proves that, of those who took active part in the struggle for religious liberty, the Baptists were the only denomination that maintained a consistent record, and held out without wavering unto the end—until every vestige of the old Establishment had been obliterated by the sale of the glebes.

It proves that, of the great political leaders of that day, Thomas Jefferson and James Madison are the men to whom must be ascribed the highest meed of praise for the establishment of religious liberty in Virginia. Patrick Henry was on the side of the Establishment.

Finally, the evidence shows that the Baptists were the only denomination of Christians that expressed any dissatisfaction with the Constitution of the United States on the ground that it did not provide sufficient security for religious liberty, and the only one that asked that it be so amended as to leave no room for doubt or fear.

FINIS.

APPENDIX.

APPENDIX.

A.

BAPTISTS AND RELIGIOUS LIBERTY.

BY REV. C. F. JAMES, D. D.

[Address before the Baptist Young People's Union of Virginia, Charlottesville, March 15, 1899.]

THIS subject cannot be treated fully in the brief space of twenty-five minutes. I must restrict myself to one or two phases.

1. In the first place, *Baptist principles furnish the only true basis and guarantee of religious liberty.* By religious liberty is meant the right of every one to worship God, or not, according to the dictates of his own conscience, and to be held accountable to none but God for his belief and practice. It differs from religious toleration, however broad and liberal, in that toleration implies the right to withhold, or to refuse license, whereas religious liberty means that the civil power has nothing to do with a man's religion except to protect him in the enjoyment of his rights. Now, let us see how this principle is grounded in certain fundamental tenets of our denomination.

(1) We hold that religion is and must be perfectly *voluntary*, that nothing except a voluntary surrender to Christ, and a voluntary service under him, is acceptable to God, and hence that no earthly power, parental, social, civil, or ecclesiastical, has any right to compel conformity to any creed, or to any form of worship. It is for this reason that Baptists have always opposed the support of religion by taxation. It is for this reason, also, that they have ever been opposed to sponsorial religion, that religion which is fastened upon the individual in unconscious infancy without his knowledge or consent, which determines one's church relations and creed before he reaches the years of accountability, and leaves him no choice except to

acquiesce in what has been done for him by his sponsors, or else, by rejecting it, involve himself in unpleasant controversy and, perhaps, persecution. Baptists are not indifferent to the spiritual welfare of children, but they hold that their real spiritual interests are best promoted by leaving them to the exercise of that freedom of choice which is essential to acceptable worship.

(2) Another fundamental principle of the Baptists is that of *a converted church membership.* This grows out of the spirituality of Christ's kingdom. When he said to Pilate, "My kingdom is not of this world," he antagonized the idea which prevailed among the Jews, that their Messiah was to be a sort of religio-political king, uniting the temporal and the spiritual, and using the civil power to bring the world into subjection to him. But our Lord disappointed their expectations. His kingdom was not of that sort. It was spiritual in its nature. It had to do with men's hearts. It was spiritually apprehended and enjoyed. Men entered it, not by outward marks, but by an inner change—by *regeneration,* a *new birth.* And the church visible, or local church, was designed to embrace all those in every community who, by regeneration, had become his loyal subjects and disciples ; and *baptism,* the initiatory rite, was designed, among other things, to distinguish his friends from his foes, a sort of badge of enlistment which proclaimed to the world their allegiance to Christ. Hence *regeneration* (including repentance and faith) and *baptism* are the only New Testament conditions of church membership, the one denoting the *inner change,* the change of character and attitude towards Christ, and the other being the outward and public profession, or declaration, of that change. As none but a voluntary service is acceptable to God, our Lord would have none to be identified with him except such as come willingly and cheerfully ; and hence his church is everywhere the company, or assembly, of those who have been baptized upon their own personal profession of repentance and faith.

(3) Another fundamental principle of Baptists is that Christ is the only king in Zion, and that his will, as revealed in the New Testament, is the only rule of faith and practice. They believe in rendering "to Cæsar the things that are Cæsar's," but they do not believe in rendering to Cæsar "the things that are God's." Hence their refusal to recognize the right of the civil authorities to regulate their faith, or their practice, or to dictate to them as to whether they

shall preach the Gospel, and if so, when and where and how. It has not been out of any rebellious or anarchistic spirit that they have ever refused to obey man rather than God. It is not sectarian bigotry, nor blind adherence to outward forms, that has ever prompted them to resist and denounce the mutilation and multiplication of the ordinances of the Gospel. It is out of loyalty to the great Head of the Church, their only Lord and Master, to whom, and to whom alone, they are accountable, that they have sought to do just what he commanded, and to oppose all taking from, and all adding to, the divine prescript.

Now, it is apparent that a people holding such views must, in the very nature of the case, be the friends and promoters of the rights of conscience. And it is equally apparent that a people holding contrary or antagonistic views cannot be really and truly the friends and promoters of absolute religious liberty.

2. I want to show, in the second place, that *the record of the Baptists has ever been consistent with their principles.* John Locke says: "The Baptists were the first and only propounders of absolute liberty, just and true liberty, equal and impartial liberty." And our own great historian, Bancroft, says: "Freedom of conscience, unlimited freedom of mind, was, from the first, a trophy of the Baptists." And it is claimed that Roger Williams founded, in Rhode Island, "the first civil government on earth which gave equal liberty of conscience." Other countries, or governments, had granted some degree of *toleration*, but none had ever recognized the principle of religious liberty. And yet, it cannot be denied that this principle is laid down in the New Testament, and that the early disciples preached it and practiced it, even to the sacrifice of property and life, rather than render to "Cæsar" "the things which were God's." How came it to pass, then, that this New Testament doctrine found no recognition among the Christian nations of the Old World—that it had to wait for recognition by civil government until the seventeenth century, and then find it in the wilds of this New World? To answer this question fully would consume more time than we have at our disposal. It is sufficient to say that the explanation is to be found in the corruption of Christianity through early departures from the simplicity of the New Testament. In the beginning there were no distinctions among ministers, and the only officers in the churches were elders and deacons. In the beginning,

the ministry was not a caste, or order, like the Jewish Priesthood, to whom belonged exclusive prerogatives. In the beginning, the churches were independent bodies—little republics, electing their own officers, receiving and disciplining their own members, transacting their own business and recognizing no lord but Christ. In the beginning, baptism and church membership were restricted to believers, and the boundary between the church and the world was clear and distinct. But this state of things did not continue. Departures set in about the second century—departures in church polity, and then departures in faith, until we have orders in the ministry, mixed membership in the churches, churches subordinate to the ministry and to one another, and baptism changed into a saving ordinance, essential to salvation. This latter change, the dogma of baptismal regeneration, led, naturally, to the baptism of the sick and of infants, and wrought a radical change in the membership of the churches. The church was no longer composed wholly, or even chiefly, of those who had been born of the Spirit, but it gradually became filled with those who had been born only of water, and who were brought up under the soul-destroying delusion that they had been regenerated in baptism and were consequently in a saved state. The world was gradually swallowed up in the church and the church was corrupted by the world. With unregenerate church-members, possessed of all the propensities and passions of unregenerate human nature, and with a Christian ministry transformed into a Christian priesthood, usurping authority over the churches and over one another, the way was open for the great apostasy, and for the rise of the Papacy, with all of its usurpations and intolerance.

It is but just to the honest and sincere persecutors, to say that they had a plausible Scriptural warrant for their acts. The apologists for infant baptism and infant church-membership took refuge in the Old Testament and the Covenant of Circumcision, and they very naturally borrowed their ideas of what a Christian community, or government, ought to be, from the Jewish Commonwealth, of which circumcision was the sign and seal of citizenship. But the Jewish Commonwealth was a *Theocracy*, in which the civil and religious were united under one government and the civil authorities punished heresy and sin. Hence, when Christianity triumphed over the Roman Empire, and the question of the relations of Church and State engaged the attention of those in authority, they did just what our Lord had forbidden, and put "the new wine" of Christianity into the "old bottles," or "skins," of the effete and cast-off system of Judaism. It was on the Old Testament that they built up their system of Pedobaptism with its union of Church and State. It was in the Old Testament that they found warrant for using the civil arm to punish and even to destroy the enemies of God. And it was Old Testament example and object lesson that inspired the honest persecutor to feel, like Saul of Tarsus, that he was verily doing God service in putting down heresy and in destroying the heretic and the infidel.

But I must hasten on. Time will not admit of my tracing the progress of apostasy and the development of the Papacy, and its use of the civil power to punish all who resisted the Papal authority, or refused to conform to the Romish creed and worship. When the Reformation began under Martin Luther, there were thousands of different names, scattered over Europe, who had long suffered persecution for conscience sake, and who now came out of their hiding places and hailed the great reformer as their leader and deliverer. But to their amazement and disappointment, Luther was as intolerant towards them as the Papists were towards him. And the Augsburg Diet, which set forth the Protestant creed, and which decreed that the German princes might choose between the Augsburg Confession and Roman Catholicism, decreed, at the same time, that the subjects of each prince must conform to his creed and practice. There was no toleration for the people, even among Protestants, but only for the princes, or rulers. Church and State continued their unholy alliance, and the church continued to use the civil power to compel conformity, and to punish nonconformists, or dissenters. Persecuted in one place, dissenters fled to another, and finally thousands of them took refuge in this New World, only to receive, in many cases, like treatment here. Among these came our Baptist forefathers, bringing with them an open Bible and an unquenchable thirst for liberty. Their peculiar principles naturally rendered them obnoxious to Pedobaptist and State churches, wherever these existed, and hence Baptists suffered persecution not only in Massachusetts and other Northern colonies, but even in Old Virginia. But history repeated itself again, and the more they were persecuted, the more they multiplied, until, at the date of the Revolution, they, together with the Presbyterians and other dissenters in

Virginia, formed about two-thirds of the population. God's hand was in all this, preparing for the deliverance of his people from ecclesiastical tyranny, and the deliverance of the Church from unholy alliance with the State. When the colonies began to show resistance to British oppression, the Baptists saw their opportunity. They, too, longed for deliverance from oppression, but it was not merely the oppression of the Mother Country, but the oppression of the Establishment, and of those laws which denied to them the rights of conscience and taxed them to support a church to which they did not belong, and in which they did not believe. And so they threw themselves into the struggle for independence, making the reasonable request that the struggle should be for religious as well as civil liberty. They did not mean to offer themselves on the altar of their country's independence, and then have that country deny to them the right to worship God according to the dictates of their own consciences. Their services were needed, their demand was reasonable, and their unquestioned patriotism won them favor and contributed to the success of their cause. It would be interesting, if we had the time to follow that struggle, in all of its details, from beginning to end—one of the most important struggles which history records. It must suffice to say here, that, of all the participants in that great struggle, the Baptists were the only ones whose principles of voluntariness in religion, of a converted church-membership and of entire separation between Church and State, marked them as the consistent friends and advocates of absolute religious liberty ; that they were the only ones whose previous history presented a consistent and unbroken record in favor of this principle ; that they were the first to strike for religious liberty in Virginia, and that, while they did not write the longest, most elaborate and most scholarly memorials, they managed to make their views and wishes known to the Legislature and to the public, and they never wavered, or broke ranks in the engagement, but maintained a brave and consistent fight to the end. The struggle began in 1775 and reached its first culmination in 1779, when the Establishment was overthrown by the repeal of all laws levying taxes for its support. But the Revolution was scarcely over before the friends of the old Establishment devised a scheme for reviving it under a modified form. Two bills were framed and presented to the Legislature, a General Incorporation Bill and a General Assessment Bill, the one providing for the incorporation of all the leading denominations of the State, including the Baptists, and the other providing for their support by taxation. It was a most subtle and plausible scheme, as it was thoroughly impartial and allowed every tax-payer the privilege of designating the denomination which should receive his tax. It had the advantage of being fathered by the "Orator of the Revolution," Patrick Henry. It was backed by all the friends of the old Establishment, and it finally won the support of the powerful and influential Hanover Presbytery, whose leaders, according to the testimony of their own historian, Dr. Foote, were won over by the influence of Mr. Henry. It seemed as though the bill would surely pass, and it was a most critical time for the cause of liberty. All denominations except the Baptists had gone over to this new and liberal scheme, which proposed to take them all in. And had *they* proven untrue to their principles, the cause would have been lost, and one of the brightest pages in Virginia's history would not have been written.

"God hath chosen the foolish things of the world to confound the wise ; and God hath chosen the weak things of the world to confound the things which are mighty ; and base things of the world, and things which are despised, hath God chosen, yea, and things which are not, to bring to nought things that are ; that no flesh should glory in his presence."

The historian tells us that when Rome was overrun by the various tribes from the forests of Germany, she was enriched rather than impoverished thereby. For while the Germans did not possess the wealth and arts and culture of the Romans, they were rich in other things which Rome lacked ; they had great capacity for civilization, love of personal freedom, and reverence for woman. And so we may say of the early Baptists of Virginia, that while they could not boast of great wealth, or culture, or refinement, they possessed some things of more real value, and which the Commonwealth greatly needed. In the first place *they had religion—genuine* religion ; not a sham, nor an empty form, but *the old time religion* of the heart. Then they had *personal worth* or *character*, that character which always follows from having genuine religion. And then, again, those early Baptists had an *unquenchable love of liberty.* The *truth* of the New Testament *makes men free* indeed, and it inspires them with a love of freedom, not for themselves only, but for all men. And it was because they possessed these traits that they resisted the temptation of the General Incorporation and General Assessment, and stood their ground amid the general desertion. They resolved to continue the fight, and asking their faithful champion, Jas. Madison, to embody their views in a "remonstrance," they took the field and re-canvassed the State for signatures to their petition. As the people read that powerful and unanswerable argument, reaction set in ; the Presbyterian laity, who had never been much in favor of the bill, got after their clergy, and there was a hastily gathered convention at Bethel, in Augusta county, where that body placed themselves on record against the Assessment, and then for the first time gave their approval to Jefferson's Bill for Religious Freedom. When the Legislature met in October, '85, the roll of signatures to the petition and remonstrance was so large that it was rolled up the aisle to the clerk's table on a wheelbarrow. The Assessment Bill was dead, and Jefferson's bill was promptly brought forward and adopted. Having led in the fight for religious liberty in Virginia, our Baptist fathers, with the help of their brethren and friends of other States, secured its incorporatian into the Constitution of the United States. And now this tree of liberty has spread its branches over this New World, and the winds and waves have wafted its seed back to the Old, to bring forth like precious fruit there, quenching the fires of persecution, overthrowing religious establishments, breaking off the shackles that bind the consciences and enslave the souls of men, and hastening the progress of our race towards that glorious day when "the kingdom of this world" shall be "the kingdom of our Lord and of his Christ."

B.

BAPTIST BEGINNINGS IN VIRGINIA.

BY REV. GEORGE W. BEALE, D. D.

In dealing with the rise of the Baptists in Virginia, it is proper to bear in mind that it occurred at a time that stood in much closer relation than our own to the preceding centuries of ignorance, intolerance, and tyranny, and was much more dominated by the force of their customs and their proscriptive spirit. There were special causes, also, at work in the colony to give edge to its temper and roughness to its manners. The planting of settlements from the sea to the mountains and beyond involved a rough battling with nature and with savage foes that was not favorable to the cultivation of the gentler and softer elements of society. The primitive and unsettled conditions prevailing in many quarters, and offering easy facilities and cover to crimes and lawlessness, absolutely demanded for the protection of life and property most rigorous laws and summary punishments. The importation and spreading over the plantations of thousands of untutored, half-savage Africans, and the severe measures necessary to their restraint and training, yet further acquainted our forefathers with scenes and methods of rigor. Many of the acts transferred from English statute books to those of the colony abounded in severest provisions and penalties of revolting cruelty. Worse than all, by virtue of the Crown and Parliament, the secular government was joined in unholy union with the religious body, and civil officers were made the guardians of men's faith, and were clothed with magisterial power to enforce obedience in spiritual matters.

Thus, when, in the providence of God, the early Baptists appeared in Virginia, the scene of their action was cumbered with peculiar difficulties and begirt with the gravest perils. A lurid reflection from the Towers, the Bedford jails, and the Smithfield fires of old England enveloped our early workmen and their work. The era of their appearance in many of its sterner aspects well suggests "The Days that Are Gone," as satirized in song by Charles Mackay:

> "The days when obedience in right or in wrong
> Was always the sermon and always the song,
> .   .   .   .
> When difference of creed was the vilest of crime,
> And martyrs were burned, half a score at a time.
>
> When Justice herself, taking Law for her guide,
> Was never appeased till a victim had died,
> And the stealer of sheep and the slayer of men
> Were strung up together—again and again."

MEETING WITH MISREPRESENTATIONS AND ABUSE.

William Fristoe, the historian of the Regular Baptists, who had personal knowledge of the facts which he relates, tells us that "at their first rise among us, and for sometime after, they were stigmatized with every name that malice could invent." Among the abusive terms and phrases with which they were commonly branded, he mentions these: "Disturbers of the peace;" "Ignorant and illiterate set;" "Poor and contemptible class;" "Schismatics;" "False prophets;" "Wolves in sheeps' clothing;" Perverters of good order;" "Callers of unlawful assemblies."

A prominent clergyman had printed and widely circulated a pamphlet, in which he called upon Christians of every name to combine in opposing the new sect, whom he styled Anabaptists, whose preachers, he said, were "going about without any license, disturbing the order of neighborhoods and churches with wild doctrines." Others of the Established clergy openly warned the people against them, and held them up to public scorn by associating them with the mad rioters of Munster and Jack of Leyden.

If the pioneers of our faith did not learn by experience the blessedness of the beatitude which says, "Blessed are the peacemakers," they must have known by a thousand experiences the comfort of that other beatitude which says: "Blessed are ye when men shall revile you, . . . and say all manner of evil of you falsely, for my sake."

MEETING THE VIOLENCE OF INDIVIDUALS.

In popular movements, when prejudices and passions are deeply stirred, and bad men are supported by the sympathy of the multitude, individuals may be commonly found ready to step forth from the ranks of the Phillistines, like Goliath of Gath, for single-handed combat. Such individual assailants sought often to throttle the gospel as proclaimed by our early preachers. Dutton Lane, at his undertaking to preach in Mecklenburg county, was rudely interrupted by a man of prominence and a magistrate and summarily commanded to desist and not to preach there again. "Father" Samuel Harriss, when preaching at Fort Mayo, was similarly interrupted and accosted thus: "Colonel, you have sucked much eloquence to-day from the rum cask; please give us a little, that we may declaim as well when our turn comes."

Robert Ware, while preaching in Middlesex, was confronted by two sons of Belial, Dr. Semple says, "who stood before him with a bottle, drank from it in his presence and then offered it to him, cursing him. They then drew out a pack of cards and began to play on the stage where he had been preaching, wishing him to reprove them, that they might beat him."

David Thomas, perhaps the most learned and scholarly of our early preachers, was seized once by a ruffian, when preaching in the northern part of the State, and dragged out of the house by his hair. On another occasion a gun was levelled at him whilst preaching and the discharge only prevented by a bystander's seizing the weapon.

Thomas Waford, a devout and zealous layman, who lived near Culpeper Courthouse, and whose delight it was to travel ahead of certain of the old preachers and arrange meetings for them, was assailed at a spring near one of the meeting-places and severely beaten. He bore the scars of this brutal violence to his grave, though he lived to be past four-score years.

Personal indignities of this character were among the bitter pains and penalties endured by the fathers, and that in various places, from the mountains to the sea.

VIOLENCE OF MOBS ENCOUNTERED.

The Apostle Paul's enemies at Thessalonica, we are told, "gathered a company." Many companies were gathered to intimidate and silence the early apostles of our faith in this State.

One of "Father" Harriss' early meetings in Culpeper ended in confusion, the congregation having been invaded by Captain Ball, at the head of a band of opposers, who, in attempting to prevent the preaching, brought on a scuffle and tumult.

Whilst John Pickett was once preaching in Fauquier a mob rushed in on the meeting, seized the preacher, and split in pieces the pulpit and communion table. In the manuscript journal of Richard Dozier, who was present at one of Lewis Lunsford's meetings in the Northern Neck, this record is made : "After he began his discourse, a shocking tumult occurred and stopped him ; some blows passed ; pistols presented, and the stage broken down. Mr. Lunsford, in the meantime, went off to Mr. Hall's house. After many of us went to the house the persecutors came there and acted very indecently." Of Jeremiah Moore, the founder of numerous churches in Virginia, as well as of one in Washington city, Mr. Semple says : "A lawless mob seized Mr. Moore and another preacher who was with him, and carried them off to duck them. After they had ducked Mr. Moore's companion they discharged them both." The biographer of David Barrow, the founder of Shoulder's Hill and South Quay churches, relates that at a meeting held by him on Nansemond river a gang of well-dressed men came up to the stage, which had been erected under some trees, and sung one of their obscene songs. They then undertook to plunge both of the preachers. They plunged Mr. Barrow twice, pressing him into the mud. In the midst of their mocking they asked if they believed. He is said to have answered : "*Yes;* I believe you intend to drown me " We are told further : "The whole assembly was shocked ; the women shrieked ; but no man durst interfere, for about twenty stout fellows were engaged in this horrid measure."

Many cases of mob violence like these, and others even more flagrant and shocking, marked the beginning of the Baptists in Virginia, and show what good reasons our early preachers had to echo from their yearning hearts the apostolic appeal : "Brethren, pray for us, that the word of the Lord may have free course and be glorified, . . . and that *we may be delivered from unreasonable and wicked men.*"

MEETING WARRANTS, ARRESTS, AND IMPRISONMENTS.

The strongest resistance which the early Baptists of Virginia encountered was the iron hand of the law, and the heaviest penalties endured by them were inflicted by magistrates and courts.

It is an important and interesting inquiry why our fathers should have been treated as offenders above all others; why, among the dissenters, they should have been singled out as the miscreants who alone deserved the pain and ignominy of arrests, bonds, imprisonments, and stripes. The reason why they were so adjudged and treated is not far to seek. The Separate Baptists, as their records show, and many General and Regular Baptists as well, believed the right to preach the gospel was inalienable and divine, and quite beyond the pale of court jurisdiction or governmental control. Therefore, whilst others took the prescribed oaths, subscribed to the necessary articles, and secured licenses from the court for certain preaching-places, many Baptist preachers proceeded to preach, as opportunities offered, without consulting the general court and regardless of legal sanction.

It was this bold and intrepid action that aroused against them the resentment of clergymen, the rage of magistrates, and the terror of courts. It was this that in so many instances on the soil of this "mother of States and of statesmen," led the fathers of our faith to suffer the stings of the cruel lash, and to preach to their fellow-men through the grated windows of our county jails.

Preaching without license was the chief count in the indictment against John Waller, Lewis Craig, and James Childs when they were sentenced to jail in Spottsylvania in 1768. It was for this alleged crime that they went to prison in Fredericksburg, singing as their guard urged them along the street:

> " Broad is the road that leads to death,
>   And thousands walk together there;
> But wisdom shows a narrow path,
>   With here and there a traveller."

It was upon this same charge that, in the winter of 1771, William Webber and Joseph Anthony were shut up within the walls of Chesterfield jail—a prison that was destined to be longer used for the incarceration of Baptist preachers than any other in the State. Here were confined, for preaching Christ and him crucified without the permit of a human court, Jeremiah Walker, John Weatherford, David Tinsley, John Tanner and Augustine Eastin. The first ministerial relief work ever done in Virginia was by the Separate Baptists at Hall's meeting-house, in Halifax, in May, 1774, when they made a contribution for the comfort of their imprisoned brethren and set apart two days of fasting in behalf of their releasement. These noble prisoners and their sympathizers formed the *bandana brigade* among the old soldiers of our faith. The money sent to Patrick Henry for his employment in behalf of their release from prison was wrapped up in a handkerchief of the above description and by that noble patriot returned in the same way. When the malice of their enemies had erected a close, high plank fence in front of the jail windows to prevent the imprisoned preachers from exhorting the crowd without, a handkerchief displayed on a pole above the screen became the signal from the waiting people that they were ready to hear, when the stalwart voice of one of the prisoners would send the truth home through the boards to the hearts of the listening company. Historic handkerchief! Never did a standard give signal in a worthier cause, or float before a nobler beleaguered band.

It was for gathering a conventicle and preaching without the license of a human court, composed largely of irreligious men, that old "Father Ireland" was called to record this piece of personal history : "At one time, preaching being over and (while) concluding with prayer, I heard a rustling noise in the woods, and before I opened my eyes to see what it was I was seized by the collar by two men. . . . They told me that I must give security not to teach, preach, or exhort for twelve months and a day, or go to jail. *I chose the latter alternative.*" The jail in which he was confined, with many attendant incidents of outrage and cruelty, was at Culpeper Courthouse, on the spot where the Baptist church now stands. He made this old prison memorable by the letters written during his confinement, which he dated from "My Palace in Culpeper." Others among the early Baptists who were confined in this jail for preaching the gospel without license, or abetting the same, were Elijah Craig, Nathaniel Saunders, William M. Clannahan, John Corbley, Thomas Ammon, Anthony Moffett, John Picket, Adam Banks, Thomas Maxfield, and John Dulany. Well might James Madison have written, in 1774, from his home in Orange, with reference to most of these men: "That diabolical, hell-conceived principle of persecution rages among some ; and, to their eternal infamy, the clergy can furnish their quota of imps for such purposes. There are at this time in the adjacent county not less than five or six well-meaning men in close jail for publishing their religious sentiments, which are in the main very orthodox.''

A famous portrait of Charlotte Corday has arrested many an earnest gaze, and her pensive and soulful face has gathered interest from the iron grating which forms its setting. The faces and forms of many of the early Baptist preachers of this State should wear in our eyes a pathetic and heightened interest as we look back through the years at them behind their prison bars. Who are those men of faith and prayer locked in the Caroline jail, as we look back to the August days of 1771? They are John Burrus, John Young, Ed. Herndon, James Goodrich, Bartholomew Choning, and Lewis Craig, under sentence for preaching Christ and him crucified without the sanction of a secular court. Who are those that preach to the crowd outside from the windows of the Middlesex jail at that same period? They are John Waller, William Webber, James Greenwood, and Robert Ware.

In the brick colonial edifice in Tappahannock, where the Centennial Baptist church now worship, four Baptist preachers were arraigned at the bar of Essex Court in 1774 as law-breakers, some of whom were consigned to prison. They were John Waller, John Shackleford, Ivison Lewis, and Robert Ware. To this list of brave and faithful men of God, who paid thus heavily for conscience sake, may be added John Alderson, Jeremiah Moore, William Loocall, and Elijah Baker, who in different counties were placed in prison and heard the iron bolts turned against them. If it had been the aim of their persecutors, during the ten years that preceded the Revolution, when the Baptists were rapidly gaining a footing in Virginia, to incarcerate as many of them as there were parishes or clergymen in the colony, we would have to concede that their purpose was fully accomplished.

If any should ask why this recurrence to the painful incidents of the buried past, the answer may be given that it may endear to us the cause and principles for which our fathers suffered. The noblest attainments and benefits of life are hallowed in veneration and affections by the pains and sacrifices which they have cost. Thoughts of Gethsemane, of the Roman soldiers, of the mocking multitude, of the thorny crown, and of the rugged cross, intensify the preciousness of the hope in Christ. The boon of civil freedom and constitutional government won for us by our patriot sires is endeared in our heart of hearts, as we remember their bleeding feet on the ice of the Delaware and amid the snows of Valley Forge. And so should the heritage of our religious equality and spiritual freedom be entwined in our glowing and grateful breasts with a thousand sacred sentiments, and hallowed by a thousand endearing memories, as we recount our fathers' wrongs and hardships, bonds and imprisonments, nobly endured for its sake.

In glancing backward at Baptist beginnings in Virginia, we may well gather inspiration and hope for the future. It ought to nourish within us a spirit of the most vigorous and healthful optimism. In the days of our fathers we beheld law as trammelled by custom and fettered by ignorance. Justice is seen to have been bigoted and blind. Before her statue, in the garb in which our fathers knew her, we would feel much as Madame Roland felt when, on her way to the guillotine, she cried out before the statue of Liberty, and our cry would be: "O Justice! what crimes are perpetrated in thy name!"

But now we exult in freedom enlightening the world and in law unfettered and just. We rejoice in the reign of Justice, whose equal scales and clear vision give promise of a coming day, when men will bow at her seat and say: "O Justice! thou art pure as the spotless ermine that wraps thy sacred form."

A review such as we now make is due the cause of historic justice. The writers of our history have not always been candid and just towards our Baptist fathers. A work widely used in our public schools today has this comment on the era of their oppression: "There was never any active religious persecution in Virginia." Another eminent Virginia writer says: "There was no terror in the law to any who chose to worship God in their own way and place, except a trivial fine for being absent from church." Again, he says: "In the history of the vestries of the Episcopal Establishment may be fairly traced that religious liberty which afterwards developed itself in Virginia."

Our venerated fathers, misunderstood, maligned, and severely dealt with in their day, have been often since passed by in silence, and have as often had their motives and actions misrepresented or perverted. They sleep in their neglected graves, with never a look to give, a hand to raise, or a word to speak in their own defence. It becomes us, who have entered into their heritage, and sit beneath the shade of the goodly tree planted by their toils and watered by their tears, to vindicate their precious memory and perpetuate in faithfulness and truth the story of their deeds and sufferings.

It would be but just to them and becoming in us to rear on the spot which we have consecrated to education, science, and religion in the capital of this State, so blessed by their deeds and hallowed by their sufferings, a fitting Memorial Hall inscribed with their honored names. What would better accord with the eternal fitness of things than that our Baptist host, who "have passed through the midst of Jordan" like Israel of old, should, like them, "take every man a stone upon his shoulder" and build on the fair shore of our deliverance an enduring commemorative pile, so that, when our children shall ask their fathers, saying, What mean these stones? then shall they answer : *These stones shall be for a memorial of the BAPTIST FATHERS OF VIRGINIA unto their children forever.*

C.

BAPTIST MEMORIALS.

*To the Honourable Peyton Randolph, Esq., and the several delegated
Gentlemen, convened at Richmond, to concert Measures conducive to
the Good and Well-being of this Colony and Dominion, the humble
Address of the Virginia Baptists, now Associated in Cumberland, by
Delegates from their several Churches:*

Gentlemen of the Convention—While you are (pursuant to the
important Trust reposed in you) acting as the Guardians of the
Rights of your Constituents, and pointing out to them the Road to
Freedom, it must needs afford you an exalted satisfaction to find
your Determinations not only applauded, but cheerfully complied
with by a brave and spirited people. We, however distinguished
from the Body of our Countrymen by appellatives and sentiments of
a religious nature, do nevertheless look upon ourselves as Members
of the same Commonwealth, and, therefore, with respect to matters
of a civil nature, embarked in the same common Cause.

Alarmed at the shocking Oppression which in a British Cloud
hangs over our American Continent, we, as a Society and part of the
distressed State, have in our Association consider'd what part might
be most prudent for the Baptists to act in the present unhappy Contest. After we had determined "that in some Cases it was lawful to
go to War, and also for us to make a Military resistance against
Great Britain, in regard of their unjust Invasion, and tyrannical
Oppression of, and repeated Hostilities against America," our people
were all left to act at Discretion with respect to inlisting, without
falling under the Censure of our Community. And as some have
inlisted, and many more likely so to do, who will have earnest Desires
for their Ministers to preach to them during the Campaign, we
therefore deligate and appoint our well-beloved Brethren in the
Ministry, Elijah Craig, Lewis Craig, Jeremiah Walker and John
Williams, to present this address and to petition you that they may
have free Liberty to preach to the Troops at convenient Times with-

out molestation or abuse ; and as we are conscious of their strong
attachment to American Liberty, as well as their soundness in the
principles of the Christian Religion, and great usefulness in the
Work of the Ministry, we are willing they may come under your
examination in any Matters you may think requisite.

We conclude with our earnest prayers to Almighty God for His
Divine Blessing on your patriotic and laudable Resolves, for the good
of Mankind and American Freedom, and for the success of our
Armies in Defence of our Lives, Liberties and Properties. Amen.

Sign'd by order and in behalf of the Association the 14th of August, 1775.   SAM'L HARRISS, Moderator.
JOHN WALLER, Clerk.

To the Honourable the Speaker and House of Delegates:

The Memorial of the Baptist Association, met at Sandy Creek, in
Charlotte, the 16th day of October, 1780, in behalf of themselves
and those whom they represent, humbly sheweth :

That a due Regard to the Liberty and Rights of the People is of
the highest Importance to the Welfare of the State; That this
heaven-born Freedom, which belongs equally to every good Citizen,
is the Palladium which the Legislature is particularly intrusted with
the Guardianship of, and on which the Safety and Happiness of the
State depend. Your Memorialists, therefore, look upon every Law
or Usage now existing among us, which does not accord with that
Republican Spirit which breathes in our Constitution and Bill of
Rights, to be extremely pernicious and detrimental, and that such
Law or Usage should immediately be abolished.

As Religious Oppression, or the interfering with the Rights of
Conscience, which God has made accountable to none but Himself,
is of all Oppression the most inhuman and insupportable, and as
Partiality to any Religious Denomination is its genuine offspring,
your Memorialists have with Grief observed that Religious Liberty
has not made a single Advance in this Commonwealth without some
Opposition. They have been much surprised to hear it said of
Things indisputably right and necessary, " It is not now a proper
Time to proceed to such Affairs ; let us first think of defending ourselves," &c., when there cannot, surely, be a more suitable Time to

allow ourselves the Blessings of Liberty, which we have in our own Power, than when contending with those who endeavor to tyrannize over us.

As the Completion of Religious Liberty is what, as a Religious Community, your Memorialists are particularly interested in, they would humbly call the attention of your Honourable House to a few Particulars, viz.: First, the Vestry Law, which disqualifies any person to officiate who will not subscribe to be conformable to the Doctrine and Discipline of the Church of England ; by which Means Dissenters are not only precluded, but also not represented, they not having a free Voice, whose Property is nevertheless subject to be taxed by the Vestry, and whose Poor are provided for at the Discretion of those who may possibly be under the Influence of Party Motives. And what renders the said Law a greater Grievance is, that in some Parishes so much time has elapsed since an Election, that there is scarcely one who was originally chosen by the People, the Vacancies having been filled up by the remaining Vestrymen. Secondly, the Solemnization of Marriage, concerning which it is insinuated by some, and taken for granted by others, that to render it legal it must be performed by a Church Clergyman, according to the Rites and Ceremonies of the Church of England ; conformably to which Sentiment Marriage Licenses are usually worded and directed. Now, if this should in Reality be the Case, your Memorialists conceive that the ill Consequences resulting from thence, which are too obvious to need mentioning, render it absolutely necessary for the Legislature to endeavour their Removal. This is an Affair of so tender a Nature, and of such Importance, that after the Restoration one of the first Matters which the British Parliament proceeded to was the Confirmation of the Marriages solemnized according to the Mode in Use during the Interregnum and the Protectorate of Cromwell. And the Propriety of such a Measure in Virginia evidently appears from the vast numbers of Dissenters who, having Objections against the Form and Manner prescribed in the Book of Common Prayer, proceed to marry otherwise ; and also that in many Places, especially over the Ridge, there are no Church Parsons to officiate. On the other Hand, if Marriages otherwise solemnized are equally valid, a Declaratory Act to that Purport appears to your Memorialists to be highly expedient, because they can see no Reason why any of the free Inhabitants of this State should be terrified by a mere Mormo from their just Rights and Privileges, or censured by others on Suspicion of their acting contrary to Law.* To these Considerations your Memorialists would just beg leave to add that those who claim this Province of officiating at Marriage Solemnities as their sole Right, undertake at the same Time to be the sole Judges of what they are to receive for the same.

Your Memorialists humbly hope that your Honourable House will take effectual measures to redress these Grievances in such a Way as may manifest an equal Regard to all the good People of this Commonwealth, however diversyfied by Appellations or Religious Sentiments; and that, as it is your Glory to represent a free People, you will be as forward to remove every just Cause of Offence as your Constituents are to complain of them; and in particular that you will consign to Oblivion all the Relicks of Religious Oppression, and make a public Sacrifice of Partiality at the glorious Altar of Freedom.

Signed by order. SAM'L HARRISS, Mod'r.

JOHN WILLIAMS, Clk.

---

*At the October session of the General Assembly, 1780, an act was passed providing: " That it shall and may be lawful for any minister of any society or congregation of Christians . . . to celebrate the rites of matrimony . . . and such marriages, *as well as those heretofore celebrated by dissenting ministers*, shall be, and they are hereby, declared good and valid in law."—Hen. Statutes at Large, Vol. X., page 363.

D.

PRESBYTERIAN MEMORIALS.

[Presented October 24, 1776.]

To the Honorable the General Assembly of Virginia:

The Memorial of the Presbytery of Hanover humbly represents: That your memorialists are governed by the same sentiments which have inspired the United States of America ; and are determined that nothing in our power and influence shall be wanting to give success to their common cause. We would also represent that dissenters from the Church of England in this country have ever been desirous to conduct themselves as peaceable members of the civil government, for which reason they have hitherto submitted to several ecclesiastical burdens, and restrictions, that are inconsistent with equal liberty. But now when the many and grievous oppressions of our mother country have laid this continent under the necessity of casting off the yoke of tyranny, and of forming independent governments upon equitable and liberal foundations, we flatter ourselves that we shall be freed from all the incumbrances which a spirit of domination, prejudice, or bigotry, hath interwoven with most other political systems. This we are the more strongly encouraged to expect by the Declaration of Rights, so universally applauded for that dignity, firmness and precision with which it delineates and asserts the privileges of society, and the prerogatives of human nature ; and which we embrace as the *magna charta* of our Commonwealth, that can never be violated without endangering the grand superstructure it was destined to sustain. Therefore we rely upon this Declaration, as well as the justice of our honorable Legislature, to secure us the *free exercise of religion according to the dictates of our consciences ;* and we should fall short in our duty to ourselves, and the many and numerous congregations under our care, were we, upon this occasion, to neglect laying before you a state of the religious grievances under which we have hitherto laboured ; that they no longer may be continued in our present form of government.

It is well known that in the frontier counties, which are justly supposed to contain a fifth part of the inhabitants of Virginia, the dissenters have borne the heavy burdens of purchasing glebes, building churches, and supporting the established clergy, where there are very few Episcopalians, either to assist in bearing the expenses, or to reap the advantage; and that throughout the other parts of the country there are also many thousands of zealous friends and defenders of our State, who, besides the invidious, and disadvantageous restrictions to which they have been subjected, annually pay large taxes to support an establishment from which their consciences and principles oblige them to dissent; all which are confessedly so many violations of their natural rights, and in their consequences a restraint upon freedom of inquiry and private judgment.

In this enlightened age, and in a land where all of every denomination are united in the most strenuous efforts to be free, we hope and expect that our representatives will cheerfully concur in removing every species of religious, as well as civil, bondage. Certain it is that every argument for civil liberty gains additional strength when applied to liberty in the concerns of religion; and there is no argument in favor of establishing the Christian religion but what may be pleaded, with equal propriety, for establishing the tenets of Mahomed by those who believe the Alcoran; or if this be not true, it is at least impossible for the magistrate to adjudge the right of preference among the various sects that profess the Christian faith without erecting a chair of infallibility, which would lead us back to the Church of Rome.

We beg leave farther to represent that religious establishments are highly injurious to the temporal interests of any community. Without insisting upon the ambition, and the arbitrary practices of those who are favored by government; or the intriguing, seditious spirit which is commonly excited by this, as well as every other kind of oppression; such establishments greatly retard population, and consequently the progress of arts, sciences, and manufactories: witness the rapid growth and improvements of the Northern provinces, compared with this. No one can deny that the more early settlement and the many superior advantages of our country would have invited multitudes of artificers, mechanics and other useful members of society to fix their habitation among us, who have either remained in their place of nativity, or preferred worse civil governments, and a barren soil, where they might enjoy the rights of conscience more fully than they had a prospect of doing it in this.

From which we infer that Virginia might have now been the capitol of America, and a match for the British arms, without depending on others for the necessaries of war, had it not been prevented by her religious establishment.

Neither can it be made to appear that the gospel needs any such civil aid. We rather conceive that when our blessed Saviour declares his kingdom is not of this world, he renounces all dependence upon State power, and as his weapons are spiritual, and were only designed to have influence on the judgment and heart of man, we are persuaded that if mankind were left in the quiet possession of their unalienable rights and privileges, Christianity, as in the days of the Apostles, would continue to prevail and flourish in the greatest purity by its own native excellence and under the all disposing providence of God.

We would humbly represent that the only proper objects of civil government are the happiness and protection of men in the present state of existence, the security of the life, liberty and property of the citizens, and to restrain the vicious and encourage the virtuous by wholesome laws, equally extending to every individual. But that the duty which we owe our Creator and the manner of discharging it, can only be directed by reason and conviction, and as nowhere cognizable but at the tribunal of the universal Judge.

Therefore we ask no ecclesiastical establishments for ourselves; neither can we approve of them when granted to others. This, indeed, would be giving exclusive or separate emoluments or privileges to one set of men, without any special public services, to the common reproach and injury of every other denomination ; and for the reasons recited we are induced earnestly to entreat that all laws now in force in this Commonwealth which countenance religious denomination, may be speedily repealed—that all, of every religious sect, may be protected in the full exercise of their several modes of worship, and exempted from all taxes for the support of any church whatsoever further than what may be agreeable to their own private choice, or voluntary obligation. This being done, all partial and invidious distinctions will be abolished, to the great honour and interest of the State, and every one be left to stand or fall, according to merit, which can never be the case so long as any one denomination is established in preference to others.

That the great Sovereign of the Universe may inspire you with unanimity, wisdom and resolution, and bring you to a just determination on all the important concerns before you, is the fervent prayer of your memorialists.

Signed by order of the Presbytery.

JOHN TODD, Moderator.

CALEB WALLACE, P. Clerk.

[Presented June 3, 1777.]

To the Honorable the General Assembly of Virginia:

The memorial of the Presbytery of Hanover humbly represents, That your memorialists and the religious denomination with which we are connected are most sincerely attached to the common interest of the American States, and are determined that our most fervent prayers and strenuous endeavours shall ever be united with our fellow-subjects to repel the assaults of tyranny and to maintain our common rights. In our former memorial we have expressed our hearty approbation of the Declaration of Rights, which has been made and adopted as the basis of the laws and government of this State; and now we take the opportunity of testifying that nothing has inspired us with greater confidence in our Legislature than the late act of Assembly declaring that equal liberty, as well religious as civil, shall be universally extended to the good people of this country; and that all the oppressive acts of parliament respecting religion which have been formerly enacted in the mother country shall henceforth be of no validity or force in this Commonwealth; as also exempting all dissenters from all levies, taxes, and impositions, whatsoever, towards supporting the Church of England as it now is or hereafter may be established. We would, therefore, have given our honorable Legislature no further trouble on this subject, but we are sorry to find that there yet remains a variety of opinions touching the propriety of a general assessment, or whether every religious society shall be left to voluntary contributions for the maintenance of the ministers of the gospel who are of different persuasions. As this matter is deferred by our Legislature to the discussion and final determination of a future Assembly, when the opinion of the country in general shall be better known, we think it our indispensable duty again to repeat a part of the prayer of our former memorial, "That dissenters of every denomination may be exempted from all taxes for the support of any church whatsoever, further than what may be agreeable to the private choice or voluntary obligation of every individual, while the civil magistrates no otherwise interfere than to protect them all in the full and free exercise of their several modes of worship."

We then represented as the principal reason upon which this request is founded that the only proper objects of civil governments are the happiness and protection of men in the present state of existence, the security of the life, liberty and property of the citizens, and to restrain the vicious and encourage the virtuous by wholesome laws equally extending to every individual; and that the duty which we owe our Creator, and the manner of discharging it, can only be directed by reason and conviction, and is nowhere cognizable but at the tribunal of the universal Judge.

To illustrate and confirm these assertions, we beg leave to observe that to judge for ourselves and to engage in the exercise of religion agreeable to the dictates of our own consciences is an unalienable right, which, upon the principles that the gospel was first propagated and the reformation from popery carried on, can never be transferred to another. Neither does the church of Christ stand in need of a general assessment for its support; and most certain we are that it would be of no advantage, but an injury to the society to which we belong; and as every good Christian believes that Christ has ordained a complete system of laws for the government of his kingdom, so we are persuaded that, by his providence, he will support it to its final consummation. In the fixed belief of this principle, that the kingdom of Christ and the concerns of religion are beyond the limits of civil control, we should act a dishonest, inconsistent part, were we to receive any emoluments from human establishments for the support of the gospel.

These things being considered, we hope we shall be excused for remonstrating against a general assessment for any religious purpose. As the maxims have long been approved, that every servant is to obey his master, and that the hireling is accountable for his conduct to him from whom he receives his wages; in like manner, if the

Legislature has any rightful authority over the ministers of the gospel in the exercise of their sacred office, and it is their duty to levy a maintenance for them as such, then it will follow that they may revive the old establishment in its former extent, or ordain a new one for any sect they think proper; they are invested with a power not only to determine, but it is incumbent on them to declare who shall preach, what they shall preach; to whom, when, at what places they shall preach; or to impose any regulations and restrictions upon religious societies that they may judge expedient.

These consequences are so plain as not to be denied; and they are so entirely subversive of religious liberty, that if they should take place in Virginia, we should be reduced to the melancholy necessity of saying with the apostles in like cases, "Judge ye whether it is best to obey God or man;" and also of acting as they acted.

Therefore, as it is contrary to our principles and interests, and, as we think, subversive to religious liberty, we do again most earnestly entreat that our Legislature would never extend any assessment for religious purposes to us, or to the congregations under our care. And your memorialists, as in duty bound, shall ever pray for, and demean themselves as peaceful subjects of, civil government.

Signed by order of the Presbytery.

RICHARD SANKEY, Moderator.

Timber Ridge, April 25, 1777.

* * *

[Presented May 26, 1784.]

To the Honourable Speaker and House of Delegates of Virginia:

Gentlemen—"The united clergy of the Presbyterian Church in Virginia, assembled in Presbytery, request your attention to the following representation. In the late arduous struggle for everything dear to us, a desire of perfect liberty and political equality animated every class of citizens. An entire and everlasting freedom from every species of ecclesiastical domination, a full and permanent security of the unalienable rights of conscience, and private judgment, and an equal share of the protection and favor of the government of all denominations of Christians, were particular objects of our expectation, and irrefragable claim. The happy Revolution effected by the virtuous exertions of our countrymen of various opinions in religion, was a favorable opportunity of obtaining these desirable objects without friction, contention, or complaint. All ranks of men, almost, felt the claim of justice when the rod of oppression had scourged them into sensibility, and the powerful hand of common danger had cordially united them against civil encroachments. The members, therefore, of every religious society had a right to expect, and most of them did expect, that former invidious and exclusive distinctions, preferences and emoluments conferred by the State on any sect above others would have been wholly removed. They justly supposed that any partiality of this kind, any particular or illicit connection or commerce between the State and one description of Christians more than another on account of peculiar opinions in religion, or anything else, would be unworthy of the representatives of a people perfectly free, and an infringement of that religious liberty which enhances the value of other privileges in a State or society.

We, therefore, and the numerous body of citizens in our communion, as well as in many others, are justly dissatisfied and uneasy that our expectations from the Legislature have not been answered in these important respects. We regret that the prejudices of education, the influence of partial custom, and habits of thinking confirmed by these, have too much confounded the distinction between matters purely religious and the objects of human legislation, and have occasioned jealousy and dissatisfaction by injurious inequalities respecting things which are connected with religious opinion towards different sects of Christians. That this uneasiness may not appear to be entertained without ground, we would wish to state the following unquestionable facts for the consideration of the House of Delegates.

The security of our religious rights upon equal and impartial ground, *instead of being made a fundamental part of our constitution as it ought to have been,* is left to the precarious fate of common law. A matter of general and essential concern to the people is committed to the hazard of the prevailing opinion of a majority of the Assembly at its different sessions. In consequence of this the Episcopal Church was virtually regarded as the constitutional Church, the Church of the State at the Revolution ; *and was left by the framers of our present government in that station of unjust pre-eminence which she had formerly acquired under the smiles of royal favour,* and even when the late oppressive establishment of that church was at length acknowledged an unreasonable hardship by the Assembly in 1776, a superiority and distinction in name was still retained, and it was expressly styled the *established church* as before; which title was continued as late as the year 1778, and never formally disclaimed; our common danger at that time not permitting the opposition to the injustice to such distinction which it required and deserved.

But "a seat on the right hand of temporal glory as the established mother church" was not the only inequality then countenanced, and still subsisting, of which we now have reason to regret and complain. Substantial advantages were also confirmed and secured to her by the partial and inequitable decree of government. We hope the time past would have sufficed for the enjoyment of these emoluments, which that church long possessed without control by the abridgement of the equal privileges of others, and the aid of their property wrested from them by the hand of usurpation, but we were deceived. *An estate computed to be worth several hundred thousand pounds in churches, glebes, etc., derived from the pockets of all religious societies, was exclusively and unjustly appropriated to the benefit of one* without compensation or restitution to the rest, who, in many places, were a large majority of the inhabitants.

Nor is this the whole of the injustice we have felt in matters connected with religious opinion. The Episcopal is actually incorporated, and known in law as a body, so that it can receive and possess property for ecclesiastical purposes, without trouble or risk in securing it, while other Christian communities are obliged to trust to the precarious fidelity of trustees chosen for the purpose. *The Episcopal clergy are considered as having a right, ex-officio, to celebrate marriages* throughout the State, while unnecessary hardships and restrictions are imposed upon other clergymen in the law relating to that subject passed in 1780, which confines their exercise of that function to those counties where they receive a special license from the court by recommendation, for recording which they are charged with certain fees by the clerk; and which exposes them to a heavy fine for delay in returning certificates of marriages to the office.

The *vestries of the different parishes, a remnant of hierarchical domination,* have a right, by law, to levy money from the people of all denominations for certain purposes; and yet these vestrymen are exclusively required by law to be members of the Episcopal Church, and to subscribe a conformity to its doctrines and discipline as *professed and practiced in England.* Such preferences, distinctions and advantages granted by the Legislature exclusively to one sect of Christians, are regarded by a great number of your constituents as glaring, unjust and dangerous. Their continuance so long in a republic, without animadversion or correction by the Assembly, affords just ground for alarm and complaint to a people who feel themselves, by the favor of Providence, happily free; who are conscious of having deserved as well from the State as those most favored ; who have an undoubted right to think themselves as orthodox in opinion upon every subject as others, and whose privileges are as dear to them. Such partiality to any system of religious opinion whatever is inconsistent with the intention and proper object of well directed government, and obliges men of reflection to consider the Legislature which indulges it, as a party in religious differences, instead of the common guardian and equal protector of every class of citizens in their religious as well as civil rights. We have hitherto restrained our complaints from reaching our representatives, that we might not be thought to take advantage from times of confusion, or critical situation of government in an unsettled state of convulsion and war, to obtain what is our clear and incontestable right.

But as the happy restoration of peace affords leisure for reflection, we wish to state our sense of the objects of this memorial to your honourable House upon the present occasion ; that it might serve to remind you of what might be unnoticed in a multitude of business, and remain as a remonstrance against future encroachments from any quarter. That uncommon liberality of sentiment, which seems daily to gain ground in this enlightened period, encourages us to hope from your wisdom and integrity, gentlemen, a redress of every grievance and remedy of abuse. And invaluable privileges have been purchased by the common blood and treasure of our countrymen of different names and opinions, and therefore ought to be secured in full and perfect equality to them all. We are willing to allow a full share of credit to our fellow-citizens, however distinguished in name from us, for their spirited exertions in our arduous struggle for liberty; we would not wish to charge any of them, either ministers or people, with open disaffection to the common cause of America, or with crafty dissimulation or indecision, till the issue of the war was certain, so as to oppose their obtaining equal privileges in religion ; but we will resolutely engage against any monopoly of the honors or rewards of government by any one sect of Christians more than the rest; for we shun not a comparison with any of our brethren for our efforts in the cause of our country, and assisting to establish her liberties, and therefore esteem it unreasonable that any of them should reap superior advantages for, at most, but equal merit. We expect from the representatives of a free people that all partiality and prejudice on any account whatever will be laid aside, and that the happiness of the citizens at large will be secured upon the broad basis of perfect political equality. This will engage confidence in government, and unsuspicious affection towards our fellow-citizens. We hope that the Legislature will adopt some measures to remove present inequality, and resist any attempt, either at their present session or hereafter, to continue those which we now complain of. Thus by preserving a proper regard to every religious denomination as the common protectors of piety and virtue, you will remove every real ground of contention and allay every jealous commotion on the score of religion. The citizens of Virginia will feel themselves free, unsuspicious and happy in this respect. Strangers will be encouraged to share our freedom and felicity, and when civil and religious liberty go hand in hand, our late posterity will bless the wisdom and virtue of their fathers. We have the satisfaction to assure you that we are steady well-wishers to the State, and your humble servants,

THE PRESBYTERY OF HANOVER.

THE PRESBYTERY OF HANOVER TO THE ASSEMBLY, IN OCTOBER, 1784.

To the Honourable Speaker and House of Delegates of Virginia:

Gentlemen—The united clergy of the Presbyterian church of Virginia assembled in Presbytery beg leave again to address your honorable house upon a few important subjects in which we find ourselves interested as citizens of this State.

The freedom we possess is so rich a blessing, and the purchase of it has been so high that we would ever wish to cherish a spirit of vigilant attention to it in every circumstance of possible danger. We are anxious to retain a full share of all the privileges which our happy revolution affords, and cannot but feel alarmed at the continued existence of any infringement upon them or even any indirect attempt tending to this. Impressed with this idea as men, whose rights are sacred and dear to them, ought to be, we are obliged to express our sensibility upon the present occasion, and we naturally direct our appeal to you gentlemen as the public guardians of our country's happiness and liberty, who are influenced we hope by that wisdom and justice which your high station requires. Conscious of the rectitude of our intention and the strength of our claim, we wish to speak our sentiments freely upon these occasions, but at the same time with all that respectful regard which becomes us when addressing the representatives of a great and virtuous people. It is with pain that we find ourselves obliged to renew our complaints upon the subjects stated in our memorial last spring. We deeply regret that such obvious grievances should exist unredressed in a Republic whose end ought to be the happiness of all the citizens. We presume that immediate redress would have succeeded a clear and just representation of them; as we expect that it is always the desire of our representatives to remove real grounds of uneasiness, and allay jealous commotions amongst the people. But as the objects of the memorial, though very important in their nature, and more so in their probable consequences, have not yet been obtained, we request that the house of delegates would be pleased to recollect what we had the honor to state to them in that paper at their last sessions ; to resume the subject in their present deliberation, and to give it that weight which its importance deserves. The uneasiness which we feel from the continuance of the greviances just referred to is increased under the prospect of an addition to them by certain exceptional measures said to be proposed to the Legislature. We have understood that a comprehensive incorporating act has been and is at present in aggitation, whereby ministers of the gospel as such, of certain descriptions, shall have legal advantages which are not proposed to be extended to the people at large of any denomination. A proposition has been made by some gentlemen in the house of delegates, we are told, to extend the grace to us amongst others in our professional capacity. If this be so we are bound to acknowledge with gratitude our obligations to such gentlemen for their inclination to favor us with the sanction of public authority in the discharge of our duty. But as the scheme of incorporating clergymen, *independent of the religious communities to which they belong,* is inconsistent with our ideas of propriety, we request the liberty of declining **any** such solitary honor should it be again proposed. To form clergymen into a distinct order in the community, and especially where it would be possible for them to have the principal direction of a considerable public estate by such incorporation, has a tendency to render them independent, at length, of the churches whose ministers they are; and this has been too often found by experience to produce ignorance, immorality and neglect of the duties of their station.

Besides, if clergymen were to be erected by the State into a distinct political body, detached from the rest of the citizens, with the express design of "enabling them to direct spiritual matters," which we all possess without such formality, it would naturally tend to introduce the antiquated and absurd system in which government is owned in effect to be the fountain head of spiritual influences to the church. It would establish an immediate, a peculiar, and for that very reason, in our opinion, illicit connection between government and such as were thus distinguished. The Legislature in that case would be the head of the religious party, and its dependent members would be entitled to all decent reciprocity to a becoming paternal and fostering care. This we suppose would be given a preference, and creating a distinction between citizens equally good, on account of something entirely foreign from civil merit, which would be a source of endless jealousies, and inadmissible in a Republic of any other well directed government. The principle, too, which this system aims to establish is both false and dangerous to religion, and we take this opportunity to remonstrate and protest against it. The real ministers of true religion derive their authority to act in the duties of their profession from a higher source than any Legislature on earth, however respectable. Their office relates to the care of the soul, and preparing it for a future state of existence, and their administrations are, or ought to be, of a spiritual nature suited to this momentous concern. And it is plain from the very nature of the case that they should neither expect nor receive from government any commission or direction in this respect. We hope, therefore, that the house of delegates share so large a portion of that philosophic and liberal discernment which prevails in America at present, as to see this matter in its proper light—and that they will understand too well the nature of their duty, as the equal and common guardians of the chartered rights of all the citizens, to permit a connection of this kind we have just now mentioned to subsist between them and the spiritual instructors of any religious denomination in the State. The interference of government in religion cannot be indifferent to us, and as it will probably come under consideration at the present session of the Assembly, we request the attention of the honorable House to our sentiments upon this head.

We conceive that human legislation ought to have human affairs alone for its concern. Legislators in free States possess delegated authority for the good of the community at large in its political and civil capacity.

The existence, preservation and happiness of society should be their only object, and to this their public cares should be confined. Whatever is not materially connected with this lies not within their province as statesmen. The thoughts, the intentions, the faith and the consciences of men, with their modes of worship, lie beyond their reach, and are ever to be referred to a higher and more penetrating tribunal. These internal and spiritual matters cannot be measured by human rule, nor be amenable to human laws. It is the duty of every man for himself to take care of his immortal interests in a future state, where we are to account for our conduct as individuals ; and it is by no means the business of the Legislature to attend to this, for *there* governments and states, as collective bodies, shall no more be known.

Religion, therefore, as a spiritual system, and its ministers in a professional capacity, ought not to be under the direction of the State.

Neither is it necessary for their existence that they should be publicly supported by legal provision for the purpose, as tried experience hath often shown ; although it is absolutely necessary to the existence and welfare of every political combination of men in society to have the support of religion and its solemn institutions, as it affects the conduct of rational beings more than· human laws can possibly do. On this account it is wise policy in legislators to seek its alliance and solicit its aid in a civil view, because of its happy influence upon the morality of its citizens, and its tendency to preserve the veneration of an oath, or an appeal to heaven, which is the cement of the social union. It is upon this principle alone, in our opinion, that a legislative body has right to interfere in religion at all, and of consequence we suppose that this interference ought only to extend to the preserving of the public worship of the Deity, and the supporting of institutions for inculcating the great fundamental principles of all religion, without which society could not easily exist. Should it be thought necessary at present for the Assembly to exert the right of supporting religion in general by an assessment on all the people, we would wish it to be done on the most *liberal plan.* A general assessment of the kind we have heard proposed is an object of such consequence that it excites much anxious speculation amongst your constituents.

We therefore earnestly pray that nothing may be done in the case inconsistent with the proper objects of human legislation, or the Declaration of Rights, as published at the Revolution. We hope that the assessment will not be proposed under the idea of supporting religion as a spiritual system, relating to the care of the soul, and preparing it for its future destiny. We hope that no attempt will be made to point out articles of faith that are not essential to the preservation of society ; or to settle modes of worship ; or to interfere in the internal government of religious communities ; *or to render the ministers of religion independent of the will of the people whom they serve.* We expect from our representatives that careful attention to the political equality of all the citizens which a republic ought ever to cherish, and no scheme of an assessment will be encouraged which will violate the happy privilege we now enjoy of thinking for ourselves in all cases where conscience is concerned.

We request the candid indulgence of the honorable House to the present address, and their most favorable construction of the motives which induce us to obtrude ourselves into public notice. We are urged by a sense of duty. We feel ourselves impressed with the importance of the present crisis. We have expressed ourselves in the plain language of freemen upon the interesting subjects which call for animadversion, and we hope to stand excused with you, gentlemen, for the manner in which it is executed, as well as for the part we take in the public interests of the community. In the present important moment we conceive it criminal to be silent, and have therefore attempted to discharge a duty which we owe our religion as Christians, to ourselves as freemen, and to our posterity, who ought to receive from us a precious birthright of perfect freedom and political equality.

That you may enjoy the direction of heaven in your present deliberations, and possess in a high degree the spirit of your exalted station, is the prayer of your sincere well-wishers,

THE PRESBYTERY OF HANOVER.

To the Honorable the General Assembly of the Commonwealth of Virginia:

The ministers and lay Representatives of the Presbyterian church in Virginia, assembled in convention, beg leave to address you.

As citizens of the State, not so by accident, but by choice, and having willingly conformed to the system of civil policy adopted for our government, and defended it with the foremost at the risk of everything dear to us, we feel ourselves deeply interested in all the measures of the Legislature.

When the late happy Revolution secured to us exemption from British control, we hoped that the gloom of injustice and usurpation would have been forever dispelled by the cheering rays of liberty and independence. This inspired our hearts with resolution in the most distressful scenes of adversity, and nerved our arm in the day of battle. But our hopes have since been overcast with apprehensions when we found how slowly and unwillingly ancient distinctions among the citizens, on account of religious opinions, were removed by the Legislature. For although the glaring partiality of obliging all denominations to support the one which had been the favorite of government was pretty early withdrawn, yet an evident predilection in favor of that church still subsisted in the acts of the Assembly. Peculiar distinctions and the honor of an important name was still continued ; and these are considered as equally partial and injurious with the ancient emoluments. Our apprehension on account of the continuance of these, which could have no other effect than to produce jealous animosities and unnecessary contentions among different parties, were increassd when we found that they were tenaciously adhered to by government, notwithstanding the remonstrances of several Christian societies. To increase the evil, a manifested disposition has been shown by the State to consider itself as possessed of supremacy in *spirituals* as well as *temporal ;* and our fears have been realized in certain proceedings of the General Assembly at their last sessions. The ingrossed bill for establishing a provision for the teachers of the Christian religion, and the act for incorporating the Protestant Episcopal church, so far as it secures to that church the churches, glebes, etc., procured at the expense of the whole community, are not only evidences of this, but of an impolitic partiality which we are sorry to have observed so long.

We, therefore, in the name of the Presbyterian church in Virginia, beg leave to exercise our privilege as free men in remonstrating against the former absolutely, and against the latter under the restrictions above expressed.

We oppose the bill—

Because it is a departure from the proper line of legislation ; because it is unnecessary, and inadequate to its professed end—impolitic, in many respects—and a direct violation of the Declaration of Rights.

The end of civil government is security to the temporal liberty and property of mankind, and to protect them in the free exercise of religion. Legislators are invested with powers from their constituents for this purpose only ; and their duty extends no further. Religion is altogether personal, and the right of exercising it unalienable ; and it is not, cannot, and ought not to be, resigned to the will of the society at large ; and much less to the Legislature, which derived its authority wholly from the consent of the people, and is limited by the original intention of civil association.

We never resigned to the control of government our right of determining for ourselves in this important article ; and acting agreeably to the convictions of reason and conscience, in discharging our duty to our Creator. And, therefore, it would be an unwarrantable stretch of prerogative in the Legislature to make laws concerning it, except for protection. And it would be a fatal symptom of abject slavery in us were we to submit to the usurpation.

The bill is also an unnecessary and inadequate expedient for the end proposed. We are fully persuaded of the happy influences of Christianity upon the morals of men ; but we have never known it, in the history of its progress, so effectual for this purpose, as when left to its native excellence and evidence to recommend it, under the all-directing providence of God, and free from the intrusive hand of the civil magistrate. Its Divine Author did not think it necessary to render it dependent on earthly governments. And experience has shown that this dependence, where it has been effected, has been an injury rather than an aid. It has introduced corruption among the teachers and professors of it wherever it has been tried for hundreds of years, and has been destructive of genuine morality, in proportion to zeal, of the powers of this world, in arming it with the sanction of legal terrors, or inviting to its profession by honors and rewards.

It is urged, indeed, by the abettors of this bill that it would be the means of cherishing religion and morality among the citizens. But it appears from fact that these can be promoted only by the internal conviction of the mind and its voluntary choice, which such establishments cannot effect.

We further remonstrate against the bill as an impolitic measure ; it disgusts so large a proportion of the citizens that it would weaken the influence of government in other respects, and diffuse a spirit of opposition to the rightful exercise of constitutional authority, if enacted into a law.

It partially supposes the Quakers and Menonists to be more faithful in conducting the religious interests of their society than the other sects—which we apprehend to be contrary to fact.

It unjustly subjects men who may be good citizens, but who have not embraced our common faith, to the hardship of supporting a system they have not as yet believed the truth of ; and deprives them of their property for what they do not suppose to be of importance to them.

It establishes a precedent for further encroachments by making the Legislature judges of religious truth. If the Assembly have a right to determine the preference between Christianity and the other systems of religion that prevail in the world, they may also, at a convenient time, give a preference to some favored sect among Christians.

It discourages the population of our country by alarming those who may have been oppressed by religious establishments in other countries, with fears of the same in this ; and by exciting our own citizens to immigrate to other lands of greater freedom,

It revives the principle which our ancestors contested to blood, of attempting to reduce all religions to one standard by the force of civil authority.

And it naturally opens a door for contention among citizens of different creeds and different opinions respecting the extent of the power of government.

The bill is also a direct violation of the Declaration of Rights, which ought to be the standard of all laws. The sixteenth article is clearly infringed upon by it, and any explication which may have been given of it by the friends of this measure in the Legislature, so as to justify a departure from its literal construction, might also be used to deprive us of other fundamental principles of our government.

For these reasons, and other that might be produced, we conceive it our duty to remonstrate and protest against the said bill, and earnestly urge that it may not be enacted into law.

We wish also to engage your attention a little farther, while we request a revision of the act for incorporating the Protestant Episcopal Church, and state our reason for this request. We do not desire to oppose the incorporation of that church for the better management of its *temporalities* ; neither do we wish to lesson the attachment of any of the members of the Legislature in a private capacity to the interest of that church. We rather wish to cultivate a spirit of forbearance and charity towards the members of it, as the servants of one common Master who differ in some particulars from each other. But we cannot consent that they shall receive particular notice or favor from government as a Christian society, nor peculiar distinctions or emoluments.

We find by the Act that the convenience of the Episcopal Church hath been consulted by it in the management of their interest as a religious society, at the expense of other denominations. Under the former establishment there were perhaps few men who did not at length perceive the hardships and injustice of a compulsory law, obliging the citizens of this State, by birthright free, to contribute to the support of a religion from which their reason and conscience oblige them to dissent. Who then would not have supposed that the same sense of justice which induced the Legislature to dissolve the grievous establishment would also have induced them to leave to common use the property in churches, glebes, etc, which had been acquired by common purchase.

To do otherwise was, as we conceive, to suppose that long prescriptions could sanction injustice, and that to persist in error is to alter the essential difference between right and wrong. As Christians, also, the subjects of Jesus Christ, who are wholly opposed to the exercise of the spiritual powers by civil rulers, we conceive ourselves obliged to remonstrate against that part of the incorporating act which authorizes and directs the regulation of spiritual concerns. This is such an invasion of Divine prerogative that it is highly exceptionable on that account, as well as on account of the danger to which it exposes our religious liberties. Jesus Christ hath given sufficient authority to his church for every lawful purpose, and it is forsaking his authority and direction for that of fallible men, to expect or to grant the sanction of civil law to authorize the regulation of any Christian society. It is also dangerous to our liberties, because it creates an invidious distiction on account of religious opinion, and exalts to 'a superior pitch of grandeur, as the church of the State, a society which ought to be contented with receiving the same protection from government which the other societies enjoy, without aspiring to superior notice or regard. The Legislature assumes to itself by that law the authoritative direction of this church in spirituals, and can be considered in no other light than its head, peculiarly interested in its welfare, a matter which cannot be indifferent to us, though this authority has only as yet been extended to those who have requested it, or acquiesced in it. This church is now considered as the only regular church, in view of the law, and it is thereby raised to a state of unjust pre-eminence over others. And how far it may increase in dignity and influence in the State by these means at a future day, and especially when aided by the emoluments which it possesses, and the advantages of funding a very large sum of money without account, time alone can discover. But we esteem it our duty to oppose the act thus early, before the matter be entangled in precedents more intricate and dangerous. Upon the whole, therefore, we hope that the exceptional part of this act will be repealed by your honorable House, and that all preferences, distinctions and advantages contrary to the fourth article of the Declaration of Rights will be forever abolished.

We regret that full equality in all things, and ample protection and security to religious liberty, were not incontestibly fixed in the constitution of the government. But we earnestly request that the defect may be remedied as far as it is possible for the Legislature to do it, by the adopting the bill in the revised law for establishing religious freedom. (Chap. 82 of the Report).

That heaven may illuminate your minds with all that wisdom which is necessary for the important purposes of your deliberation, is our earnest wish. And we beg leave to assure you, that however warmly we may engage in preserving our religion, free from the shackles of human authority, and opposing claims of spiritual denominations in civil powers, we are zealously disposed to support the government of our country, and to maintain a due submission to the lawful exercise of its authority.

Signed by order of the Convention.

JOHN TODD, Chairman.

Attest :—Daniel McCalla, Clerk, Bethel, Augusta County, 13th August, 1785.

E.

REVIEW OF PRESBYTERIAN MEMORIALS, IN REPLY TO MR. HENRY.

[*Religious Herald.*]

Bro. Editor—The Hon. Wm. Wirt Henry, in his article of October 7th, says : "Up to this date, the adoption of the Virginia Constitution in 1776, it thus appears that the views of the Presbyterians and Baptists in Virginia, on the subject of religious liberty, coincided, and Dr. James cannot point to a single expression of any representative body authorized to speak for the Presbyterians which indicated the contrary."

I accept the challenge, and will meet it, first, by referring him to the record of the Presbyterians, on that subject, from their origin, under Calvin, down to the time when many of them fled from persecution, in the old world, to America ; and, secondly, by a review of Dr. Foote's Sketches and the Memorials of the Hanover Presbytery, given by him.

It will certainly not be claimed that, at the time of their settlement in this new world, they were in harmony with the Baptists on the question of soul liberty. That they should have learned some wholesome lessons from their own sufferings, is not to be wondered at. The wonder is that they did not learn more—that they did not learn better than to use the civil power for the oppression of others, as they did in the Northern Colonies, wherever they had control of the civil arm. Their course was different in Virginia, but why? Was it because they were constitutionally and unequivocally opposed to any sort of union between Church and State, and opposed to the use of the latter to sustain the former, and to suppress what they might be pleased to call heresy? If we, like Patrick Henry, are to be "guided by the lamp of experince," and if we are "to judge the future by the past," we shall find it extremely difficult to answer this question in the affirmative. The record of the Presbyterians up to that time—the time of their settlement in Virginia—would seem to require a negative answer. Who will dare say that, had they been in the position of the Episcopalians, they would not have done here what they had done elsewhere? But they were few in Virginia, at that time, while Episcopacy was the established religion.

It is not difficult to understand why they should have sided with the Baptists, the most numerous and powerful body of dissenters, as against the oppressive Establishment. Nor is it difficult to see that the result of this alliance was to bring Presbyterians and Baptists into closer sympathy and into greater unanimity of opinion on the vital question of freedom of conscience. Hence we are prepared to admit that the Hanover Presbytery was in advance of their denomination in America, and that they occupied higher ground than had hitherto been occupied by any other Presbyterian body. But we do not believe that, at the date of the Revolution, they were in full accord with their Baptist brethren on that question. And we will now undertake to sustain this opinion by a review of Dr. Foote's "Sketches," a standard Presbyterian authority.

We have already discussed Dr. Foote's meaning when he spoke of the contest in Virginia "for an ill-defined liberty of conscience." He was then describing the state of things when the principle of religious liberty was incorporated in the Bill of Rights in 1776. We are willing to grant "that Dr. Foote, in this passage, is speaking of the growth of the principle of religious liberty among the people at large." But we are not willing to grant that he "has no more reference to Presbyterians than to any others." It is manifest from his history that he is chiefly concerned about the attitude of his own people, for while he touches upon the proceedings of the Baptists and others, he gives a most elaborate account of the proceedings of the Hanover Presbytery, quoting in full their Memorials to the General Assembly, from 1776 to 1785, concerning the last of which he says : " *This paper expressed the true feeling of the Presbyterian church, after much private and public discussion.*"

Now, I maintain that all along, from 1775 to 1785, Dr. Foote is "tracing the growth of the principle of religious liberty" among his own people, and that he means, in the language above quoted and which I have *italicized*, to assert, that, *after much* private and *public discussion*, running through that Revolutionary period, the Presbyterians of Virginia reached the goal, at last, in the unanimous adoption of the Memorial of August, 1785, in which, *for the first time*, they asked that Jefferson's Bill for the Establishment of Religious Freedom might become the law of the State. If that is not Dr. Foote's meaning, then I have failed to understand him.

But Mr. Henry would point to the Memorials of the Hanover Presbytery as telling a different story, and he quotes from them largely to sustain his view. Unfortunately for his view, there are some things in those Memorials which he does not quote, and which I will now give to your readers, and which will enable them to decide between Mr. Henry and Dr. Howell.

In order to appreciate the Memorials in question, and the attitude of the Hanover Presbytery in that transition period, we must keep in mind the very important distinction between the church polity of Episcopalians, Presbyterians, and Baptists—the three principal denominations then in Virginia. Episcopacy is "the government of the church by bishops or prelates." Presbyterianism is "that form of church government which invests presbyters, or elders, with all spiritual power, and admits no prelates over them." The Baptist church polity, known as the independent or republican, lodges the government in the hands of the members of the local church. Now, supposing that all three of these sects were in favor of an establishment, and of the support of the church by taxation, it would be impossible for them to agree as to the particular form of the establishment. The Episcopalians would want the clergy incorporated, independently of the congregations; the Baptists would insist upon the incorporation of the members of the church as such, without distinction between clergy and laity; while the Presbyterians, occupying a middle ground, would oppose both of these schemes, and insist that the act of incorporation should be so framed as to leave the government in the hands of the elders, but not so as to make the *preaching elders* independent of their congregations. In the nature of the case, an establishment which would suit either of the extremes would destroy Presbyterianism as a system of church polity. Let us keep this well in mind, as we scan the Memorials of the Hanover Presbytery, and let us remember that, at the date of the Revolution, Episcopacy was the established religion in Virginia, that the Baptists were the most numerous body of dissenters, and that the Presbyterians, though a very respectable and influential body, were too few in numbers to hope for such an establishment as would accord with their views. The best that they, the Presbyterians, could do was to coöperate with the Baptists in the effort to pull down the existing establishment and to place all upon an equal footing before the law. Now to the Memorials which they sent up to the Legislature from 1775 to 1785.

The first Memorial is that of November 11, 1774, which was presented to the House of Burgesses June 5, 1775, and which places them alongside of the Baptists as against the toleration act and against any legislation which did not give to them equal rights, etc., with their fellow-citizens.

The next is that of October, 1776, to which reference has been made in former articles. That was a noble production, written, doubtless, by their ablest men. The quotations made by Mr. Henry would leave little room for doubt that the Hanover Presbytery was, by this memorial, fully and unequivocally committed to the broadest religious liberty and the most entire separation between Church and State. But the following extract, towards the close of the memorial, raises a little doubt. After discussing the questions in hand at some length, they say : "And for the reasons recited we are induced earnestly to entreat, that all laws now in force in this Commonwealth, which countenance religious domination, may be speedily repealed—that all, of every religious sect, may be protected in the full exercise of their several modes of worship ; *and exempted from all taxes for the support of any church whatsoever, further than what may be agreeable to their own private choice or voluntary obligation.*" Mark those italicized words. We will hereafter see how those words may be construed when the Establishment is torn down and the time for readjustment comes.

The next memorial is that of April, 1777, which refers to the *variety of opinions touching the propriety of a general assessment,* and calls the attention of the Legislature to their prayer in their former memorial : "That dissenters of every denomination may be exempted from all taxes for the support of any church whatsoever, further than what may be agreeable to the private choice or voluntary obligation of every individual ; while the civil magistrates no otherwise interfere, than to protect them all in the full and free exercise of their several modes of worship." Now, weigh well the following from the latter part of the same memorial : "These things being considered, we hope we shall be excused for remonstrating against a general assessment for any religious purpose. As the maxims have long been approved, that every servant is to obey his master ; and that the hireling is accountable for his conduct to him from whom he receives his wages ; in like manner, if the Legislature has any rightful authority over the ministers of the gospel in the exercise of their sacred office, and it is their duty to levy a maintenance for them as such; then it will follow that they may revive the old Establishment in its former extent; or ordain a new one for any sect they think proper; they are invested with a power not only to determine, but it is incumbent on them to declare who shall preach, what they shall preach; to whom, when, at what places they shall preach; or to impose any regulations and restrictions upon religious societies that they may judge expedient." *The question will come up, as one reads this, whether they objected to an assessment, per se, or whether they were afraid that any assessment bill, which could be adopted, would give the State the right to interfere in the government of the church.*

I find no other memorial until May, 1784; but Mr. Henry finds, in April, 1780, the following record : "A memorial to the Assembly of Virginia from this Presbytery, *to abstain from interfering in the government of the church,* was prepared, and being read in Presbytery, is appointed and directed to be transmitted to the House." You will observe that their great concern was *lest the State should interfere in the government of the church.* The establishment had been virtually destroyed the year before, and Jefferson's bill for establishing religious freedom had been reported the same year, 1779, but this memorial of 1780 ignores it. Why did not the Presbyterians rally to the support of that bill? Was that, too, "*accidental*" ? The sequel will show.

There is an ominous silence for four years, until May, 1784, when the Hanover Presbytery is heard from again, in a lengthy memorial, covering two pages of Dr. Foote's book, the burden of which is a protest against certain peculiar privileges which were still granted the Episcopal church, and demanding that the Legislature should be impartial. *Not one word about the assessment, nor a word about Jefferson's bill.* What's the matter? We think their long silence on these topics was due to the fact that there was division among them. They were not agreed. They had started out in October, 1776, with "their faces as though they would go to Jerusalem," but there was a side door in that memorial, through which they might turn aside and stop at Samaria. There was a growing sentiment in favor of "the new theory of an establishment," which would "take them in," and in October, 1784, that theory gets a majority vote in Presbytery.

Let me here introduce the testimony of Semple, "in whose accuracy as a historian" the Hon. Mr. Henry "has great confidence."

Semple says, p. 73 : "The Baptists, we believe, were the only sect who plainly remonstrated [against the assessment]. Of some others it is said that the laity and ministry were at variance upon the subject, so as to paralyze their exertions either for or against the bill· These remarks, by the by, apply only to religious societies, acting as such. Individuals of all sects and parties joined in the opposition."

Let us now examine the memorial of the Hanover Presbytery of October, 1784. I will quote at length, that your readers may the better comprehend its nature. After referring to their former memorial (May, 1784), and expressing regret that "immediate redress" had not been granted, they say : "The uneasiness which we feel from the continuance of the grievances just referred to, is increased under the prospect of an addition to them by certain exceptionable measures said to be proposed to the Legislature. We have understood that a comprehensive incorporation act has been and is at present in agitation, whereby ministers of the gospel, as such, of certain descriptions, shall have legal advantages which are not proposed to be extended to the people at large of any denomination. A proposition has been made by some gentlemen of the House of Delegates, we are told, to extend the grace to us, amongst others, in our professional capacity. If this be so, we are bound to acknowledge our obligations to such gentlemen for their inclination to favor us with the sanction of public authority in the discharge of our duty. But as the scheme of incorporating clergymen, *independent of the religious communities to which they belong*, is inconsistent with our ideas of propriety, we request the liberty of declining any such solitary honor, should it be again proposed. To form clergymen into a distinct order in the community, and especially where it would be possible for them to have the principal direction of a considerable public estate by such incorporation, has a tendency to render them independent, at length, of the churches, whose ministers they are ; and this has been too often found by experience to produce ignorance, immorality, and neglect of the duties of their station." The memorial then goes on to show how the tendency of this measure would be to make "the Legislature the head of a religious party," composed of ministers, and "the fountain head of spiritual influences to the church," etc. It proceeds : "Religion, therefore, as a spiritual system, and its ministers in a professional capacity, ought not to be under the direction of the State." . . . "Should it be thought necessary at present for the Assembly to exert this right of supporting religion in general by an assessment on all the people, we would wish it to be done on the most *liberal plan.* A general assessment of the kind we have heard proposed is an object of such consequence that it excites much anxious speculation amongst your constituents. We therefore earnestly pray that nothing may be done in the case inconsistent with the proper objects of human legislation, or the Declaration of Rights as published at the Revolution. We hope that the assessment will not be proposed under the idea of supporting religion as a spiritual system, relating to the care of the soul and preparing it for its future destiny. We hope that no attempt will be made to point out articles of faith that are not essential to the preservation of society ; or to settle modes of worship ; or to interfere in the internal government of religious communities ; or *to render the ministers of religion independent of the will of the people whom they serve.*"

Along with this memorial—which your readers can criticise for themselves—was sent up to the Legislature " a plan, agreeably to which alone Presbytery are willing to admit a general assessment for the support of religion by law." The leading principles of this plan, as given by Dr. Foote, are as follows : " 1st. Religion as a spiritual system is not to be considered as an object of human legislation, but may, in a civil view, as preserving the existence and promoting the happiness of society. 2d. That public worship and public periodical instruction to the people be maintained, in this view, by a general assessment for this purpose. 3d. That every man, as a good citizen, be obliged to declare himself attached to some religious community, publicly known to profess the belief of one God, his righteous providence, our accountableness to him, and a future state of rewards and punishments," etc., etc. I need not quote any further. It is manifest that the Hanover Presbytery were not unconditionally opposed to incorporation and assessment bills ; but that, while irreconcilably opposed to any bill which would be acceptable to Episcopalians, in that it incorporated the clergy to the exclusion of the laity, and thus made them independent of their congregations, etc., they were quite willing for the Legislature to pass an incorporation act on the "*plan*" which they proposed—a plan which, among other things, required every citizen to belong to some religious society, and to profess faith in a certain creed.

The General Assembly met in October, 1784, and steps were taken

looking to the passage of incorporation and assessment bills. The
journal for the House of Delegates has, for November 18, the following entry : "A petition of John Todd and John B. Smith, . . .
explaining so much of the memorial of the Hanover Presbytery as
respects the incorporation of religious societies, and praying that the
distinction therein stated may be preserved." On the 24th of
December, the vote on the assessment bill was postponed until the
fourth Thursday in November, 1785, and the bill was ordered to be
printed and distributed among the people. The Hanover Presbytery
met at Bethel, Augusta county, May 19, 1785, and "a petition
was presented to the Presbytery from the session of Augusta congregation, requesting an explication of the word '*liberal*' as used in the
Presbytery's memorial of last fall ; and also the motives and end of
the Presbytery in sending it to the Assembly." *Trouble in the camp !*
"A committee was appointed to prepare an answer and report. On
motion, the opinion of Presbytery was taken—whether they do
approve of any kind of an assessment by the General Assembly for
the support of religion. *Presbytery are unanimously against such a
measure.*" *Madison's " Remonstrance " was after that measure dealing it
deadly blows, and the tide of opposition was swelling every day.* The
Presbyterians issued a call for a "General Convention of the Presbyterian body," to be held at Bethel, August 10, 1785, where they
again fell into line with the Baptists on a *right about march !* The
memorial of this Convention was *the first Presbyterian memorial which
asked for the passage of the "bill for Establishing Religious Freedom."*
And it was this memorial which Dr. Foote said "*expressed the true
feeling of the Presbyterian church, after much private and public discussion.*" Their otherwise satisfactory memorials of '76 and '77, which
were sent up while the Establishment was in force, were open to
criticism, and left some room for doubt whether they would be unwilling to accept a modified form of Establishment, *i. e.*, an Establishment which would not be destructive of their own system of
church polity. And when we duly consider two significant facts—
viz., (1) the almost unbroken silence of the Presbytery from that
time (1777) down to the year 1784, when they exposed themselves
to severe criticism at the hands of Jefferson and Madison and others,
and (2) the fact that Jefferson's bill for establishing religious freedom, though before the Legislature from '79 to '85, never received
the approbation of their official body, but only of that unofficial and

hastily called Convention of August, 1785, I think we are justified in concluding that Dr. Foote, in the language above quoted, means to say that not until 1785 did the Presbyterians of Virginia reach solid standing ground on the great question of soul liberty. Both he and Dr. Baird speak of the action of Presbytery in 1784 as a "*wavering*" in the fight, and they very naturally put the most liberal and charitable construction upon it by attributing it to a conviction, on the part of Presbytery, that some sort of assessment would be made anyhow, and to a desire to render it as unobjectionable as possible. But let us see how their action was viewed by others. I have already (August 12) given the opinions of James Madison and Dr. Hawks. There are two or three others whose testimony ought to be heard.

Thomas Jefferson, in giving an account of the struggle from 1776 to 1779, over the question "whether a general assessment should not be established by law, on every one, to the support of the pastor of his choice, or whether all should be left to voluntary contributions," says : "Some of our dissenting allies, having now secured their particular object, went over to the advocates of a general assessment." Jefferson's Works, Vol. I., p. 39.

Prof. Tucker, in his Life of Jefferson, Vol. I., p. 98, says of the same struggle : "The advocates of the latter (voluntary) plan were only able to obtain, at each session, a suspension of those laws which provided salaries for the clergy—the natural progress in favor of liberal sentiments being counterbalanced by the fact that *some of the dissenting sects, with the exception of the Baptists*, satisfied with having been relieved from a tax which they felt to be both unjust and degrading, had no objection to a general assessment; and, on this question, voted with the friends of the church."

Rives, in his Life and Times of Madison, Vol. I., p. 602, says of the assessment bill : "What is specially remarkable is, that in a memorial presented by the united clergy of the Presbyterian church, a body which had hitherto distinguished itself by its zeal in favor of the principle of unlimited religious freedom—an opinion was now expressed, as cited in the journal of the House of Delegates, that '*a general assessment for the support of religion ought to be extended to those who profess the public worship of the Deity.' It is, perhaps, not to be wondered at, that, among a people accustomed from the earliest times to see religion lean for support on the arm of secular power, an apprehension should have been felt of its decline upon the withdrawal of that support.*"
(Italics mine).

With the evidence thus given by these several witnesses, I submit the case to the jury—your readers. I feel confident that their verdict will be that, "at the date of the Revolution," "the views of the Presbyterians did *not* fully coincide with the views of the Baptists on the subject of religious liberty." Whether they will agree with Dr. Howell, that "the new theory of an Establishment" was of Presbyterian parentage, I am not quite so sure. Really, Bro. Editor, I am beginning to have a touch of sympathy for that cast-off child. It seems now to have been like Melchisedec, "without father or mother." Had it not fallen into disrepute and come to an "end of life," it would have been quite different. The real parents would have been willing to own their offspring. We read in "an old book" of a contest between two women, both of whom had become mothers in the same house, and about the same time. One of the infants having died, its mother disowned it and set up a claim to the living child of her neighbor, and the case came before a very wise judge for adjudication. We will not say that Dr. Howell was a Solomon, but we will venture the opinion that he succeeded quite well in determining the true parentage of two other offspring, which were born during the night of the Revolution—viz., the "bill for Establishing Religious Freedom," and the "New Theory of an Establishment." It is certain that the Presbyterians of Virginia never asked for the former until the latter was dead.

C. F. JAMES.

Culpeper, Va.

F.

PRESBYTERIANS AND RELIGIOUS LIBERTY.

BY REV. C. F. JAMES, D. D.

[Central Baptist, July 26, 1888.]

Some of your readers know that, ever since the struggle for religious liberty in Virginia was ended in 1785, by the defeat of the "General Assessment" and the passage of Jefferson's "Statute for Religious Freedom," many of our Presbyterian friends have been trying to get rid of the reproach of having broken ranks in the midst of that fight, and to make it appear to the world that the Presbyterians did equally valiant and faithful service with the Baptists. In some respects, at least, their case is similar to that of a certain company of the Eighth Virginia Infantry in the battle of Ball's Bluff. Soon after the battle opened in earnest, this company, for some cause, not necessary to explain here, fell back and did not stop until they had cleared the woods in which the battle was raging. Finding that the other companies had not followed their example, but were holding their ground against the enemy and beating them back, the captain rallied his men, faced them about and marched them back at double-quick to rejoin their comrades. Fortunately for their reputation, they got back into line just in time to join in the final charge with those who had borne the heat and burden of the day. They had the modesty and discretion, however, not to claim equal credit with those *who did not fall back.*

The Presbyterians of Revolutionary times went into the fight as allies of the Baptists and others, as against the Establishment and apparently in favor of absolute religious freedom. But when the first shock of the battle resulted in the overthrow of the existing Establishment, they broke ranks and went over to the Episcopalians and Methodists in favor of the General Incorporation and General Assessment Bills. But the Baptists never wavered. Solitary and alone of the religious sects of that day, they held their ground against every proposition which had any squint towards a union of

Church and State and the support of religion by taxation. With Madison's "Remonstrance" in one hand and their petitions to the General Assembly in the other, they canvassed every county until the Presbyterians, ashamed of themselves, and convinced that Madison and the Baptists were going to win the day, ordered a "right about" in their Convention of August, 1785, and came in with the opposition before the legislature which met in October. They are to be congratulated that they did *right about* and join the Baptists in the final charge. And had they been content with the credit which was their due, it would have been far more honorable and creditable to them. But they are not content with their just meed of praise. Many of them claim equal credit with the Baptists and have been doing so for years. But your readers, while somewhat accustomed to hearing the cry, will be amazed to learn that the *Presbyterians* and *not the Baptists* were the *pioneers* in that struggle for religious liberty in Virginia, and that "the largest part of the credit of this great work" belongs "to the Hanover Presbytery." And yet such is the claim now set up in the year of our Lord, 1888. The basis of the claim is an old manuscript of a memorial of the Hanover Presbytery dated November 11, 1774, discovered by the Hon. Wm. Wirt Henry, published for the first time in the *Central Presbyterian* the 16th of last May. Some unknown friend did me the kindness to send me a copy of the paper which gives the memorial in full, together with a prefatory note from the discoverer and a lengthy notice from the editor. It is claimed for this long-hidden document, which, according to Mr. Henry, eluded the search of the diligent investigator, Dr. Foote, that it antedated all other petitions to the Virginia Assembly claiming equal rights for dissenters, that it was "the advance guard of that army of remonstrances which so vigorously attaked the Establishment, and finally overpowered it, and established perfect religious liberty on its ruins;" and that it, "taken in connection with the able memorial of Hanover Presbytery of 1776 and 1777," was actually the source whence Thomas Jefferson "got his views of religious liberty." The Baptists are no longer to stand at the head of the religious liberty class, but must yield that place to the Presbyterians. Such is the result of this recent discovery; that is, if Mr. Henry and the editor of the *Central Presbyterian* are correct in their reading and interpretation of this manuscript. But, unfortunately for them, this manuscript, like the New Testament, will not read the way they want it to read. Let us look at it for a moment and see what it says in behalf of the Presbyterians of 1774.

It seems that "in 1772 a bill was introduced into the House of Burgesses, having for its professed object the better security of the religious liberty of Protestant dissenters in the colony, but really contrived for their oppression in several particulars." For example, the bill required dissenting ministers to preach only at regularly licensed preaching places, never to hold services with closed doors, and never to receive and baptize servants without the consent of their masters. These restrictions were doubtless aimed chiefly at the Baptists, but they applied to all dissenters alike. And this memorial of the Hanover Presbytery in 1774 is simply a respectful and well written protest against those provisions of the bill which they regarded as "grievous and burdensome," and an appeal to the Assembly for all the privileges which were granted to dissenters under the "English Toleration Act." The *ground* of their protest and appeal was "an instrument of writing under the seal of the colony, containing the most ample assurances that they (the Presbyterians who came from Pennsylvania to Virginia) should enjoy the full and free exercise of their religion and all the other privileges of good subjects." This agreement was made by Governor Gooch about the year 1738, and "for the encouragement of all Presbyterians who might be inclined to settle in the colony." The fact of such agreement is stated in the beginning of the memorial and urged as a sufficient reason why they should not be harassed by oppressive and restrictive legislation. But there are always two sides to such a contract, and, if the Colonial Government was bound by this agreement of 1738 not to oppress the Presbyterians who claimed protection under it, so were the Presbyterians bound to acquiesce in and submit to the existing establishment in Virginia and not to seek its overthrow. Accordingly there is not the slightest intimation given in this memorial of any disloyalty to the establishment, or of any desire even to be relieved of taxation for its support. They accept in good faith the existing order of things, and only ask that "*faith,*" as to that agreement of 1738, "*be fully kept.*" What makes this doubly certain that this memorial is no "advance guard" of "remonstrances against the establishment," and no religious liberty document, is the fact that, towards its close, they referred to the

"English Act of Toleration," and ask for dissenters in Virginia the same privileges as are granted under that act to dissenters in England. This is the sum and substance of their memorial. No protest against the Establishment; no appeal for anything more than the broadest toleration, and no hint that they recognized any difference between *toleration* and *liberty*; and if we are to judge Mr. Henry and the editor of the *Central Presbyterian* by their comments upon this document, we must say that *they* have not yet learned the difference, and need that some one should instruct them in the way more perfectly. It is not at all surprising that the Presbyterian historian, Dr. Foote, in giving a full and detailed account of what the Presbyterians did for religious liberty in Virginia, did not see any reason for laying this memorial before his readers. And when we come to think about it, it should not be a matter of surprise to us that men who can so read the New Testament as to find *infant baptism* and *sprinkling* there, should be able to find the great doctrine of *religious liberty* in this memorial of the Hanover Presbytery.

It would have been a little more generous in the editor had he been content with claiming too much for the Hanover Presbytery as to their achievements in that memorable struggle. But he must detract from the Baptists, by reiterating, in the face of the testimony of Semple and that of the Journal of the Convention of '75, the statement that "the first Baptist memorial of 1775 simply asked 'for the liberty of preaching to the troops at convenient times without molestation or abuse;'" and also by informing his readers that the Presbyterian memorials "far surpass in ability and learning those of the Baptist Association," whose ministers were "without learning and without patronage." All the greater shame, then, upon the Presbyterians of that day, that they did not really lead in the fight for religious liberty, but came in behind the Baptists, as the records clearly prove, then broke ranks in the midst of the contest, and allowed the "unlearned" Baptists to go down in history as "the only sect" that never deserted the standard of Jefferson and Madison in that memorable struggle which culminated in 1785.

On one occasion, during the Revolution, the famous Tarleton, in marching through the Carolinas, stopped at the house of a patriot lady and called for dinner. Forgetful of the proprieties of the occasion, he began to criticise Colonel Washington, saying to his hostess,

"I hear that he is so illiterate that he cannot write his name.'' The high-spirited dame retorted that he could at least "*make his mark*"—referring to a recent encounter between Washington and Tarleton, in which the latter came off second best and with *the mark* of Washington's sword upon his person. Granted that the Baptists of those Revolutionary times could not talk and write as well as their Presbyterian allies, they succeeded quite well in making the political leaders of that day understand the meaning of religious liberty, as distinguished from mere toleration, and they made a mark on the page of Virginia's history which can never be effaced —a record of courage, and piety, and unfaltering devotion to the principles of civil and religious liberty which no faithful historian will ever assail. The Baptists of the present day, though more learned and cultivated, have no cause to blush at the mention of their fathers of the Revolution.

Culpeper, Va.

G.

MADISON'S REMONSTRANCE.

To the Honorable the General Assembly of the Commonwealth of Virginia:

We, the subscribers, citizens of the said Commonwealth, having taken into serious consideration a bill, printed by order of the last session of General Assembly, entitled "A bill establishing a provision for teachers of the Christian religion"; and conceiving that the same, if finally armed with the sanctions of a law, will be a dangerous abuse of power, are bound, as faithful members of a free State, to remonstrate against it, and to declare the reasons by which we are determined. We remonstrate against the said bill:

Because we hold it for a fundamental and unalienable truth, "that religion, or the duty which we owe to the Creator, and the manner of discharging it, can be directed only by reason and conviction, not by force or violence."* The religion, then, of every man must be left to the conviction and conscience of every man; and it is the right of every man to exercise it as these may dictate. This right is, in its nature, an unalienable right. It is unalienable, because the opinions of men depending only on the evidence contemplated by their own minds, cannot follow the dictates of other men. It is unalienable, also, because what is here a right towards man is a duty towards the Creator. It is the duty of every man to render to the Creator such homage, and such only, as he believes to be acceptable to him. This duty is precedent, both in order of time and in degree of obligation, to the claims of civil society. Before any man can be considered as a member of civil society he must be considered as a subject of the Governor of the Universe. And if a member of civil society who enters into any subordinate association must always do it with a reservation of his duty to the general authority, much more must every man who becomes a member of any particular civil society do it with a saving of his allegiance to the Universal Sovereign. We maintain, therefore, that in matters of religion, no man's right is abridged by the institution of civil society, and that religion

---

*Declaration of Rights, Article XVI.

is wholly exempt from its cognizance. True it is that no other rule exists by which any question which may divide a society can be ultimately determined but by the will of the majority. But it is also true that the majority may trespass on the rights of the minority. Because, if religion be exempt from the authority of the society at large, still less can it be subject to that of the legislative body. The latter are but the creatures and vicegerents of the former. Their jurisdiction is both derivitive and limited. It is limited with regard to the coördinate departments ; more necessarily is it limited with regard to the constituents. The preservation of a free government requires not merely that the metes and bounds which separate each department of power be invariably maintained, but more especially that neither of them be suffered to overleap the great barrier which defends the rights of the people. The rulers who are guilty of such encroachment exceed the commission from which they derive their authority, and are tyrants. The people who submit to it are governed by laws made neither by themselves nor by an authority derived from them, and are slaves.

Becouse it is proper to take alarm at the first experiment on our liberties. We hold this prudent jealousy to be the first duty of citizens and one of the noblest characteristics of the late revolution. The freemen of America did not wait until usurped power had strengtnened itself by exercise and entangled the question in precedents. They saw all the consequences in the principle, and they avoided the consequences by denying the principle. We revere this lesson too much soon to forget it. Who does not see that the same authority which can establish Christianity in exclusion of all other religions may establish with the same ease any particular sect of Christians in exclusion of all other sects ? That the same authority which can force a citizen to contribute three pence only of his property for the support of any one establishment may force him to conform to any other establishment in all cases whetsoever.

Because the bill violates that equality which ought to be the basis of every law, and which is more indispensable in proportion as the validity or expediency of any law is more liable to be impeached. "If all men are by nature equally free and independent,"* all men are to be considered as entering into society on equal conditions, as relinquishing no more, and therefore retaining no less, one than

---

*Declaration of Rights, Article I.

another of their natural rights ; above all are they to be considered as retaining an "*equal* title to the free exercise of religion according to the dictates of conscience."* Whilst we assert for ourselves a freedom to embrace, to profess and observe the religion which we believe to be of divine origin, we cannot deny an equal freedom to those whose minds have not yielded to the evidence which has convinced us. If this freedom be abused it is an offence against God, not against man. To God, therefore, and not to man, must an account of it be rendered.

As the bill violates equality by subjecting some to peculiar burdens, so it violates the same principle by granting to others peculiar exemptions. Are the Quakers and Menonists the only sects who think a compulsive support of their religions unnecessary and unwarrantable? Can their piety alone be intrusted with the care of public worship? Ought their religions to be endowed, above all others, with extraordinary privileges, by which proselytes may be enticed from all others? We think too favorably of the justice and good sense of these denominations to believe that they either covet preëminences over their fellow-citizens or that they will be seduced by them from the common opposition to the measure.

Because the bill implies either that the civil magistrate is a competent judge of religious truths, or that he may employ religion as an engine of civil policy. The first is an arrogant pretention, falsified by the extraordinary opinion of rulers, in all ages and throughout the world ; the second, an unhallowed perversion of the means of salvation.

Because the Establishment proposed by the bill is not requisite for the support of the Christian religion. To say that it is, is a contradiction to the Christian religion itself, for every page of it disavows a dependence on the power of this world ; it is a contradiction in fact, for it is known that this religion both existed and flourished, not only without the support of human laws, but in spite of every opposition from them ; and not only during the period of miraculous aid, but long after it had been left to its own evidence and the ordinary care of Providence : nay, it is a contradiction in terms, for a religion not invented by human policy must have preëxisted and been supported before it was established by human policy ; it is, more-

*Declaration of Rights, Article XVI.

over, to weaken, in those who profess this religion, a pious confidence in its innate excellence and the patronage of its Author, and to foster in those who still reject it a suspicion that its friends are too conscious of its fallacies to trust it to its own merits.

Because experience witnesses that ecclesiastical establishments, instead of maintaining the purity and efficacy of religion, have had a contrary operation. During almost fifteen centuries has the legal establishment of Christianity been on trial. What have been its fruits? More or less in all places pride and indolence in the clergy ; ignorance and servility in the laity ; in both, superstition, bigotry and persecution. Enquire of the teachers of Christianity for the ages in which it appeared in its greatest lustre. Those of every sect point to the ages prior to its incorporation with civil policy. Propose a restoration of this primitive state, in which its teachers depended on the voluntary rewards of their flocks, many of them predict its downfall. On which side ought their testimony to have greatest weight, when for or when against their interest?

Because the Establishment in question is not necessary for the support of civil government. If it be urged as necessary for the support of civil government, only as it is a means of supporting religion, and it be not necessary for the latter purpose, it cannot be necessary for the former. If religion be not within the cognizance of civil government, how can its legal establishment be said to be necessary to civil government? What influence, in fact, have ecclesiastical establishments had on civil society ? In some instances they have been seen to exact a spiritual tyranny on the ruins of civil authority ; in more instances have they been seen upholding the thrones of political tyranny ; in no instance have they been the guardians of the liberties of the people. Rulers who wished to subvert the public liberty may have found an Established clergy convenient auxiliaries. A just government instituted to secure and perpetuate it needs them not. Such a government will be best supported by protecting every citizen in the enjoyment of his religion with the same equal hand which protects his person and his property ; by neither invading the equal rights of any sect, nor suffering any sect to invade those of another.

Because the proposed Establishment is a departure from that generous policy which, offering an asylum to the persecuted and oppressed of every nation and religion, promised a lustre to our country and an accession to the number of its citizens. What a melancholy mark is the bill of sudden degeneracy. Instead of holding forth an asylum to the persecuted, it is itself a signal of persecution. It degrades from the equal rank of citizens all those whose opinions in religion do not bend to those of the legislative authority. Distant as it may be, in its present form, from the inquisition, it differs from it only in degree; the one is the first step, the other the last in the career of intolerance. The magnanimous sufferer under the cruel scourge in foreign regions must view the bill as a beacon on our coast, warning him to seek some other haven, where liberty and philanthropy in their due extent may offer a more certain repose from his troubles.

Because it will have a like tendency to banish our citizens. The allurements presented by other situations are every day thinning their number. To superadd a fresh motive to emigration, by revoking the liberty which they now enjoy, would be the same species of folly which has dishonored and depopulated flourishing kingdoms.

Because it will destroy that moderation and harmony which the forbearance of our laws to intermeddle with religion has produced among its several sects. Torrents of blood have been spilt in the old world by vain attempts of the secular arm to extinguish religious discord by proscribing all differences in religious opinion. Time has at length revealed the true remedy. Every relaxation of narrow and rigorous policy, wherever it has been tried, has been found to assuage the disease. The American theatre has exhibited proofs that equal and complete liberty, if it does not wholly eradicate it, sufficiently destroys its malignant influence on the health and prosperity of the State. If, with the salutary effects of this system under our own eyes, we begin to contract the bounds of religious freedom, we know no name that will too severely reproach our folly. At least let warning be taken at the first fruits of the threatened innovation. The very appearance of the bill has transformed that "Christian forbearance, love and charity,"* which of late mutually prevailed, into animosities and jealousies which may not soon be appeased. What mischiefs may not be dreaded should this enemy to the public quiet be armed with the force of a law?

Because the policy of the bill is adverse to the diffusion of the

---

* Declaration of Rights, Article XVI.

light of Christianity. The first wish of those who ought to enjoy this precious gift ought to be that it may be imparted to the whole race of mankind. Compare the number of those who have as yet received it with the number still remaining under the dominion of false religions, and how small is the former! Does the policy of the bill tend to lessen the disproportion? No; it at once discourages those who are strangers to the light of truth from coming into the regions of it, and countenances by example the nations who continue in darkness in shutting out those who might convey it to them. Instead of leveling, as far as possible, every obstacle to the victorious progress of truth, the bill, with an ignoble and unchristian timidity, would circumscribe it with a wall of defence against the encroachments of error.

Because attempts to enforce by legal sanctions acts obnoxious to so great a proportion of citizens tend to enervate the laws in general and to slacken the bands of society. If it be difficult to execute any law which is not generally deemed necessary or salutary, what must be the case where it is deemed invalid and dangerous? And what may be the effect of so striking an example of impotency in the Government on its general authority?

Because a measure of such singular magnitude and delicacy ought not to be imposed without the clearest evidence that it is called for by a majority of citizens; and no satisfactory method is yet proposed by which the voice of the majority in this case may be determined or its influence secured. "The people of the respective counties are indeed requested to signify their opinion respecting the adoption of the bill to the next session of the Assembly," but the representation must be made equal before the voice either of the representatives or of the counties will be that of the people. Our hope is that neither of the former will, after due consideration, espouse the dangerous principle of the bill. Should the event disappoint us, it will still leave us in full confidence that a fair appeal to the latter will reverse the sentence against our liberties.

Because, finally, "the equal right of every citizen to the free exercise of his religion according to the dictates of conscience" is held by the same tenure with all our other rights. If we recur to its origin it is equally the gift of nature; if we weigh its importance it cannot be less dear to us; if we consult the "Declaration of those rights which pertain to the good people of Virginia as the basis and foundation of government,''* it is enumerated with equal solemnity, or rather with studied emphasis. Either, then, we must say that the will of the Legislature is the only measure of their authority, and that in the plentitude of this authority they may sweep away all our fundamental rights, or that they are bound to leave this particular right untouched and sacred ; either we must say that they may control the freedom of the press ; may abolish the trial by jury ; may swallow up the executive and judiciary powers of the State ; nay, that they may annihilate our very right of suffrage and erect themselves into an independent and hereditary assembly ; or we must say that they have no authority to enact into a law the bill under consideration. We, the subscribers, say that the General Assembly of this Commonwealth have no such authority ; and that no effort may be omitted on our part against so dangerous a usurpation, we oppose to it this remonstrance, earnestly praying, as we are in duty bound, that the Supreme Lawgiver of the universe, by illuminating those to whom it is addressed, may, on one hand, turn their councils from every act which would affront his holy prerogative or violate the trust committed to them, and on the other guide them into every measure which may be worthy of his blessing ; may redound to their own praise, and may establish most firmly the liberties, the property, and the happiness of this Commonwealth.

*Virginia Bill of Rights.

H.

JEFFERSON'S ACT FOR ESTABLISHING RELI-
GIOUS FREEDOM IN VIRGINIA.

"Be it enacted by the General Assembly, That no man shall be compelled to frequent or support any religious worship, place or ministry whatsoever; nor shall be enforced, restrained, molested or burthened in his body or goods, nor shall otherwise suffer on account of his religious opinions or belief; but that all men shall be free to profess and by argument to maintain their opinions in matters of religion, and that the same shall in no wise diminish, enlarge or affect their civil capacities."

INDEX.

* The word "Assembly" is used often for the " House of Burgesses,"
which passed away with the Revolution, and for the " House of Delegates," which is the lower house of the present General Assembly.

---

*The "Establishment," or "Established Church," is the same as "Church of England" in Virginia, of which the "Protestant Episcopal Church" is the successor.